Adventure in Business

An **I.M.M.E.R.S.I.O.N**
Approach to Training and Consulting

Ann Smolowe, Steve Butler and Mark Murray
with Jill Smolowe

and contributions from Dick Prouty, Paul Radcliffe and Moe Carrick

A Project Adventure Publication

Published in Conjunction with

PEARSON
CUSTOM PUBLISHING

Printed in the United States of America

10 9 8 7 6 5 4 3 2 1

Please visit our website at www.pearsoncustom.com

ISBN 0–536–02216–X

BA 98804

PEARSON CUSTOM PUBLISHING
160 Gould Street/Needham Heights, MA 02494
A Pearson Education Company

Contents

Acknowledgments

Collaborating on a book with a team of people requires a high degree of mutual respect and trust. When we began the process, we acknowledged it would take the collective and synergistic talents of individual specialists to complete the product.

While the team approach was a given, we realized we needed to balance the need for a dedicated book team with the need for a dedicated consultant team who would remain focused on our current and past clients.

We are grateful to Peter Aubry and Ellen Zwart for their unwavering commitment and support while graciously managing a heavier than usual consulting schedule during much of the development of this publication. We also appreciate Tom Zierk and Lisa Furlong for their Project Adventure publications experience which helped guide us through the collaborative and editing processes.

We are particularly grateful to the five generous non-PA people who reviewed an earlier manuscript serving as our first line of readers. Rick Tette provided unflagging support and helpful insights, gently reminding us to believe in ourselves and encouraging us to actively acknowledge Project Adventure's specific contributions to the field. Beverley Whitehead was kind enough to offer a global perspective while in the midst of her first two weeks of motherhood. Pam Jaeger kindly reviewed the manuscript with a specific client system lens of scrutiny. Lou Provato supported much of our breakthrough work in recent years, offering trenchant, useful criticisms that have kept us in good stead ever since. Kate Douglas contributed to the review process with constructive feedback, excellent advice and appropriate words of caution about representing the field.

Finally, we realize that an attempt to acknowledge everyone who has helped us along the way is impossible. We are indebted to numerous individuals who have provided us with opportunities to craft and test many of these ideas. To our colleagues internally who have served in powerful mentor roles on the innovative and fun side of the business, we remain in deep awe and admiration for what you bring to the table. For those who have shared their specific creative ideas in the areas of design and delivery, we've grown tremendously. Our past, present and future clients, for whom this book is written, have provided us with pioneering opportunities to learn, grow, test and challenge ourselves professionally. To our partners, colleagues and clients who have offered feedback, criticism and bluntness, we're better for it. Some have provided humor along the way, helping us always see, and enjoy, the lighter side of life. Others have offered ease and support in difficult situations which we'll forever appreciate and never forget. Hopefully, you all know who you are. Thank you.

Introduction

For years, the corporate market team at Project Adventure has wanted to write a book about the exciting and expanding uses of adventure in the corporate arena. This is important, we told each other, and we can do it. PA has already produced a number of books for the school, therapeutic, recreational and community markets that we also serve. All we have to do is carve out the time, put our minds to it and . . .

Suffice it to say, as with some of our adventure initiatives, so with this book project: what initially looked simple and straightforward had many unsuspected risks and challenges lurking beneath the surface.

Identifying goals was not a problem. From our first effort back in 1990, the corporate market team had a fairly clear sense of what we hoped to achieve. We wanted our book to:

- Present a clear picture of how adventure-based learning can serve as a central vehicle for change in the corporate arena;
- Dispel some of the misconceptions and myths about adventure, particularly the ones that confuse adventure with wilderness training;
- Contribute a quality introductory text to the adventure field;
- Offer information, not instruction, about the versatile applications of adventure;
- Showcase our experience, not our expertise.

That first effort lasted a few months, then got buried beneath a series of back-to-back intensive client contracts. A year later, we dusted off those pages and tried again. This time, the effort extended for six months, then got lost in the excitement of some large client rollouts.

Finally, we had to face two hard truths. First, our consulting schedule, happily congested with a wide assortment of fascinating clients—among them

AT&T, Apple Computer, Bell South, BMW of North America, BMW of South Africa, Digital Equipment Incorporated, Eastman Kodak Company, Esso Singapore, Exxon International Company, Exxon Shipping Company, First Union Bank, General Electric, General Motors Corporation, Hasbro, Progressive Insurance Company, Nintendo of America Inc., Nissan, Starbucks, Transportation Displays, Inc. and Westinghouse—was not going to give us the breathing space we needed to produce the book we had in mind. Second, we're adventure consultants, not writers.

This second "truth" was both hard—and liberating. Most of us, I think, believe that we can write. All we need, we tell ourselves, is some time, some privacy, some quiet. Who knows. Maybe it's true. Maybe we all *can* write. But it's also true that a busy work schedule does not permit for that time, privacy and quiet. And here's one more truth: a professional writer brings certain skills and talents to the task that the rest of us don't have.

This was brought home to me in 1991 when I was facing a tight deadline for an article I was writing for *Zip Lines*, PA's quarterly magazine. Stuck and unable to make the article say what I wanted it to say, I began to have a meltdown. In near panic, I called my sister Jill Smolowe at *Time* magazine, where she was a senior writer.

"Help!" I groaned.

Calmly, methodically, she grilled me about the content of the piece. She asked lots of questions, pressed for clarification when she wasn't sure what I meant, and refused to let me hide behind professional jargon.

"That's mumbo jumbo to me," she kept saying. "Put it into English."

After that interview, she asked me to fax her the draft I was working on, plus any earlier versions of the article. About an hour later, she faxed me "my" article. Darn! It was just what I meant it to say—only better. When I asked how she'd been able to turn the piece around so fast, she said, "This seemed very familiar because the way you and I worked was a lot like how we produce articles at a newsweekly."

Intrigued, I asked her to explain what she meant. The "group journalism" process, she explained, typically involves several people on a story. Usually, three or more correspondents report an event, then write "files," which are sent to New York, where a writer works from those reports to produce a single, seamless story. Often, the writer will "interview" a correspondent to make sure she understands the reporter's intent, or to draw out certain points.

"The correspondents provide the reporting and expertise," she said. "The writers focus on telling the story." I stored that information in my memory bank and came away from the experience with the feeling that I'd learned something valuable about knowing when it is time to turn to an outside "expert" for help.

Five years later, when the corporate market team reached a decision to take a third stab at a book, Jill came to my mind immediately. She expressed interest in writing the book using a newsweekly process, then described what would be needed. In addition to our consultants filing reports, there would have to be a "chief of correspondents" to monitor the flow and content of the files and assume responsibility for managing the project.

All of this struck me as very similar to PA's "core team" approach, which involves several consultants and specialists, both internal and external to PA, working closely together to manage large client systems and product development. The "chief of correspondents" sounded like a PA "client representative," who takes the lead in working with client management, guides the overall design process and bears responsibility for the final results. I felt ready to volunteer for the role.

My PA colleagues shared my enthusiasm for trying this new process. All agreed that it was in keeping with the thrust of our corporate work, which actively promotes a partnership between consultant and client. In this case, however, *we* would be the client.

We had no trouble assembling an enthusiastic core team: Steve Butler, Mark Murray, Dick Prouty, Paul Radcliffe and me. Getting our schedules in sync, however, was another matter. Finally, in January 1997, we sat down with Jill at PA's headquarters in Hamilton, MA, to rearticulate our goals.

"So," Jill asked, "who's your audience?"

That proved to be a more interesting question than we'd imagined. Initially, we assumed we'd be writing to the same audience addressed by most books in the adventure field—the practitioner. We saw this audience as having two distinct components: (1) traditional consultants, who work comfortably in corporate environments, but are unfamiliar with the full range of adventure techniques; and (2) nontraditional adventure practitioners, who are well-versed in the techniques of experiential learning, but have done little or no work in a corporate environment. This audience made sense. We work with them regularly in our train-the-trainer programs, a staple of the PA curriculum.

But the more we talked, the more we realized that in order to address a practitioner audience effectively, we would need to produce a how-to book. And that was not what we had in mind.

"Say it again," Jill pressed. "What is it you want to accomplish here?"

First and foremost, we agreed, we want to make vivid how adventure can be integrated into a traditional corporate setting to address real business problems and issues. We want to dispel the notion that adventure is a mere warm-up for more serious stuff. We want to make it transparently clear that adventure is fun and challenging *and* serious stuff, too.

What we want, we finally realized, is to illuminate the legitimacy and credibility of adventure consulting by bringing the experience alive for the potential recipients of our services. Aha!

This book, then, is addressed primarily to corporate audiences. For our colleagues in the adventure and consulting fields, we offer some particulars about the delivery of adventure programs in both the narrative and the appendix. But those who seek more how-to material about specific initiatives and activities might want to take a look at other PA books, particularly *Cowstails and Cobras II* or *Silver Bullets* by Karl Rohnke, and *Quicksilver* by Rohnke and Steve Butler.

Section I defines "adventure" in the corporate community and its application to the key themes driving corporate change in the '90s; explores the rapid growth of adventure consulting globally; and presents a historical overview of corporate adventure. Section II describes and shows applications of the three operating principles that undergird all of Project Adventure's work: the Experiential Learning Cycle, Challenge by Choice and the Full Value Contract.

In Sections III and IV, we strive to make vivid our corporate work and its transformative qualities by following the adventure consulting process from needs assessment, to program design, to delivery, to outcomes. To further demystify our work and make it as transparent as possible, we include a look at the hardware (activities) and software (leadership style) of the adventure toolkit.

PA sees learning as a core value. Our values state that "learning is viewed as a continuous process and is the lifeblood of our organization. It includes the individual demonstrating a willingness to engage in an active process of reflection, questioning, gathering, applying and sharing ideas."

The writing of this book proved an effective vehicle for honoring that commitment. After 15 years of delivering programs to corporate audiences, this was the first time that we paused to systematically discuss, dissect and digest what—exactly—it is that we do. The self-examination proved eye-opening, enlightening and, yes, fun. (After all, we are *adventure* consultants.)

Though our initial intention had been to write generically about corporate adventure, as we got deeper into the process, we found that the book often required a specific focus on Project Adventure's work. Such PA-centricity is uncomfortable for us. Historically, the focus of PA consultants has been to disseminate information, not to call attention to ourselves. But obviously, we know our own work best. And clients have repeatedly advised us that our failure to speak forthrightly about our pioneering work undermines their own efforts to advocate for wider use of adventure training in their respective companies.

Thus, while our intention is to showcase our experience, not to flaunt our expertise, the use of mostly PA examples reflects our standing in the adventure field as leaders in the areas of: designing corporate programs; collaborating and partnering with corporate clients; integrating clients' products into our designs; providing adventure training to consultants, both internal and external to corporations. When we speak of "adventure consultants," we are reflecting our own understanding and practice of adventure consulting.

Jill wants you to know that her use of "he" and "she" throughout is random, and that any seemingly sexist lapses are unintentional. I want to express Project Adventure's gratitude to the following companies for giving us permission to share and attribute their stories: Hasbro Games Group, Eastman Kodak Company, BMW of North America, BMW of South Africa, Hartford Life, Inc., EG&G Electro Optics Division and Nintendo of America Inc. We are also grateful to our many other clients not mentioned by name in this book, who, through the years, have offered us such wonderful consulting and learning challenges.

That's it. We hope your reading experience will be as insightful, entertaining and rewarding as we found the experience of putting this book together.

—*Ann Smolowe*

Writer's Note

For years, I'd listened with fascination when my sister spoke about her work. Her consulting challenges were always interesting, and often shed light on personnel situations I encountered in my own profession.

Particularly riveting were Ann's descriptions of the Project Adventure culture. She and her colleagues seemed to invest as much time and energy in each other as they did in their clients. For them, it was routine to discuss, dissect and diagnose the ways in which they worked both individually and collectively. The people at Project Adventure seemed to feel that the *way* they worked was every bit as important as the work itself.

Coming from the field of journalism, which takes a perverse pride in caring more about meeting deadlines than managing people, I found this constant focus on people and process startling. It sounded so healthy, so open. So connected. "I can't believe you guys work that way," I said over and over.

So, when Ann approached me with the idea of collaborating on this book, I was intrigued. What, I wondered, would it be like to work for a company that in essence regards the management of people as an art, and elevates the process of work to an art form?

The answer is that it was fascinating and altogether satisfying. Sure, there were days when it was a bit of a slog getting through the material. But rarely in my professional life have I felt so supported and valued. By making their appreciation of my skills transparent, Ann and her colleagues made me aware (perhaps for the first time in my 20-year writing career) of what it is exactly that I bring to the table.

Some of that, of course, was simply the result of working with people outside my usual field. But it also reflected Project Adventure's acute interest in and appreciation of people and "process." Among journalists, it is standard to meet outsiders, particularly consultants and new managers, in a 3-D stance: Distrust (is this person going to hurt me?), Doubt (who is this person to think he has anything to teach me?), Defend (things are fine the way they are, so why are you bothering me?).

So, it was a revelation to work with people who operate from an assumption that they stand to learn and benefit from an outsider. Indeed, their open interest and delight in the "newsweekly process" made me newly aware and appreciative of this elegant apparatus that I'd worked with first at *Newsweek*, then at *Time*. Frankly, until Project Adventure came calling, I'd never even thought of it as anything so lofty as a "process."

It was also a treat to see PA in action after hearing about the company for so many years. Both BMW of North America, Inc., and Eastman Kodak Company graciously allowed me to attend trainings run respectively by Steve Butler and Mark Murray. In each instance, the PA staff made every effort to share their thinking with me and to make the process of adventure-based learning as clear as possible.

When the team on this book sat down for the first time in January 1997 to discuss whether this project was feasible, I told Ann, Steve, Mark, Dick and Paul, "There will be a book. I don't know if it will be the book that each one of you has in mind, but I'm in the business of meeting deadlines. So, be assured, there *will* be a book."

It was a truth with a fair tint of bravado. While I was confident that I could deliver my part of the equation, I had no way of knowing if the PA folks could deliver what I was asking of them. They are, after all, adventure consultants, not newsweekly journalists. In the ensuing months, they delivered their "files" in a timely fashion. When I requested additional information, their responses were prompt, helpful and seemingly ego-free.

As collaborations go, this one was nothing short of remarkable.

—*Jill Smolowe*

Some Challenges While You Read ...

As you, the reader, move through the content of this book, you will come across several activities to challenge your mind. Since experiences are the foundation of our work, we wanted to include a few sample problems you could actually do while reading the book. The activities are found directly after the page marking the beginning of each section. All the information you need to solve the problems is on the page with the activities.

If you take the challenge and either want to verify your own answer or want to know what the solution is, you may turn to page 313 in the back of the book for the answers.

We invite you to try these problems and hope you will enjoy this mini-immersion.

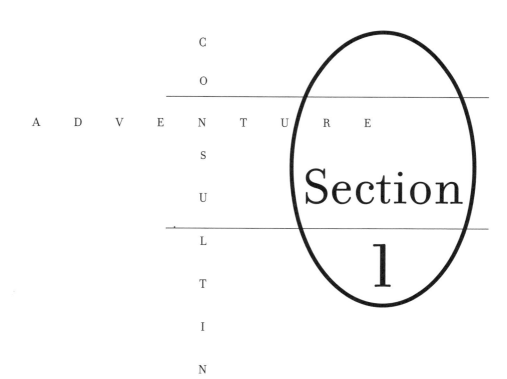

A D V E N T U R E

C O N S U L T I N G

Section

1

Word Puzzle #1

Spell the longest word possible by tracing
one line from one letter to an adjacent letter
moving up, down, horizontally or diagonally.

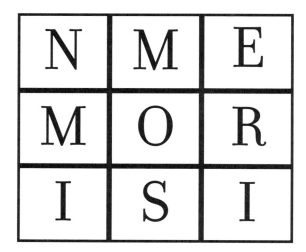

N	M	E
M	O	R
I	S	I

Wordles

Find a common word or phrase contained in each box.

XSELLNNN

*Photo of dimes courtesy of
Prentice-Hall, Inc.*

*Photo of building courtesy of the
New York Convention and Visitors
Bureau, photo of team courtesy
of PhotoDisc, Inc.*

I n this section, we set out to address three fundamental questions about adventure consulting in the corporate sphere:

- What is adventure, and what does it mean in a business context?
- How are business interests served by this method of consulting?
- How and why did adventure consulting enter the corporate field?

An appreciation of the nature of adventure is an important first step toward understanding its potential applications in a business context. Toward that end, adventure is defined here as I.M.M.E.R.S.I.O.N. in an intense experience, with each of the related qualities—interactive, meaningful, mirthful, experiential, risky, supportive, introspective, out-of-the-box, natural—speaking to a different aspect of the adventure experience.

To shed further light on the techniques that distinguish this unique approach to consulting from other methods, the adventure consultant's tasks are broken into three roles—consultant, trainer, facilitator. Each role is then explored for what is particular to that function.

The lens next shifts to the client to explore how these various consulting functions serve the interests and needs of corporate clients. The intersection of business needs and adventure consulting services is examined through the prism of five common challenges in today's international marketplace: building teamwork, strengthening leadership, sharpening customer focus, cultivating learning organizations and developing values-driven corporate cultures.

The final chapter of this section puts the rapid and strong spread of adventure consulting into historic context, looking both backward at its emergence on the corporate scene, and forward to the evolving business trends that point toward its continued strong performance in the decade ahead.

All along the way, we draw on specific consulting experiences to illustrate particular points. This is in keeping with the spirit of adventure consulting, where the emphasis is on immersion in an experience.

1 Defining Adventure Consulting

"Y our task," says the consultant, laying 13 nails on the table, "is to balance all of these nails on the head of one vertical nail. The solution is freestanding, which means you can't rely on any other props. It's achievable. And you have 10 minutes to do it."

Without need of further coaxing, the partner and his three associates hunch over the 30-penny nails and set to the challenge, intrigued and engaged. As they talk with each other and ask the consultant questions, they move the nails around, building effectively on each other's ideas. An impressive two minutes before the deadline, they successfully conceptualize how the nails need to interlock, then lay nails out accordingly. All that remains is to lift the interwoven nails onto the head of the vertical nail, and do a mental victory lap.

But they don't. Instead, the partner begins to re-analyze the problem. The others chime in. By the time the 10-minute work period elapses, they have talked themselves out of the solution. Talked themselves out of it, that is, without ever having tried to lift the interlocked nails onto the head of the vertical nail.

"Since you've spent some time and energy configuring the nails," suggests the consultant, "why don't you try lifting it onto the vertical nail."

"There's no way to lift it without the nails rolling," says Tom, the partner.

"But you've identified this as the best and perhaps only solution."

"Yeah, but it won't work," he answers emphatically. "There's got to be a trick."

"I'm not so sure," the consultant prods. "Go ahead and try it."

Everyone holds their breath as Tom slowly lifts the interlocked design and places it on the vertical nail. As he lets go, there's a spontaneous burst of applause and high-fives.

When asked what strengths contributed to the success, the group offers several possibilities. When asked what got in their way, the group grows silent. Turning to Tom, the consultant asks, "What prevented you from lifting up those nails and placing them on the vertical nail?"

He reflects a moment, than answers, "Risk. I simply didn't want to take the risk." The others nod.

"I observed a reluctance on your part to take the risk," the consultant affirms. "Do you tend to be conservative taking risks with your clients or making recommendations?"

After another reflective moment, Tom says, "I am conservative. In our line of work, we don't like to make mistakes. But I often think I'm too conservative." He turns to his associates. "What do you guys think? Am I too conservative?"

Reluctantly, they nod their heads.

"Well, in my opinion," the consultant says, "you just modeled one of the *highest* levels of risk-taking. As a partner of this firm, to sit around this table

with your colleagues and be open to looking at your potential liabilities as well as your strengths exemplifies your ability to be an extreme risk-taker, even though you may not leverage these skills as frequently or consistently as you feel your day-to-day situations might warrant."

Welcome to adventure in the corporate arena.

That's right.

Adventure.

What's that? Not quite what you were expecting? Oh. You're wondering what's become of the blizzard-locked mountains, the treacherous white-water rapids, the precarious ropes courses. Well, certainly, those props are part of the adventure toolbox. In fact, this particular moment arose during a meeting called by a leading Big Eight consulting firm to explore the possible uses of a ropes course. The intent was to integrate a ropes course component into a training planned for 100 employees.

But like most corporate audiences, these clients had a fairly static notion of what is meant by adventure. To them, adventure and physical risk were pretty much synonymous. Adventure could help set a tone, break down a silence, present an interesting or fun challenge, create a "warm, fuzzy feeling," all in the interest of creating a mood to move on to the "real" business at hand.

But could adventure offer something directly transferable back to the workplace? At this meeting, it was immediately apparent the client hadn't considered that possibility.

The consultant had taken out the nails aiming simply to offer a hands-on encounter with the experiential learning process that would show some linkages, connections and transferences back to the workplace. "Porcupine Progression," the activity just described, can be an effective tool for dramatizing team dynamics as people work together against a tight deadline. What she hadn't anticipated was how quickly and deeply this simple exercise would cut to the core of behaviors blocking the team's ability to produce the results they desire. When she saw the opening for self-discovery, she prodded. The clients ran with it, and what emerged was eye-opening, even profound, for the management consultants.

That is adventure in the corporate arena. Dynamic. Unpredictable. Mind-opening. Playful, yes, most definitely. But it is fun with a serious agenda. An adventure activity is not an end in itself. Rather, it is a beginning.

Used effectively, adventure becomes a key for unlocking closed minds, stimulating fresh thinking, encouraging meaningful dialogue, triggering learning that is transferable to the workplace. Removed from familiar work surroundings and presented with challenges where participants know neither what to expect nor what is expected of them, they are free simply to participate. An adventure experience then holds up a mirror to reflect back information about personal styles, modes of interaction, options, choices and potential. The result is often jolting, usually surprising and sometimes transformational.

The I.M.M.E.R.S.I.O.N. Experience

"This adventure kind of training can really change your life. I have guys who still think about things they did back in 1995. The hard part is breaking through the mindset of 'This is just games.'"

—Lou Provato, BMW of North America, Inc.
Manager, Performance Development Group

Adventure, of course, means different things to different people. And it varies, depending on the setting. In the business world, there is still a tendency in some quarters to view adventure as a mood-setting prelude to the real business at hand. It's the warm-up, the entertainment, the diversion from business-as-usual. The props—kayaks, bungee cords, belay ropes—are seen as a diversion rather than a teaching tool. And the bigger the prop, the bigger the potential entertainment.

But, frankly, an egg can also do quite nicely. Or a piece of paper. Or simply an engaged imagination. In an authentic adventure environment, activities serve as a springboard to lead from engagement to exploration to enlightenment. Whether the challenge is improving relationships with a client's customer base (either internally or externally), reinforcing corporate values, examining leadership styles, identifying work norms or building more effective teams, adventure is a potent tool for exploring, learning, discussing, sharing. And all of these are important precursors to sustainable change in the workplace.

Adventure consulting utilizes an interdisciplinary approach that blends organization development (OD) practices; experiential learning techniques; intellectual and emotional challenges that invite risk-taking; and process intervention skills. It also utilizes skills and tools, unique to adventure environments, that make seemingly risky physical challenges an exciting and safe option.

The result is a wonderful versatility. Adventure consulting can be tailored to enhance a corporate training effort. It can be configured to work in partnership with a company's in-house training staff. Or it can be the primary vehicle for change. Moreover, the activities and challenges can be custom-tailored to speak to, engage and ignite the thinking of a particular audience.

Whatever the configuration of players, whatever the appearance of the activities, what defines and sets an experience apart as *adventure* is a particular set of qualities. During our quarter century of work in the corporate arena, Project Adventure (PA) consultants have come to regard the hallmark of adventure as I.M.M.E.R.S.I.O.N. in an intense experience that has the following qualities:

INTERACTIVE. Relying on activities that compel participants to interact, adventure highlights how people work together. Sharpened awareness of

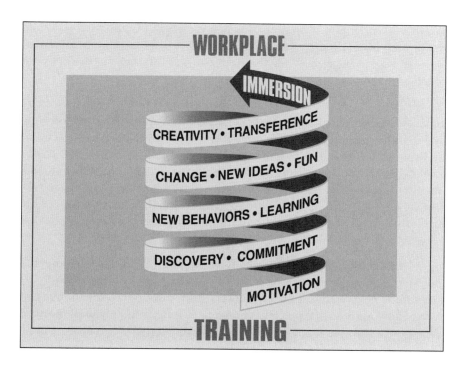

these interactive styles leads to exploration of new and more effective ways of learning, thinking and cooperating. As a result, trust is often developed at an accelerated rate.

MEANINGFUL. People embark on an adventure conscious that something different, unusual, important is about to happen. Because adventure activities demand effort and commitment beyond the routine, people tend to invest more energy in the experience—and thereby extract more value, insights and awareness from it. Adventure activities trigger innovative thinking, reawaken creativity and foster a sense of discovery.

MIRTHFUL. Fun is hard to manufacture, but easy to recognize. It's contagious, spontaneous, laughter-filled and magical. Fun both invites active involvement and signals that it's okay to relax. It creates a sense of joyfulness, camaraderie and openness to new possibilities that is essential to any successful group process. It can also be liberating for people who have been mired in cynicism to see that it is more fun to be positive. Adventure learning can help challenge the assumption that work should not be fun.

EXPERIENTIAL. Adventure learning is experiential. It increases a group's learning power by appealing to a variety of learning styles. While people can learn by sitting and listening, most learn best when all five of their senses are engaged. When the emphasis is on "doing," the lessons tend to be more memorable, the messages more enduring.

RISKY. Adventure almost always involves risk, be it physical or emotional. That element of risk, which takes a participant out of his comfort zone and deposits him in unfamiliar territory, is usually what engages attention and sustains excitement. When emotional risk-taking is managed effectively, there is low consequence for "failure" and high potential for valuable outcomes that can be sustaining. When physical risk-taking is managed effectively, safety is actively monitored and maintained. Actual risk runs higher on the emotional spectrum than the physical one, but a perception of physical risk heightens the sense of unpredictability.

SUPPORTIVE. Whether the challenge is physical, intellectual or emotional, the bedrock conditions of the adventure environment are support and safety. These conditions, engendered and cultivated by the unique nature of adventure initiatives, encourage participants to defy preconceived notions of success and failure, and to feel emboldened to "go for it." Along the way, people learn to value input from individuals they may not have sought out in the workplace. They also gain a better appreciation of their own strengths as they find themselves assuming roles they don't usually play in the work environment.

INTROSPECTIVE. Though adventure accentuates hands-on group experiences, the "aha!" that comes with introspection is often highly individual. Adventure initiatives compel people to look in the mirror and see how their own behaviors and actions impact an organization. They also expand participants' understanding and appreciation of what they can, do and might contribute. This reflective process promotes critical thinking that enables people to achieve new awareness about not only their own behavior, but its effect on others.

OUT-OF-THE-BOX. If you want to stimulate fresh, out-of-the-box thinking, you've got to take people out of the box. Adventure does that in two ways—by removing people from the physical walls that surround them and by helping people to see the walls they "put up," the walls that keep them from contributing to the success of the company. Good-bye offices, good-bye cubicles, good-bye assembly lines. Adventure levels the playing field, creates opportunities to invite new participation and opens up possibilities for multiple outcomes. As people seek common ground through adventure initiatives, skillful debriefings guide them toward seeing, recognizing and better understanding the patterns of relationships and processes that affect their work environment. Adventure becomes a particularly powerful tool when the activities involve metaphors that allow participants to see and feel the whole business entity and when effective facilitation guides participants to capture and apply new insights.

NATURAL. Adventure is organic. It feeds and builds on what transpires. While adventure activities are often outfitted with playful, memorable props, the real business of adventure revolves around eliciting authentic behaviors that serve to provide a rich exploration of human nature. Through the constant probing, dissecting and debriefing that attends each activity, a learning community begins to emerge that then builds on itself, paving the way for ever-deeper exploration.

Once participants are immersed, adventure becomes a powerful vehicle for taking a group's pulse, breaking through stale assumptions, identifying barriers to communication, cooperation and effectiveness, and opening minds to new ideas, roles and possibilities.

What Is an Adventure Consultant?

The appearance of adventure is the unfamiliar, intellectual and physical challenges that draw participants into a group. The essence of adventure is what is done with that attention once it is engaged. Both components are the work of the adventure consultant.

In the hands of a skilled adventure consultant, for instance, the simple "Porcupine Progression" does not end with 12 nails configured on the head of another nail. Instead, as we saw in the example above, it can be a powerful vehicle for:

- probing the group's approach to problem-solving,
- illuminating a barrier to risk-taking,
- understanding how such an obstacle can limit a group's effectiveness.

And the potential from this one small, quiet activity does not stop there. As the partner and his associates grasped instantly, the learnings from 10 minutes of tinkering with 13 nails are transferable back to the workplace.

Such moments of intense insight are neither unusual in a corporate adventure experience, nor do they arise out of a vacuum. Adventure consultants appreciate that adventure can produce surprising insights at any time. Its value lies at the intersection between emotional involvement and unexpected outcomes. Adventure consulting involves a constant attention to and awareness of the opportunities for probing and learning that can arise at any time during group activities.

Whether performing solo or in tandem with other consultants, the seasoned adventure consultant shifts fluidly among three roles: consulting, training, facilitating. Though these three roles overlap, each taps a distinct set of skills and has a different perspective on the experience that is unfolding. Broadly speaking, the consultant keeps an eye on the metaview, the trainer monitors the macroview, and the facilitator handles the microview.

The Consulting Role

The consulting role is the one that most business executives know, recognize and relate to most comfortably. In corporate vernacular, this is the outsider who has been brought in to troubleshoot, brainstorm, conduct a needs assessment, fashion and design a plan. In consulting terms, this is the strategist whose main task is transactional.

Responsible for big-picture thinking, the consultant has the first interaction with the client. He conducts the needs assessment, eliciting the information that will clarify the client's goals and provide the basis for the conceptualization and design of a training program. The consultant constantly walks a fine line between gaining an education and offering one.

In this role, the work between adventure consultant and client is highly collaborative. While the consultant arrives with a contextual knowledge of the company and its place in the larger industry, he lacks the crucial particulars surrounding needs and goals that will dictate the design of a training. He involves the client in self-diagnosis and a collaborating effort to identify a remedy that fits his unique set of needs.

The consultant also represents another set of eyes on the situation. He can offer insight into what he sees going on around him in the client's environment, identify obstacles and help to establish achievable guidelines, parameters and goals.

From there, the consultant immerses quickly in the client's corporate culture. His ability to intuit, delineate and appreciate what is unique and particular to the client's culture helps him to gain a clear understanding of the client's learning objectives, goals and desired outcomes. When the client is not clear on these critical points, as is common, the consultant elicits information that identifies, clarifies and illuminates.

As the consultant is gaining an understanding of the practices and concerns of the client, and building trust with this invaluable partner in the consulting process, he is also advancing the client's appreciation of how adventure can be leveraged to meet corporate goals. Often, clients have a preconception—fueled by media misrepresentations and Dilbert comic strips—that, at its most extreme, still limits adventure to wilderness training. Moreover, like any external consultant, the adventure practitioner must be prepared for and able to break through the resistance and resentment that understandably greets an outsider brought in to "fix" internal problems.

Many adventure consultants now embrace an approach, championed by Project Adventure since its inception, that seeks to demystify adventure methodology. Instead, the consultant strives to make all parts of the unfolding experience vivid and transparent for the client, while still maintaining a necessary element of surprise.

During the needs assessment process that precedes an adventure training, the consultant illuminates the linkages between workshop and workplace that foster transfer of learnings from the adventure environment to the office. During the design and delivery phases, he makes the connections between people, content and goals that help clients to consider new approaches and alternatives. After a training, he is the advisor and confidant with the external vantage point that helps the client to assess what changes have been set in motion, how they are unfolding and what further work might be required.

As the vital link between the adventure consulting concern and the client, the consultant maintains enough distance to keep an eye on the big picture, yet moves in close enough to establish an effective collaboration with the client.

The Training Role

The trainer, who delivers the content of the program, is the role probably most familiar to employees. When employees have encountered trainers in the past, usually they are people from the company's human resources or training department who have been brought into a particular field office or department to work on developing a specific set of skills.

The trainer's main task is informational as she walks participants through the program contents. In many traditional training environments, this is the person who stands in front of the room, providing information and instruction, often utilizing such tools as overhead transparencies, flip charts, workbooks and videotapes.

In an adventure environment, trainers place an emphasis on setting the mood, engaging the participants both as individuals and as a group, and monitoring emotional and physical safety as they guide participants through the series of activities. Responsible for making the activities connect and make sense to participants, the trainer works from a deep conceptual and practical knowledge of adventure methodologies. Her skill set, as also required in a traditional training environment, includes the abilities to communicate, educate and improvise effectively.

Her interpersonal skills are crucial to a training's success. At the outset of a training, her aim is to engage the participants quickly and begin fashioning them into a learning community. Indifference, apathy or resistance, however, may stand in the way. When compliance is not forthcoming, it is up to the trainer to work with the resistance and redirect the mood.

The trainer's improvisational skills are exercised constantly. If an unexpected result or perspective presents itself during the course of an activity, a skillful trainer has the knowledge and ability to incorporate the insight into the discussion. Always, the trainer is prepared to adjust the program in response to changing and evolving needs, not to mention unforeseen challenges. (Despite the best-laid plans, training sites are often not quite what was expected; equipment gets lost in transit; the sequence of events is disrupted by late-arriving participants or keynoter speakers whose planes were delayed by weather, mechanical failure, whatever.)

As the vital link between the program design and the participants, the trainer is responsive to the group's particular needs, yet manages the training design's broader agenda.

The Facilitating Role

In business circles, "facilitating" usually means to assist a group through an agenda. Participants in traditional training settings can expect facilitators to create "parking lots" of action items and to drive decision-making when appropriate. In adventure circles, it has a deeper meaning and purpose that is often unfamiliar to corporate audiences.

The roots of adventure-based facilitation lie in the therapeutic community, where group dynamics are a subject of intense scrutiny. The group is used both as a vehicle to test and elicit certain behaviors, and as a mirror to reflect back to participants resulting information and insights about themselves. This debriefing component is what lifts an adventure activity beyond the immediate experience. By intervening in the activity to engage and challenge the participants, the facilitator helps guide participants toward a deeper appreciation and understanding of how they actually interact.

The facilitator's main task is observational. He listens, watches and senses the patterns of interaction, then helps participants enlarge their understanding and perception of what has transpired. What the facilitator thinks he sees may or may not be accurate, so he is as much on a journey of discovery as the members of the group.

The facilitator's primary role is to help participants mine the experiences of the here and now for observations, insights and lessons that will be useful in the future when transferred back to the workplace. The intent is to get beneath the skin of the activity, and into the marrow of what transpired between people.

The debriefing role constantly views and reviews the unfolding experience, asking, in essence, "What just happened? What did we learn from it? Where do we go next?" But sitting down with a group to discuss "what it all means" can be difficult and intimidating for those involved. For many people, self-reflection does not come easy in a business-related setting, nor does open dialogue with colleagues about issues touching on performance or feelings.

The art of debriefing, therefore, is the facilitator's ability to keep it connected to the whole of the adventure activity, and not allow it to become positioned as separate and potentially more threatening. In a skillful debriefing, the process itself becomes an adventure initiative, conducted in an environment that feels safe and invites the group to share observations, perceptions and conflicts.

As with all parts of an adventure experience, the aim during a debrief is to explore and comb for meaning so that individual and team learning can take place. At various stages of group development, participants tend to want the adventure consultant to be the expert. Experts are safe to be with; they have all the "answers." The group doesn't have to think when experts are willing to step in. It keeps them comfortably distanced from the burden of interpretation and responsibility.

The facilitator is adept at getting participants to do their own thinking, to dig into their feelings, to build up their own collection of observations and to provide an atmosphere to act on them. He prods when the discussion does not go deep enough, intervenes when it veers off track, mediates when it turns combative.

As the vital link between the content of the program and the participants' true grasping and internalizing of it, the facilitator moves in close to manage resistance, engender introspection and explore learning situations, yet maintains enough distance to remain an effective observer.

The Three Roles at (Inter)Play

So, how does this work when all three roles are in play? Let's go back to the example that started this chapter. The Big Eight consulting company had been preparing for its annual off-site retreat involving its entire office staff and their spouses. The primary goals involved building trust, deepening mutual understanding and creating a learning community among the employees and their "partners" outside the company. PA consultant Ann Smolowe had been called in to explain the potential uses of a ropes course that was permanently on-site at the five-star resort facility where the three-day program was to be held.

Through four months of phone and mail communication, the company had communicated its aim of finding a vendor that could run all 100 conference participants through a ropes course component in a single day. By the time of this first face-to-face meeting, it was clear that the company had a preconceived notion of what could be done with a ropes course and what was meant by adventure.

As a consultant, then, Ann entered the meeting with a full agenda. She hoped to begin developing a good rapport and trusting relationship; to provide the client with a deeper understanding of Project Adventure's work methods and the experiential process; to expand the client's view of ropes courses and adventure in general.

More essential, however, she knew she needed to gather more information concerning the company's learning objectives and desired outcomes; understand clearly the client's perspective of how an adventure component would fit with their larger vision for the three-day program; and educate the client on the pros and cons of static versus dynamic ropes courses so they could consider the full range of possible uses in the overall design.

Ann probed, discussed, listened. About an hour into what would prove to be a four-hour meeting, she sensed that a quick "hands-on" experience with adventure learning would bring her explanations to life.

Shifting into the training mode, she pulled the 13 nails out of her briefcase and explained the activity. As the group members worked on the problem, they kept looking to Ann to step in and provide the solution. As a consultant seeking to solidify a contract, it was risky business to stay in a trainer role. But Ann knew that there would be no sense of discovery if she intervened.

When the 10 minutes were up, she shifted into the facilitator role. Sensing their need to know the solution first, she gently prodded them to complete the task. Then she headed into the debriefing, the critical process that holds the potential for making an activity meaningful and memorable.

As a consultant, Ann found herself silently assessing the risks and rewards of trying to pull out direct insights and learnings from the experience. She knew she could build on the positive things they'd identified, facilitate some general observations that would speak to their team work, and build on their theoretical understanding of the adventure learning process. That low-risk approach, she knew, would legitimize the experience—but it might not have much personal or professional impact.

As a facilitator, she felt the potential to pull some powerful learning from the experience. But making a behavioral connection to their work setting was risky from the consultant vantage point; perhaps this wasn't their agenda. Perhaps this would cost her a contract. Ann's consultant headset assessed the risks and rewards, then opted to stay in the facilitator mode. And so the adventure unfolded.

In the end, engaging the client in an adventure activity proved a powerful strategy. It both deepened the client's understanding of adventure and leveraged the adventure work. Had Ann stayed in the consultant role throughout, it is unlikely the client would have gained the enhanced appreciation of adventure learning that enabled them to expand their understanding of its potential uses and power.

After they engaged in a brief adventure experience, their perspective shifted. The ropes course, they now understood, could be more than a recreational device for emphasizing individual challenge. Instead, with modification it could be used to cultivate the learning community they were seeking to establish. In her training role, Ann was able to detail a variety of potential uses that would offer varying levels of challenge and choice.

In *Flawless Consulting,* Peter Block writes, "It is a mistake to assume that clients make decisions to begin projects and use consultants based purely on rational reasons. More often than not, the clients' primary question is: 'Is this consultant someone I can trust? Is this someone I can trust not to hurt me, not to con me, someone who can both help to solve the organizational and technical problems I have, at the same time be considerate of my position and person?'"

The fluid shifting among the three roles worked toward building that critical element of trust. Instead of playing it safe by remaining in the consultant mode, Ann was true to the spirit of adventure when she shifted into the riskier facilitation mode. With that shift, she subtly modeled both the risk inherent in an adventure activity and its potential value. That authenticity, which quietly resonated throughout the experience, helped to begin the critical process of building trust between consultant and client.

Summary

More than an approach, more than a sequence of activities, adventure is a process informed by a set of qualities that educate, provoke and stimulate. The hallmark of the adventure experience is I.M.M.E.R.S.I.O.N. in an intense experience that is interactive, meaningful, mirthful, experiential, risky, supportive, introspective, out-of-the-box and natural.

In the corporate arena, adventure consulting blends adventure techniques with OD consulting skills and tools in order to speak effectively to a wide range of learning styles. The result is a versatility that enables adventure consultants to custom design programs that alternately can enhance existing client programs or serve as the primary vehicle for change.

Beyond the unfamiliar activities and challenges he has to offer, the adventure consultant is distinguished by the fluid shifting of its practitioners among three overlapping, but distinct, roles:

- Consultant. In this role, he establishes and maintains contact with the client, jointly assesses the client's situation, elicits information, designs programs, serves as confidant and advisor to the primary client contact.

- Trainer. In this role, he sets the tone of the training, then communicates, educates and improvises as he orchestrates and delivers the content through a sequence of activities and facilitated group discussion.

- Facilitator. In this role, he leads the debriefings, engaging and challenging participants to dig for deeper meaning, mediating disagreements and pushing for ever-greater clarity and understanding.

2 The Thematic Drivers

Change is rarely easy in any dimension of our lives. When a business organization initiates change, people often feel threatened. Fearful of being marginalized, left out or let go, they tend to react defensively with resistance, distrust or cynicism. Thus, asking people to review, rethink and retool the way they approach or conduct business can be a particularly difficult challenge for an organization.

Yet fundamental change is the hallmark of the technological era. At the core of this change is a human dimension relatively new to the world of business. Interpersonal and interactive, this human component creates attendant issues and challenges that are more concerned with stirring hearts, minds and loyalties than making and moving products.

Indeed, as information proliferates and becomes ever more accessible in this evolving technological age, often what sets a company apart from its competitors has less to do with the product than the human elements that drive and support service: a company's culture, character, customer practices, capacity to flex, respond and change.

"There's no avoiding it. The eternal search for sustainable competitive advantage is leading us straight into the squishy softness of culture and character," *Fortune* magazine summarized in November 1997. "Many business people won't like it. They won't be comfortable talking with colleagues about trust, honesty, purpose, values." The article went on to warn, "They will have to face the fact that they will likely be eaten alive by competitors who confront these issues with relish."

Adventure consulting excels at lifting such seemingly ephemeral concepts off the page and bringing them first to light, then to life. Why? Adventure consultants are, in effect, architects of behavioral change, who focus on engaging groups in the discovery of their own purpose, process and skills.

The elements that make an adventure experience distinct—experiential learning activities overlaid by components that create a perception of risk— are purposefully designed to engage the emotions, as well the intellect. Inherently, they speak to the "human" side that can cause discomfort.

Project Adventure's corporate experience has evolved to support the development of a learning community. Whether we are working with business or education professionals, therapists or community groups, the creation of learning teams informs and permeates every aspect of our work. Our foundational tools (see Section II) emphasize a commitment to challenge, risk-taking and collaboration, all within a safe environment that shifts the focus away from individual successes and failures and toward an ongoing process of growth.

This theoretical framework appreciates that individual learning does not occur in isolation. Rather, it acknowledges the role of the community in an individual's learning experience and attends to that community as the context within which the learning occurs. The interactive adventure experience throws into sharp relief the degree to which a person's "success" or "failure" is integrally connected to the involvement of and contributions made by the other participants.

Five Themes That Drive Change in the '90s

In today's corporate world, the problems that most frequently lead a company to consult external specialists all speak to the ongoing struggle to sustain competitive advantage in the face of rapid change. Over the last decade, corporate requests for training programs have tended to arrange around one of five themes:

- Team Development
- Leadership
- Customer Focus
- Learning Organizations
- Values

Let's first take a quick and broad look at how adventure techniques are harnessed to address each of these themes. Then, we'll take a closer look at some adventure applications.

Team Development

A team approach appreciates not only that the synergistic sum is greater than its component parts, but that all parts are influenced by the rest. Teams are created as a way of increasing performance by emphasizing the combined skills of many people, rather than the unique contributions of just one. Effective teams have long been a component of successful organizations. And recently organizations are faced with teams that present unique issues that are the result of a restructuring that has involved layoffs, buy-out packages and job reductions.

Adventure is a powerful tool for breaking through self-protective instincts and beginning the process of building trust. Team-development training focuses on creating an environment where individuals see directly that they can achieve quicker and better results by pooling skills, sharing information and working closely together. The team skills targeted and strengthened by activities include communication, active listening, feedback, conflict management, risk-taking, effective support and decision-making, as well as identifying behaviors that can undermine effective team performance.

Key to any such effort is clarification of what is meant by "team." In the '90s, team has become a catch-all word for cooperative effort, loosely applied to anything and everything from small service groups to entire organizations. In reality, intact teams are quite different from self-managed teams; natural work teams bear little resemblance to working groups; real teams, while similar, are different from high-performance teams; project teams and product teams share some, not all, characteristics and so forth.

Bringing clarity to a team's self-definition is part of the adventure consultant's task. Once that clarity is achieved, a team is better positioned to understand the dynamics that do or can inform the team's operations. With expectations more closely aligned the team is better poised to begin moving along the team-performance continuum that ranges from pseudo team to high-performing team (Katzenbach & Smith, 1993).

Leadership

Leadership is, and has always been, a function of relating to others. In the changed business environment of the last decade, however, the challenges of the leadership role have diversified. Once upon a time, a strong directing hand was enough. In today's marketplace, a premium is placed on leaders who understand that their employees are a company's most valuable asset and know how to motivate their people accordingly. Thus, the new leader needs to be more visionary, more communicative, more invested in the people that make up her organization, more open to new approaches, more responsive to change.

Again, clarity is required to design the most effective training program. When the concept of leadership is being explored within the context of team development, the emphasis is generally on the relational slant. If, for instance, a training involves elements of Ken Blanchard's popular Situational Leadership approach, the related adventure activities might focus on making participants aware of how a given situation can affect our choice of style. Training emphasis would therefore be on creating different situations that elicit a range of different styles.

Newer models influenced by consultant Margaret Wheatley, president of The Berkana Institute, view leadership through the prism of context. "Leadership," writes Wheatley, "is always dependent on the context, but the context is established by the relationships we value. We cannot hope to influence any situation without respect for the complex network of people who contribute to our organizations" (Wheatley, 1991).

Within the team context, leadership trainings may emphasize helping individuals understand how to make sense of the complexity of relationships. The effect on others of particular leadership styles may be explored or team leader skills may be illuminated by the decision-making process elicited by activities.

If, alternately, the focus is on the journey toward becoming a leader, the emphasis becomes the dynamic qualities of leadership. Here, the learning community might be designed to allow for greater introspection or to enable participants to use the group as a leadership lab. Participants might develop a personal leadership profile, based on a rich combination of feedback from work colleagues, self-discovery inventories and feedback from the training's adventure-based learning community.

Whatever the particular focus, adventure training can utilize a range of theoretical models, views and perspectives to help participants give definition and structure to the concept of leadership. It can frame activities that enable participants to practice being leaders and see vividly the effects of different leadership responses. These responses can be explored and discussed in various contexts, including but not limited to leadership effectiveness, the role leadership responses play in developing a company culture, delineating leadership behaviors from management responses and leading by values.

Customer Focus

With the globalization of the economy, quality products have proliferated. If a company hopes to remain competitive, it must abandon the one-size-fits-all model of customer service and differentiate clients, catering directly to specific needs, demands and priorities. Key to providing what a client wants is the ability to listen and learn from the customer.

Customer service is an attitude fostered within a work culture. At its best, it anticipates as well as attends to the needs of others in the production and delivery of goods and services. A customer-focused attitude understands how to manage the expectations of others while at the same time discovering and attempting to deliver what will delight the client and ensure continued business.

Adventure training accentuates the learning aspects of the customer relationship. It shows how soliciting client input and valuing feedback not only invites the customer's foresight and insights, but lends to an interactive process that builds and tightens the relationship. The dynamics of adventure training foster the development of relationships based on respect, caring, listening, honesty and trust—all key components of customer satisfaction.

Learning Organizations

Systems thinking is a discipline that strives to see business entities as wholes. Within this conceptual framework, interrelationships are of greater concern than lines of authority. As theorized and popularized by Peter Senge, the goal is to become a "learning organization," by which Senge means environments where "new and expansive patterns of thinking are nurtured, where collective aspiration is set free, and where people are continually learning how to learn together" (Senge, 1990).

Adventure training provides a laboratory for examining how work flow processes unfold and function. People explore patterns of communication, how decisions are made, why obstacles arise, how they might be averted. As participants analyze a company's inner workings from an organizational viewpoint and seek to identify means of improving efficiency and performance, they also set in motion the dynamic that lends to the building of a true learning organization.

Key to the development of a learning organization is an appreciation that teams and organizations are living systems, always in the process of becoming something more. As groups work together during adventure activities, they gain insight into the dynamic quality of relationships within a system, and how those ever-changing relationships affect performance, attitude and outcomes.

Values

"I look for the same kind of qualities most look for in choosing a spouse: integrity and passion," writes Howard Schultz, the CEO of Starbucks, one of the decade's great corporate success stories. "I want to work with people who don't leave their values at home, but bring them to work, people whose principles match my own" (Schultz, 1997).

Back in 1987 when Schultz purchased Starbucks, many in the business world thought him a maverick and his approach fanciful. Today, "values" is rapidly becoming the corporate watchword. Companies that continue to dismiss such concepts as irrelevant risk having their competitive edge shaved by businesses that step up to the challenge of improving interpersonal communications and relationships.

Increasingly, companies are coming to regard values as a conceptual organizer that creates alignment of activity within a team or organization. A values-based approach extends well beyond executive formulations of mission statements. In companies where values are well-articulated and embraced, there is heightened attention to how people relate to each other. The values represent fundamental beliefs that state what is important to an organization, then guide interactions both with colleagues and clients.

Adventure consultants work with organizations at different stages of values development, from identification and articulation to meaning and alignment. Adventure's central focus on interpersonal skills, and its emphasis on valuing others' ideas and opinions, make it uniquely positioned to help illuminate what is meant by "values." In an adventure lab, participants come to understand how these intangible concepts play out in very concrete ways in the workplace.

Before we look at how adventure consultants work with clients to design and deliver programs, let's get a more detailed view of what an adventure experience might look like in the service of these thematic drivers. Between them, the following three touch on all five thematic drivers. The first anecdote illustrates an adventure initiative custom(er)-tailored to customer focus issues, and touches tangentially on related leadership issues. The second addresses the building of learning organizations and team development, two areas that inevitably overlap. The final example takes a look at a small segment of a cutting-edge values curriculum.

Meet the Atwells

During a three-day training for BMW retail center owners, the challenge for Project Adventure is to breathe life into two of the client's goals: to explore the dynamic nature of the company's "Best Practices" in regard to its clients, and to enhance understanding of how a dealership owner's leadership style can impact those Best Practices.

At the closing of the first day, PA consultant Steve Butler says to the 60 participants, "I'd like to remind you that the Atwells will be joining us in the morning."

Attention is then called to a fax in the participant manual, which reads: "This fax is to confirm my appointment for tomorrow at your dealership. I spoke with a Service Advisor to schedule a drop-off at about 8:15 a.m. and pickup at 2:45 p.m. I'm including a list of all the repair work that I need done. Please let me know now if there will be any problems completing this work on time." The group is then divided into seven "dealerships."

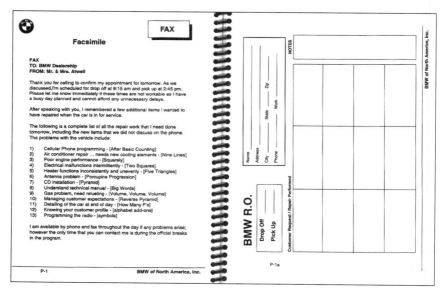

The next morning, Steve further explains, "The Atwells will be one of many customers who will need your attention today. We ask that you be attentive with each customer that is presenting up front throughout the day." In other words, the time and attention paid to the Atwells must be interspersed with the other program activities scheduled throughout the day.

The Atwells (adventure consultants decked out in business garb) then enter, talking a mile a minute and demanding to see the Service Advisor. As they approach the various dealerships, Mrs. Atwell burbles, "I'm sorry I'm late but my daughter had a conniption this morning when she was packing for her weekend trip to Skidmore because she realized her favorite jeans were dirty and . . ."

Some of the dealerships offer responses in line with the company's Best Practices policies, greeting the Atwells promptly and having a pre-prepared repair order in hand. Others have ignored the exercise, and now must scramble to designate who will handle the voluble Atwells. The Atwells take their cues from the dealers. If the dealership attempts to establish a cordial relationship, the Atwells respond in a friendly, easy-going fashion. If the dealership ignores them or seems indifferent to their demands, the Atwells grow angry and vocalize their frustration.

As the Atwells depart, each dealership is left with a box cut in the shape of a car containing 13 puzzles and exercises, each of which corresponds to one of the repair problems. The metaphoric problems range from a CD player that was installed incorrectly to poor engine performance. Mrs. Atwell's parting remark is a reminder that the car must be ready promptly at 2:45.

"It's a three-hour drive to Skidmore," she rambles, "and my daughter's orientation starts at 7:00, which means . . ." She leaves her cellphone number and asks to be contacted if there are any questions or problems.

The day progresses, with no formal time set aside to address the 13 repair problems. But between presentations and during lunch, the participants involve themselves with the tasks, which range from the relatively simple to the very complex. (In addition to the customer focus, the initiative is also designed to explore whether the dealers will attempt to share information and answers across groups. Typically, dealerships regard one another as competitors, a practice not always in the manufacturer's or dealer's best interest.)

When Mrs. Atwell returns at 3 p.m., again talking a blue streak, the dealerships' state of preparedness mirrors the spectrum of responses a real client might encounter. Some groups have solved all the problems and are awaiting the Atwells, completed paperwork in hand. Some have solved all the problems but have not completed the paperwork. Others have not solved all the problems, but take a proactive approach to informing the Atwells when and how the work will be completed. And some groups have continued to disregard the Atwells and most of the problems are unfinished. As the consultants and participants role-play their parts, a typical exchange goes:

Dealer: "Mrs. Atwell, we've got your car. Fortunately we were able to repair all of your problems except the CD, which . . ."

Mrs. Atwell: "I can't believe you didn't get the CD installed. You knew I was taking my daughter to Skidmore this weekend and that it's a three-hour drive. How am I going to listen to her for three hours? Why didn't you call and give me an update on the status?"

Dealer: "We tried to reach you, but your cellphone was busy." (He squirms uncomfortably, then whispers to his colleagues.) "If you let us keep the car over the weekend, we'll have it ready for you first thing Monday morning. We can give you a loaner . . ."

Mrs. Atwell: (voice rising) "I don't want a loaner. I'd like to see the re-pair order and what the costs are running."

Dealer: (annoyed) "Mrs. Atwell, the paperwork isn't ready yet because the car isn't done . . ."

The role-playing becomes increasingly heated, continuing for another 5 to 10 minutes until Mrs. Atwell finally agrees to accept a loaner, then leaves in a huff. The activity is then brought to a close and the participants are asked to evaluate their performance, based on BMW's Best Practices, among them quality of repair work, respectful and courteous treatment, and explanation of the service work performed.

In the post-activity debriefing, this exercise, delivered at 22 different training sessions to handle over 300 retail centers, elicited a fascinating array of responses—again, all of them mirroring real-life transactions. Some groups offered fair and accurate assessments of their performance. Others, who had not entirely satisfied the Atwells, projected the problems onto the customer: too many problems to be solved, not enough time, cus-tomers who were too pushy. One of the most memorable debriefs ended this way:

Dealer A: "Well, we didn't fix all of the problems, so I rated us good on the quality of the repair work and having the problems fixed on time as promised."

Dealer B: (sounding defensive) "I rated us excellent right down the list. We did the best we could, especially since there was no time built into the day to work on the problems. This wasn't real-istic. In our business, we'd assess the problems and allocate appropriate time." (His agitation building) "And our cus-tomers know us. They'd be more reasonable."

Facilitator: "Do you always have the time to accurately assess the problems and the time to fix them? What do others think?"

Dealer C: "Come on, guys, let's own up to what happened here. This happens all the time. We have customers come in, but we have lots of other work to do. We lose our focus, or make mistakes or even do our best but it isn't good enough. We often fall short of keeping our customers apprised of the status of their repairs during the course of the day. And when the customer arrives at the end of the day, we're often caught up in the rush of completing the paperwork.

"It doesn't matter really if we were right or wrong in what we did. We have to acknowledge that the customer is upset and respond. We have to recover the situation or we risk losing their business."

That stark admission prompted a candid discussion about breakdowns in customer service. The debriefing soon shifted to strategies for service recovery, with the various dealership owners sharing insights and specific strategies that could be transferred back to the workplace.

The next morning, when a PA trainer asked the group if there were any lingering thoughts, insights or reflections from the prior day's activities, Dealer A said, "Actually, we'd like to request Mrs. Atwell's presence one last time."

Dealer B then entered the meeting room, dressed in a pinstripe suit, and handed a dozen roses to a blushing and rather stunned Mrs. Atwell. "Mrs. Atwell," he said, "I hope you'll accept these roses as an acknowledgment that we disappointed you yesterday. Your business is truly important to us and I hope the loan won't put you out too much this weekend . . ."

As Dealer B modeled many of the key elements to effective service recovery identified by the group the day before, it was clear that the Atwell experience had brought home the meaning of Best Practices far more vividly than any lecture or video presentation.

The honest give and take also galvanized the participants to engage more actively, openly and enthusiastically in the remainder of the training. "It's important to use all five senses," one dealership owner said in praise of the experience. "It's important in the showroom, too."

Group Juggling to Warp Speed

Group Juggling is a simple activity that quickly shows groups what it means to be a learning organization. When Project Adventure CEO Dick Prouty leads this activity, he invites a group of 8 to 12 people to stand in a circle. He throws a fleece ball to someone, and asks that the ball be passed on, with the people remembering the order of the pass. The exercise is then repeated and timed, typically clocking in at about 12 seconds. With a little practice, the time is chopped to 8 seconds.

Dick then introduces two or three more balls, and asks how many seconds the group thinks it will take to pass all the balls in the same order. Fifteen seconds is a typical guess. Usually, the first effort, filled with flubs, frustration and laughter, is well in excess of that. After much brainstorming, the group gets it down to about eight seconds.

Just as everyone is beginning to look pleased with themselves, Dick throws another curve: "The customer has asked us to improve our efficiency by at least 50%—and we have only 15 minutes to accomplish the task. I also want to assure you that we would never ask you to do something that is not achievable by a high-performing team."

What! Stares. Incredulity. Confusion.

Then the questions begin. "What exactly is the request?" (That you pass the balls around the group in the same order.) "What's a pass?" (The ball must go from one person to another, touching everyone in the proper sequence.) Then, finally, someone gets an idea. "Do we have to stay in a circle?" (No, that was never part of the instructions.)

Aha! "Restructuring" solutions proliferate, and the group begins to generate lots of energy. Usually within the 15-minute time frame, the group gets the time down to a "warp speed" juggle of under two seconds.

The action offers numerous opportunities for looking at systems and change. Depending on how the initiative has been introduced and the particular dynamics of the individuals involved, groups see a wide variety of workplace assumptions and behaviors mirrored back through the activity. Among the insights gleaned by groups engaged in this popular activity over the years:

- "The whole of us is smarter than any one of us." This is made obvious by the rapid succession of ideas that quickly merge into a solution. The fusion of intellectual capital as the group brainstorms can be astounding—and eminently transferable back to the workplace.

- "Change is easier and more likely to occur when individuals understand the whole process." Too often in our work lives, we get caught up in the detail and complexity of change without having a sense of the whole. In this activity, "restructuring" becomes easier because the group can see the whole process and flow of work in front of them.

- "Change is easier to embrace when the affected team plays a role in the decision-making." Even in group juggling, the routes to warp speed can breed conflict. But the group often concludes that compromises were easier because the team had some control over the process.

- "Challenging goals encourage us to achieve the seemingly impossible." Repetition, lack of receptivity to new ideas and trammeled expectations are so often the norm in a workplace that change becomes perceived as "impossible." This initiative gives people a sense of the creative possibilities unleashed when a group believes in the possibility of achieving high goals.

- "Cynicism afflicts everyone on a team." Almost invariably, someone in the group balks that the goal is a "trick" or manipulation. Often, as new attempts are made, someone will push to return to the circle formation. People usually see the metaphor: old ways are more comfortable—challenging assumptions about the way we've done things for many years is hard intellectual and emotional work.

The list of learnings attached to this one relatively simple activity goes on and on. Among the other ideas transferred back to the workplace: when change produces an outcome that is successful it enhances a group's ability to pursue new ideas; stagnant assumptions impede improvement; blaming individuals (who drop balls) is counterproductive; and creativity is fun.

Finding ways to make the complex more simple and patterns more obvious is a fundamental challenge in the business arena. Indeed, it can be argued that key to effective leadership is helping everyone see the fundamental processes of the group so that all members can add the maximum value possible. When debriefed effectively, activities like Group Juggling and Warp Speed make the importance of these concepts vivid and transparent.

Values: From Concept to Concrete Action

"The most important thing a leader has to do is set the values. Not the least."

—*George Fisher, Chairman and CEO, Kodak*

In recent years, the Eastman Kodak Company has placed increasing emphasis on its five guiding values: Respect for Individual Dignity, Uncompromising Integrity, Trust, Credibility, Continuous Improvement and Personal Renewal. Lest anyone forget, these values are printed on posters that are prominently displayed throughout Kodak facilities around the world.

Kodak's leaders understand, however, that these values risk being reduced to little more than glib buzzwords if employees are not given the chance to explore and internalize their meaning and application. Only then can the process begin of transforming the values from mere words to shared beliefs, from vague concepts to concrete actions. Though it's a task easier said than done, an illustration will help to show the potential power of values-based adventure training.

During an ongoing program that Project Adventure conducts in partnership with Kodak, an exercise called "Stepping Stones" has proved effective at addressing Kodak's goal of "Bringing the Values to Life." On this particular day at Kodak's Education and Development Center in Rochester, NY, PA consultant Mark Murray divides the group of 20 line supervisors in two, then explains that each team must retrieve five "Kodak Values" from various points in a "river" that they must then traverse as a group. The guidelines for the activity are complicated; any number of missteps can send the teams back to square one.

As the groups move through the activity, the light-hearted competitiveness that inevitably sets in exposes multiple opportunities for winking away infractions, looking the other way, not giving full credence to "uncompromising integrity." The way in which the players interact highlights "respect for individual dignity."

That much seems obvious. More intriguing are the side dramas that evolve. Mark, for instance, has informed the group that he will play the role of "an obstinate team member." He has not spelled out what functions he can or can't perform, and his body language is charged; both the way he constantly looks down or away, and his moody demeanor, invite distrust.

Both teams quickly come to regard Mark as a pariah, and respond by trying to distract or sideline him. Their key ploy, in other words, is to remove him from the activity. The basic assumption is that he cannot be counted on or trusted.

As it happens, Mark is a valuable resource. Though taciturn, he has useful ideas for completing the crossing. Moreover, contrary to people's assumptions, he is both reliable and trustworthy. It will take both teams a long time to figure this out.

In the debriefing that follows, Mark notes that no one asked him such key questions as, "Are you committed to the success of this team? What would you like to do? What can you do?" As the discussion evolves, the participants observe that those who assumed leadership roles in the exercise had designated Mark as a pariah, and that no one else had thought to question that assumption.

"Instead of shunting me aside," Mark observes, "you could have tried to draw me in, or at least ascertain my position by asking me direct questions."

As a group, the participants begin to see how their conduct toward Mark failed to reflect either "trust" or "respect for individual dignity." Building on that recognition, they probe why they assumed Mark was an obstruction. Is this the usual operating assumption when someone seems less than a team player, let alone behaves unsociably or antagonistically? Do we typically marginalize someone if we don't like their manner, mood or body language? Do we make attempts to test whether our visceral distrust may be misplaced? Do we make attempts to work with this person? Do we try to encourage their best work?

The activity proves an unthreatening vehicle for looking at other workplace behaviors, as well. Why, for instance, did it take several attempts for a group member to make her idea heard, one that ultimately proved critical to solving the challenge? Why was the person who offered that solution unwilling or unable to speak up louder and more forcefully? Why are new ideas, when introduced, so fragile? How does this all relate back to "continuous improvement"?

Other exercises then build on these ideas, helping participants to identify what behaviors would attend specific values, and what those behaviors might look or sound like in a work context. Walking the talk is more than a buzz phrase at Kodak; managing by values is a real goal.

Summary

In today's competitive work environment, excellence of product is assumed. Increasingly, what gives a company its competitive edge is its attention to the human part of the business equation. This has led business executives to focus increasingly on issues that guide and propel corporate interactions with clients and employees. Today's leading concerns involve team development, leadership, customer focus, learning organizations and values.

The art of adventure consulting is its ability to bring these concepts to light and life. Adventure learning addresses these concerns by offering activities and metaphors that precipitate behaviors that mirror interactions in the workplace. Free from fear of reprisals or work-related consequences, participants are freed to engage wholly in the activity, then to analyze the impact of individual and collective behaviors.

As architects of behavioral change, adventure consultants focus on helping groups to identify, understand and improve their purpose, process and skills. Once an effective adventure community is forged, ideas and observations fuel off each other. Whatever the particular focus of the training, the excitement engendered by and the interactive skills nurtured and practiced in this learning community become a model for transfer back to the workplace.

Three Views of the Atwells

As an adventure activity unfolds, the needs, goals and challenges of the consultant are, of course, different from that of the client. Here is an up-close view of the Atwell activity, as seen through the three-pronged lens of the adventure consultant:

Consultant: We needed an activity that would illuminate the complex issues of customer response and satisfaction. But given BMW's needs, the flow of the three-day training did not permit for a separate activity module. The challenge was to sculpt an activity that could breathe life into the practices within a retail center, yet fit in the design between other initiatives and presentations by the BMW staff. We decided to take an existing activity known as "Mastermind," which typically involves a variety of problem-solving tasks and brainteasers, and adapt it to the needs of our client. The modifications included expanding the time frame, customizing the activities to reflect car repair problems and role-playing to enhance the framing of the activity.

Throughout the activity, there was constant checking in with the BMW trainers to assess and identify what behaviors exhibited by the dealership teams needed to be addressed in the debrief. There were many factors—the dealership's relationship to the BMW organization, the current state of the dealership's operation, the commitment and motivation of that dealership's leadership to accept and adhere to Best Practices—that influenced how issues were raised and addressed in debriefs.

Trainer: From the trainer's perspective, it was a challenging activity to present because of the extended time parameters and the distractions that occurred during the course of the daily agenda. The added element of role-playing was a particular challenge, because you were required to slip in and out of the "Atwell" roles as participants approached you with questions. At those points, the task was to respond "in the relationship" and emotionally to participant behaviors—quite the inverse of the trainer's usual role.

Facilitator: Managing the closing debrief to the Atwell experience required strong facilitator skills prompted by the high level of emotion and often defensiveness that emerged. Holding up a mirror to the participants' behavior and transferring it back to the workplace challenged the facilitator to probe unsettling behaviors with their customers, manage resistance and model the appropriate sharing of observations. The activity was intended, and proceeded, to produce highly charged emotions. This further required the facilitator to use his honed ability to turn "failures" into "successes," put to use good assessment skills and feel confident in his ability to read the group accurately, and manage the range of emotions and reactions in a large group setting.

The Evolution of Corporate Adventure

3

Immersion, Adventure's signature characteristic, was on prominent display when the experiential learning movement got launched in the early days of World War II—literal immersion in the cold North Atlantic, that is.

Back then, there was a pressing need for high-intensity survival training, born of a peculiar finding: British merchant seaman in their 40s and 50s were surviving ship sinkings at a higher rate than seemingly healthier, more robust men in their 20s. Interviews with survivors identified the chief difference as the older men's prior sail training, with its exposure to wind and sea. That experience, it appeared, had left the men more self-reliant and better able to cope with the shock of a sinking ship.

To equip England's younger generation with comparable fortitude and survival skills, Kurt Hahn founded Outward Bound in 1941. Hahn, an innovative German educator who had been exploring experiential learning techniques before he fled to England to escape the Nazis, developed a one-month course that used the sea as his lab. From this wilderness base, he developed individual and group activities in small boats that worked on strengthening young sailors' courage, commitment and collaborative skills.

Three decades later, around the time that four lads from Liverpool invaded US shores, Outward Bound did the same, transported across the Atlantic by a Boston educator named Joshua Miner. While the Beatles set about revolutionizing American culture, Outward Bound set about revolutionizing American education. Though quieter, the revolution launched by Outward Bound proved more enduring.

Through the '60s, Outward Bound schools proliferated across the US. Though these early wilderness programs focused primarily on building self-esteem in troubled youths, there were also programs for adults. Most who attended the latter were educators interested in exploring the contours and wider potentialities of experiential learning.

By the mid-'80s, Outward Bound was tailoring programs to attract new audiences, including business groups. Though exciting, these courses had two built-in limitations: they required a sizable chunk of time and a wilderness setting. The challenge for others in the emergent adventure field was to develop programs that could transfer the principles of experiential learning from wilderness to facilities-based settings, and to work within the time constraints of a standard school or business day.

Hundreds of vendors, both large and small, would emerge to tackle the challenge. Of those, Project Adventure would earn and sustain a leading reputation for designing and customizing adventure experiences that could be delivered to the doorstep of the widest variety of clients: schools, therapeutic communities, recreational and civic organizations, corporate groups.

Bringing the Adventure Home

From its founding in 1971, Project Adventure has had a philosophical mission and practical commitment to "Bring the Adventure Home." After establishing roots in the early '70s in the educational sphere (primary and secondary schools, colleges, universities), Project Adventure branched out through the late '70s into the therapeutic community (drug and alcohol treatment centers, psychiatric hospitals, children's homes, juvenile detention facilities), the civic and recreational areas in the early '80s (Boy and Girl Scouts, camps, state agencies), the US corporate arena in the mid-'80s (Fortune 500 companies, small and mid-size firms) and the international market in the early '90s (companies in Africa, Asia, Australia, Europe, South America).

While adventure consultants have found multiple challenges in each of these sectors, the corporate audience, with its pressing schedules and exacting demands, has produced the adventure field's swiftest evolution in design and delivery. In rapid succession, the original singular focus on wilderness programming shifted first to fixed-site ropes courses, then to a facilities-based mix of indoor and outdoor initiatives and on to the current emphasis on portable adventure experiences that can be delivered anytime, anywhere: work sites, office buildings, conference centers.

Project Adventure's flexibility and inherent fascination with high-risk challenges has enabled us both to ride and guide these changes. Our commitment to "Bring the Adventure Home," however, extends beyond direct service to clients. From our inception, we have been uniquely dedicated to disseminating adventure education by training, coaching and empowering others to run their own adventure programs. Through our train-the-trainer programs, we reach independent trainers, who work on a contract basis, and internal trainers, who work full-time for organizations. Our programs both introduce traditional consultants to adventure techniques and augment the skills of adventure specialists.

This long history of serving as goodwill ambassadors for adventure learning prepared PA well for the direction that corporate consulting is now taking and is likely to maintain well into the next century: partnering. Before we look forward, however, let's take a quick look back at how corporate adventure got to this moment.

Highlights from a Rich History

By the late '70s, PA's innovative school-based project had been designated a model program by the US Department of Education and over 400 schools had become adopter sites. At Boston University's College of Education, faculty members Tony Langston and Jim Gillis tapped the expertise of the two PA staffers who were teaching graduate courses in adventure education to devise an adventure-based curriculum for BU business students.

In 1978, Boston University launched Executive Challenge, one of the first corporate training programs designed around adventure learning. Executive Challenge offered three-day, on-site programs that typically progressed through an increasingly complex series of trust and initiative problems. Ropes courses and flip charts were both in evidence as groups set about building team and communication skills.

The program found a ready audience in the innovative high-tech companies of the Northeast, and quickly became a leader in working with corporate clients in a nonwilderness setting. By 1980, when Boston University transferred Executive Challenge from the College of Education to its School of Management, the program had already served a wide variety of companies, among them General Foods, Merrill Lynch, Honeywell and Walt Disney World.

The impact of Executive Challenge played a visible role as increasing numbers of companies began exploring how to tailor adventure programs to meet their particular needs. Among the first such programs was one created by Jim Hassinger, a former consultant with Executive Challenge. Later, as a manager at Norton Company, a manufacturer of industrial abrasives based in Worcester, MA, Jim added an outdoor component to Norton's traditional training strategy. It was around this same period that Project Adventure began to receive requests from other consultants to assist in developing corporate programs.

PA's first serious step into the emerging corporate arena came in 1984, when the human resources group at Digital Equipment Corporation in Concord, MA, requested that we design and deliver a team-building program for a 10-person, multi-purpose work group. The three-day workshop, conducted on-site at PA headquarters in Hamilton, MA, produced enduring improvements in the group's communication, trust and confidence levels.

Encouraged by the DEC results, PA launched Executive Reach in 1985 with the aim of developing a portfolio of programs that would accommodate the full range of business interests, from small family enterprises to Fortune 500 corporations. Reflecting the times, most of the early programs focused on team-building, leadership development and improving communication skills across multiple teams.

A typical effort was the program PA delivered to Exxon Shipping in Houston in 1986, to further the aims of the company's "EXCEL" program. At the time, Exxon was grappling with the fallout from deep labor reductions. Extensive retraining and cross-training was underway for the remaining employees who were going to staff the company's new generation of high-tech supertankers. The heart of the company's problems was that the combination of new technology and stiff staff cuts had rendered the traditional top-down mode of communication and decision-making ineffective. Now that supertanker captains no longer had a working knowledge of all potential problems, much less all the answers, flexible work-team strategies were becoming essential.

"We want to provide opportunities to bring ideas forward and have upward input," John Tompkins, the EXCEL project executive, explained in an in-house newsletter. "We will be using task forces more to tackle problems or major objections and to generate ideas for management consideration. Such task forces will be cross sections of the employees in the organization."

Initially, PA delivered a one-day management training program that focused on both driving decision-making down into the system and cultivating team strategies. The effort was so well received that eventually most company employees, both seagoing and shoreside, went through a training, staffed by in-house trainers who had been trained by PA.

The Houston results were so strong that two years later PA was approached by the managing director of the Esso Singapore Refinery, Paul Revere, to develop a two-day program for the refinery operation's 500 employees. The aim was to offer a team-building workshop to a staff plagued by low productivity, low morale and a host of related personnel problems.

First, PA had to figure out how to bridge the geographic distance between Boston and Singapore, and the cultural one as well. While the tensions between the refinery's managers and union employees felt familiar, the tensions born of Singapore's unique culture and Esso Singapore's

ethnically diverse work force—Buddhist and Christian Chinese, Islamic Malays and Hindu Indians—were new to us.

Though the risk was high and PA's learning curve steep, the program proved so effective at augmenting trust, communication and effective teamwork that it was eventually presented to the entire staff of the Singaporean support center for Esso Asia-Pacific. The program also put PA at the vanguard of the consulting world's effort to introduce adventure learning to the international corporate marketplace.

Portable Adventure

Back home, the corporate market was exploding. With demand growing exponentially, the pressure was on to find ways to serve this fast-growing clientele more efficiently and more effectively. In the late '80s, Pecos River pointed the way with a strategy that made adventure more portable.

The original Pecos River Learning Center, founded in 1985 by motivational speaker Larry Wilson, was situated on a resort ranch outside of Santa Fe, NM. Wilson's initial approach was to use the site to host four-day programs that offered CEOs and human resource directors two days of ropes-course training, followed by two days of traditional classroom work that related the adventure experience and concepts back to the workplace. Each workshop involved hundreds of participants, who were moved through the stations of a challenge course by a crew of "adventure technicians."

From that base, Pecos pioneered an approach that now routinely puts adventure providers into partnership with conference centers and hotels around the country. Under this strategy, adventure providers build permanent ropes courses at existing facilities, then bring in clients for trainings. The arrangement is mutually beneficial: the facility gains both an adventure site and the clients supplied by the adventure company; the adventure provider gains an attractive site with quality accommodations to host its clients.

Today, a conservative estimate of roughly 30% of all corporate conference centers and hotels have an on-site adventure challenge course. PA alone, the world's leading provider of ropes courses, has designed and installed over 3,000 ropes courses, including many at company headquarters and training centers, as well as hotels and conference centers. This portability has left adventure consultants well-poised to help individual companies looking to strengthen performance in a fast-changing international market to address their specific needs, among them effective teamwork, leadership and customer service. It also gives adventure specialists the flexibility to pursue new approaches that may better serve emerging business needs.

Future Trends

The corporate worldwide market for adventure learning is estimated by the *Wall Street Journal* to generate about $100 million in annual revenues. That figure is likely to continue climbing well into the next century. Some of the issues that drive today's adventure programs—team development, leadership, customer service—promise to be central in the decade ahead. While attention to these fundamental needs remains constant, the context in which they play out is already shifting. Five distinct but interrelated business trends suggest that adventure consulting can be instrumental to companies' future efforts to navigate, ride and leverage rapid shifts.

- Shifting Paradigms
- Partnering
- Core Values
- Teaching Organizations
- Globalization of Adventure

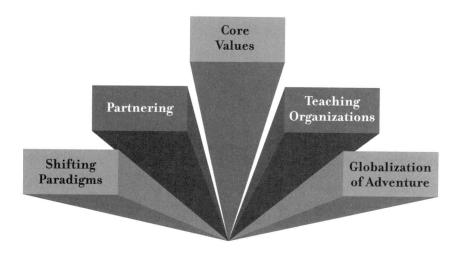

Shifting Paradigms

For almost 300 years, man's understanding of the nature of the world has been dominated by the work of Sir Isaac Newton. Mathematician, philosopher and physicist all rolled into one, Newton seemed capable of explaining just about anything. By the time he finished discovering the law of gravitation, developing calculus and dissecting the component parts of white light, he'd pretty much convinced his fellow Homo sapiens that the world operated much like a machine: it could be pulled apart, examined, understood, then predicted, directed and controlled. Under this construct, effect followed cause in a linear, rational manner.

In recent decades, that paradigm has gradually shifted to allow for a more subtle, less reductionist understanding of the natural forces that surround, affect and embrace us. As talk of chaos, synchronicity, flow and alignment has entered the popular vernacular, society has shifted to a greater appreciation of the complexity and interrelationship of individuals, systems and forces. Interestingly, this theoretical shift has been most steadily explored and most readily embraced not by academicians and educators, but by business leaders and management consultants.

Under this new construct, the emphasis has shifted from predicting and controlling to harnessing and expanding. It has shifted, in other words, from a static state of *being* to a dynamic process of *becoming*. Correspondingly, the skills that speak to synergy—communication, collaboration, systems thinking, teamwork, continual learning—have achieved prominence. If sweat was the currency of the world-as-machine view, ideas are the currency of this new paradigm, which regards the world as a living system that is always growing and changing.

Adventure is well-suited to address the business needs emerging from this new paradigm. With its open-ended approach to learning and outcomes, and its holistic melding of mind, body and emotions, the adventure methodology meshes comfortably with the new corporate emphasis on continual learning and perpetual re-creation.

Partnering

The same financial pressures that gave rise to downsizing, belt-tightening and merging have more recently produced outsourcing. Today, businesses of all sizes parcel out work that was formerly handled in-house by full-time employees.

When companies contract out work in the training and human resource areas, the strategies are many. An executive hires a consultant to assume full responsibility for the design and delivery of a training program; yet the executive may also want to play a central role in delivering the program. The executive may choose to divide the pieces of a training among various consulting groups in order to bring different strengths to the program (which may have been designed entirely in-house, in tandem with one consultant, or collaboratively with a variety of consultants); or she may choose to rely upon the skills of one consultant for the design, but want the company's internal trainers to handle delivery (either solo or collaboratively with the consulting company's trainers).

In short, the emphasis these days is on partnering. Companies are less inclined to sign on to the "expert" model, where consultants ride in and provide fixed solutions, then ride back out. Instead, savvy companies are looking for creative ways to satisfy their training and consulting needs. Many of the solutions, such as insourcing, co-sourcing, share-sourcing and strategic sourcing, rely on partnerships or alliances that demand a synergistic mindset and collaborative skills.

Consultants increasingly need the ability to work in partnership not only with clients, but with other consultants as well. Optimal effectiveness requires an understanding of and familiarity with the particular strengths, expertise and tools that each consulting approach (organization development, process, adventure, etc.) brings to program design and delivery.

As a direct outgrowth of our extensive background in training consultants, including our colleagues in the adventure field, Project Adventure came to corporate partnering early. Over the last decade we have delivered programs in any number of configurations, among them: serving as the primary vehicle for change by designing and delivering entire corporate programs; acting in the service of someone else's design; leading a design where we've enlisted the services of other consultants; co-designing and co-delivering full programs with in-house training staffs; designing around other consultants' design needs; providing a mood-setting opening stage-setter, then stepping out of the way; designing a program, then training a company's internal staff to deliver the program.

All of this makes clear that clients' needs increasingly require a versatility from both consultants who are external and those who are in-house. The potential for what may result from this evolving synergy is as exciting as the challenge is steep.

Core Values

In today's demanding business environment, it is no longer enough for a consultant to be able to shift fluidly between the roles of adviser and diplomat, facilitator and confidant. Increasingly, he must also be able to show that he is attentive to and in alignment with the client's core values.

At Starbucks, with whom PA has collaborated on several trainings since 1996, CEO Howard Schultz asserts that he won't hire anyone in whom he perceives "a mismatch or vacuum where values should be." He includes in that statement such external partners as investment bankers and consultants. "Much can be gained," he maintains, "by enlisting partners and colleagues who are committed to the same goals" (Schultz, 1997).

While Starbucks has been a pioneer in championing a values-driven corporate culture, it is hardly alone. Many industry giants, including Eastman Kodak Company, Levi-Strauss and Symantec Corporation, have made a commitment to identifying core values, then creating a shared understanding of those values among employees. Some of these efforts have received so much attention and achieved such promising results that corporate "values" programs may well drive management efforts in the decade ahead.

Acknowledged or not, values are the conceptual organizer around which enterprises form and operate. "Organizations are value systems," writes Peter Vail (1995). "They are relatively stable expressions of human priorities...of what people want and don't want, value and don't value, attach meaning to and don't attach meaning to." An organization's success, maintains Dee Hock, has "more to do with clarity of a shared purpose, common principles and strength of belief in them than with assets, expertise, operating ability, or management competence" ("Writings for the Chaordic Alliance," The Systems Thinking Action Conference).

Though the new corporate emphasis on values seemed radical when it first emerged in the early '90s, it actually is a return to a very old theme. Back in the days when the economy was agriculturally based and people worked close to home, personal values and work values were so closely linked that people tended to invest their entire selves—hands, head and heart—in their work. It was only as the Industrial Revolution took hold that workers were essentially told to leave their brains and passion at home, and bring only their hands to work. In exchange for blind loyalty and passive compliance, workers got lifelong job security.

The competitive pressures of the global economy that dawned after World War II provoked a rethink. Management experts like W. Edwards Deming began to promote the notion that those closest to the product could provide some of the most creative and innovative ideas. Now, workers were expected to bring their heads, as well as hands, to work.

The bumpy transition into the Information Age, with its layoffs and belt-tightenings, mergers and buy-outs, forced another reevaluation. As malaise, insecurity and flagging loyalty permeated corporate cultures around the globe, employers came to perceive workers' character and commitment as essential to high performance and a sustained competitive edge. Today, employers want workers to bring hands, heads and hearts to work.

Employees want to feel passionate about their work. "The organizations that people love to be in are ones that have a sense of history, identity and purpose," notes Margaret Wheatley. "These are things that people want to work for" (Wheatley, 1997). Optimally, such passion means that workers invest the best of themselves in their work.

Too often, though, workers' enthusiasm is smothered beneath layers of procedures, rules and roles. A primary challenge for today's corporation is to revive and renew the spirit that fosters commitment to and excitement about work. Increasingly, the avenue of choice is a values curriculum.

Adventure consulting is pioneering the way with programs that address the various stages of values development. The introspective qualities of adventure provide a good starting point for helping executives and employees to identify, articulate and clarify values. The interactive qualities of adventure help to breathe life into those values so that people can see how they play out in a work setting. None of this is a singular event. Corporations that lead with their values know that close attention to values is a continuing and evolving process.

Teaching Organizations

In a recent *Training & Development* article, Noel Tichy and Eli Cohen, both of the University of Michigan Graduate School of Business Administration, assert that learning organizations have been surpassed by a new model: teaching organizations. "Teaching organizations," they state, "are more agile, come up with better strategies, and are able to implement them more effectively" (*ASTD*, July 1998).

Within teaching organizations, the emphasis is on developing leaders throughout the corporate ranks. Adventure offers an enticing and legitimate approach for such transfers of learning. It helps to create a playing field where all participants have an opportunity to exercise leadership, regardless of their standing in the hierarchy. Learning from each other and the pooling of knowledge capital and resources are crucial to achieving success.

Innovative teaching methods are being pursued across the country. At Walt Disney World, a manager of one of the park's premium restaurants takes a new dishwasher through a unique training experience. On the employee's first day, the manager places him in front of an actual place setting. When the employee seems distracted, the manager asks, "What's wrong?" The hiree points out that a glass had lipstick stains, the dishes had crusts of food on the rims and the silverware was spotted.

"Imagine," says the manager, "that you are a guest who will spend $100 for that meal."

Why this immersion approach? Grasping Disney CEO Michael Eisner's message that Disney World is driven by an "emotional engine" rather than an "economic engine," the restaurant manager aims to immerse his new employees in the "guest experience" before addressing any job's specific tasks (*ASTD*, July 1998).

By offering unique experiences with their products, organizations are helping employees to see their roles in a whole new way. In the case of Disney, the employee experiences the product from the customer's point of view, rather than as a dishwasher. Using the organization's product as a teaching tool can be a highly effective way to design an adventure program and models for the organization strategies for viewing their product as a learning opportunity. In pioneering a three-day program, co-designed and co-delivered by Project Adventure and BMW of North America, consultants took the nation's 350 BMW retail center owners to a designated paved area often referred to as the "tarmac" for a series of adventure initiatives that gave new meaning both to putting the client in the driver's seat and to bringing the adventure home. The leading twin goals of the training were to explore the importance and dimensions of leadership and to strengthen the partnership between retailers and corporate executives through discussion and commitment to a consistent set of business practices.

From a design standpoint, the design team wanted to provide an immersion experience with the product that the retailers dealt with daily, yet remove them from their usual frame of reference. BMW NA wanted the program design to showcase the product's special features, among them interior ergonomics, responsive braking and turning dynamics. For both partners in this training collaboration, there was the need to ensure safety, since we would be out on a tarmac where there would be many moving vehicles. And, of course, the training's main issues and goals needed to be met.

The resulting design incorporated a number of challenges that achieved all of the above. Through most of the tarmac activities, the retailers were divided into four-member teams to navigate BMWs through tight patterns of cones.

In one exercise, four people were assigned to a 528i vehicle and served in the driver or front-seat and back-seat passenger roles. In one instance, the driver was blindfolded and had to rely on verbal instruction from his three teammates to navigate the course. In another, the front-seat passenger, from a position of obstructed vision, steered the wheel, while the driver worked the foot pedals and the back-seat passengers gave directions. In a third, a filled champagne glass was placed on the car roof, and the passengers had to alert the driver to all potential bumps and cones that might jar the fluid as he steered the car. While this particular exercise dramatized the importance of clear communications, teamwork and strategy, it also cast light on how leadership might be defined in the retail environment—illuminating the fact that the designated "drivers" might not necessarily always be the "leaders" in particular situations.

Such tarmac initiatives sought to connect leadership behaviors to the fundamentals and unique qualities of the product itself. If leadership excellence is about unleashing creativity and capturing and implementing ideas whenever and wherever they occur, then teaching organizations will be on the constant lookout for innovative approaches that unleash creativity and energy. Adventure is one such tool.

Globalization of Adventure

The globalization of the world economy has meant the internationalization of management and training techniques. Both American and international companies are working to adapt the trends, programs and services of other cultures to their own. Adventure consulting is among those tools that has effectively crossed the geographical and cultural boundaries to help organizations profit from global opportunities.

Singapore offers an instructive illustration of how other countries are taking adventure programming and tailoring it to domestic needs. In a parallel of the US experience, adventure in Singapore began with Outward Bound's wilderness programs. PA's work with Esso Singapore then offered a new possibility that intrigued the country's business leaders, while PA's donation of a challenge ropes course to the local Boy Scout Camp whetted the appetite of civic groups for adventure activities.

Today, Singapore is a hotbed of adventure learning. Beyond the corporate trainings offered by a variety of adventure providers, the Singapore Association of Training and Development (STADA) has developed a $2 million branch that provides adventure training to Singapore-based corporations, including Singapore Airlines and Compaq Computer. The Singapore Outward Bound School now offers a multifaceted adventure curriculum that features a large Challenge Ropes Course as well as more traditional wilderness programming, and serves corporate as well as community audiences.

The government is now an enthusiastic booster of adventure education for the community in general, and for Singapore's youth in particular. Officials

see adventure programming as an effective way to tackle the *kia soo* phenomenon. Kia soo, a Chinese phrase that means "afraid to fail," describes the too conservative attitude of the newly affluent classes of Singapore. Concerned that entrepreneurism won't flourish in a kia soo environment, Singapore's officials have embraced adventure as a means of fostering a bolder attitude toward risk-taking.

Today, Singapore, Japan and Taiwan are among the pioneers of corporate adventure in Asia. The adventure consulting happening in these countries shows the facileness of the I.M.M.E.R.S.I.O.N. approach for creating learning in a wide variety of cultures. The trend is for more and more global collaboration. Adventure consulting offers tools to make that collaboration a reality.

Summary

From its inception in the late '70s, corporate adventure has evolved in directions that are responsive to the ever-changing needs and demands of the international marketplace. Along the way, adventure training has shifted from one-size-fits-all designs, offered in limited numbers of venues, to custom-tailored designs whose portability enables the consultant to bring services to the client. As venue locations have multiplied, adventure programming has diversified to address an ever-expanding and ever-shifting menu of needs.

In the decade ahead, five trends can be anticipated that will inform both clients' needs and consultants' practices:

- a process-oriented paradigm that recognizes change as a constant and synergy as a requirement;

- a partnering approach that requires clients and consultants, both internal and external to companies, to work collaboratively;

- an approach that revolves around the identification, elucidation and practice of core values;

- a marketplace dominated by teaching organizations;

- a continuing spread of adventure techniques that will affect how business is conducted internationally.

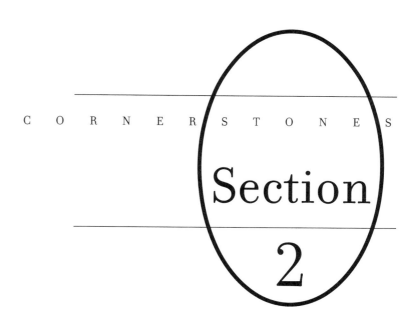

Section

2

CHALLENGES # 2

Word Boxes

> Using every space, fill in both lines of horizontal boxes
> with a key concept described in this text.

The letters to the right are all that is needed to complete
each line. A black space in the line means no letter.

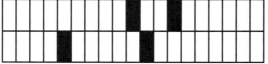

YHLNGEOILCCBACEEH

TTUUELLFLAAVNRCCO

Letter Equations

> Each problem is an "equation" that can be solved by
> substituting the appropriate words for the letters.
> EXAMPLE: 26 = L. in the A. (26 = Letters in the Alphabet)

1) E. + R. + G. + T. = F. S. of E.L.C.
2) C. + C. + C. + C. + C. = F. C.'s of T.
3) P.A. + B.P. + S.Y.T. = T. of the F.V.C.
4) C.B.C. = The R. to C. – W. and at W. L. to P.

How Many F's?

> Excluding this question, how many
> F's are included in this one activity?

THE FULL VALUE CONTRACT IS THE RESULT OF
YEARS OF CREATIVE THINKING COMBINED WITH
THE EXPERIENCE OF WORKING WITH GROUPS

The adventure experience, as approached by Project Adventure consultants, has three theoretical cornerstones: the Experiential Learning Cycle, the Full Value Contract and Challenge by Choice. These three operating norms, which guide and inform all interactions in a PA learning community, provide the foundation for creating an environment within which people feel safe to leave their comfort zones and take risks that are variously intellectual, physical and emotional in nature.

The first of these foundations, the Experiential Learning Cycle, has a rich history, both in theoretical literature and in practical application. Its four-phase cycle—experience, reflection, generalization, transfer—provides a framework for moving fluidly from a concrete activity to processing the learnings from that experience to new activities that reinforce and deepen insights and learnings.

The Full Value Contract attends to the relationships within a training group. It establishes norms that respect the integrity, diversity and strength of individuals, and support the collective effort of the group. Its primary tenets speak directly to issues of emotional and physical safety, and help to ensure that each group member has the opportunity to learn. Implicitly, the tenets address the issue of trust, an ingredient critical to the construction and maintenance of an effective learning community.

Challenge by Choice, like the Full Value Contract, is a Project Adventure contribution to the field of adventure learning. This foundation attends primarily to the individual, encouraging risk-taking that will promote personal growth and learning. Its tenets also work on building collective trust by heightening awareness and respect for others' needs, ideas and choices.

These three guiding constructs, which are intentionally and consistently integrated throughout the adventure experience, are matched with traditional consulting techniques and tools to create a unique consulting approach that specializes in triggering meaningful and enduring behavioral change in the corporate community.

4 The Experiential Learning Cycle

E xperiential learning is learning by *doing*. It is the way humans learn best. As an ancient Chinese proverb eloquently and succinctly notes: "What I hear I forget; what I see I remember; what I do I understand."

"Texts and lectures are actually recent developments, relative to the long history of humankind. Up until about 150 years ago, most education was experiential in nature, relying on apprenticeships and on-the-job training in guilds to transmit information from one generation to the next."

—*Henry Ford, The Henry Ford Museum*

Today, biologists and neuropsychologists argue that humans are "hard-wired" to learn this way. It has been estimated that while we remember only 20% of what we hear and 50% of what we see, that we retain fully 80% of what we do. As a result, there is great momentum for understanding the nature and power of experiential education, and how it can make use of the way the human nervous system is wired to learn.

The bedrock of all Project Adventure programs is the Experiential Learning Cycle (ELC). Based on four-phase theoretical models developed by educators over half a century, from John Dewey's work in the 1930s to David Kolb's in the '70s and '80s, the four-phase Experiential Learning Cycle provides a foundation for developing learning situations that emphasize experience, reflection, generalization and transfer.

During this cycle, activities flow from hands-on initiatives to a processing that engages the mind, and often the emotions as well. A well-structured debrief mines for insights and learnings that can then be transferred to the next activity—and back to the workplace.

Intuitively, this process makes sense. Activity-based experiences have greater sticking power than traditional-style trainings where participants sit and receive information via lecture, overhead and video. Think about it. Which do you remember better? The first time you cracked open a driver's manual—or the first time you turned the key in the ignition, shifted from park to drive and accelerated?

Before tackling the theoretical research that undergirds the experiential style of learning, let's first take a look at how the ELC process actually works. To illustrate the four phases of the continuous Experiential Learning Cycle, we'll use a popular adventure activity called "Corporate Connection," in this instance tailored by PA for a group of automotive retail operators.

Experience

A group of as few as 20 and as many as 50 is subdivided into four groups and dispatched to the four corners of a room. Each group is given a bag filled with a dozen foam balls of a single color. In the center of the floor are eight containers, two each marked with a color that corresponds to the respective team's balls.

"Each of the four groups represents a different area of a retail operation," the trainer explains. "As experts in your respective areas, your primary goal is to leverage as many successful customer connections as possible for the whole operation in the time allotted. As is true in any business operation, each area delivers services to its own group of customers—both internal and external. It is these customer connections, represented by these different colored foam balls, that matter.

"Every time a ball successfully enters a can matching its color, it represents a successful customer connection. Those that land in the corresponding bucket placed closest to a team are worth 10 points each; those that land in the basket placed farther away are worth 20. Any ball that lands in another team's container has no point value. Each team is responsible for getting its balls into the appropriate cans. Finally, I'd like to ask each group to please designate a leader and meet me outside."

As they select a leader, the groups react spontaneously and begin to show their particular character. Some stand and exchange ideas, brainstorming on possible strategies. Some immediately begin throwing the balls, wanting to get in quick practice time. Others stand looking amused or baffled or

skeptical. Occasionally, someone will think to ask the sort of question that proves pertinent to maximized performance. Invariably, such suggestions get lost in the din.

During a brief "leadership summit," the four designated leaders are told, "You are responsible and accountable for the overall success of the whole operation, and for your own area's performance. As the designated leaders, you have the ability to call a leadership summit at any time in order to confer for up to three minutes."

(It's amazing how focused a person can become when she is selected by a team to serve as the leader. The most disengaged or reluctant participant can begin to feel responsible for the team's performance and the activity's outcome. Even in play—particularly in front of colleagues—the role of designated leader, and all that it implies, carries weight.)

More rules are laid out. Among them, the teams learn that a ball must bounce at least once before entering a container (to ensure safety). They also learn that they can designate members as retrievers, to fetch misfired balls and throw them back to the other team members for another try. Then the first round, which lasts two minutes, begins.

In the ensuing chaos, balls whiz, voices yell, excitement builds—and scores are usually disappointingly low. The teams are allotted five minutes of discussion and planning. Then comes Round 2. This time, the teams learn they can designate members as backboards, separate from retrievers, to assist getting the balls into the buckets. Another five minutes of planning, then the final Round 3. Between the first and last rounds, each team's score multiplies three-fold to 100% success.

Why? Because along the way, in the hail of balls and "leadership summits," the teams come to see that collaboration and cooperation serve their needs and interests more effectively than isolation and competition. As they realize that the rules don't bar cooperation, they will exchange balls so that the team nearest to another team's distant containers can easily score those baskets. In the end, a collective effort will serve the needs of both the individual teams and the umbrella retail organization.

Reflection

This phase, which asks, "What happened?," presents an opportunity to explore what just transpired, both collectively and individually. Although some groups may immediately make the leap to insights that can be applied back to the workplace, the natural tendency for most groups is to review what the group just accomplished, in effect replaying the sequence of events that unfolded. Sharing such perceptions gives participants a chance to recap their actions and feelings. This reflective stage paves the way for illuminating the differing views and perceptions that participants may have of the experience, and augments the chance to capture deeper insights and learnings.

So, in this adaptation of Corporate Connection, the sequence is reviewed to examine the leadership characteristics which led to the intermediary steps that enabled the groups to triple their scores. When the activity is cast in this light, the debriefing questions tend toward: What captured your attention as a leader? Was your primary focus on people, seeking broad participation and relating to others? Or were you more focused on task accomplishment, wanting to meet the challenge head-on and get immediate results? When it came to strategizing, were you more inclined to listen to others and analyze their opinions, or follow your own internal instincts and barometer? How did you regard and respond to your leader's style?

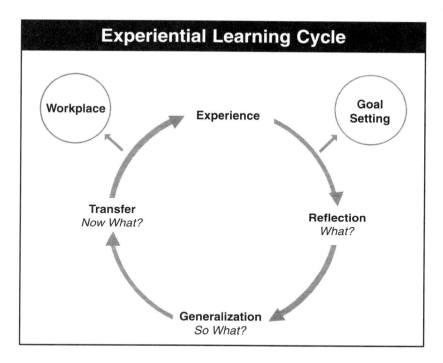

Generalization

The third phase of the Experiential Learning Cycle asks, "So what?" as it examines abstract concepts and makes connections between ideas and experience. Here, the group looks at the meaning of the experience and searches for patterns that emerged during the successive rounds of the activity.

In the Corporate Connection example, participants tend to conclude quickly that their efforts improved exponentially after they stopped to brainstorm and share ideas. As discussion deepens, the facilitator probes such questions as: If your primary focus was on relating to people, how were you able to balance the challenge of task accomplishment and tending effectively to your people? If your focus was task-oriented, how did you keep people interested and involved? If you were an expert, how did it feel when your ideas weren't heard? What types of relationships evolved between the four areas of the retail operation? As leaders, why was the first impulse to adopt a competitive stance? What factors changed to promote cooperation? How did it feel to be involved in a collaborative effort?

Transfer

In this phase, the question is, "Now what?" As participants connect the exercise back to the workplace, they mine for insights that might be useful on the job. Because of the nonthreatening environment and the activity's remove from the actual workplace, participants often feel comfortable enough to address issues of leadership performance and group dynamics more openly and honestly than they might in a work context.

As the Corporate Connection "dealers" explore the advantages and drawbacks of their particular leadership tendencies and styles, they often speak to such issues as their overall impact on their retail operation's performance, the challenges of promoting collaboration and the obstacles they face in building trust.

Depending on the level of openness and trust in the room, a facilitator may guide the conversation toward such questions as: If your leadership tendency is to focus on doing whatever it takes to accomplish a goal, what strategies allow you simultaneously to accept mistakes when they occur and learn from them? Do you tend to assume a competitive posture? If so, how does it impact your culture? Does it, in the long run, impede or enhance overall performance in your retail operation?

For participants to increase the chance of retaining the insights from this experience, the learnings need to be applied to a new experience—the sooner the better. Depending on the overarching goal of the particular training, a leadership inventory might follow, or another activity that deepens awareness and appreciation of various leadership characteristics and their impact on teamwork.

That's the beauty of the Experiential Learning Cycle. Experience follows learnings follows experience follows . . . Moreover, research supports that learning can begin in any one of the four quadrants in the cycle. This is a particular advantage from a design perspective, as all program experiences do not begin with activity. Designs may be launched at the "reflective" stage of the cycle, if, for example, a goal-setting component is used to build on the *workplace* experience and provide further structure for the program the group is about to embark on. Conversely, lunchtime discussion of a morning activity may point towards re-engaging participants in the "generalization" phase of the cycle.

Framing the Experience

The ELC process tends to be most vivid and effective when an activity is tailored to grab the attention and interest of a specific audience. Such framing goes beyond helping the group to focus on an activity and understand, even visualize, the series of events that are about to transpire. It establishes a context that speaks to the group's communal interest, enhances its relevance and meaning and joins them in a common effort, if not (yet) common cause.

With corporate groups, context is particularly critical if they are to begin making the connections that will enable them to first open themselves to the experience, then transfer the learnings back to the workplace. A skillful introduction can frame the activity to speak to a group's own work experience, conjuring a metaphorical fantasy that summons the actual work environment, with its inherent tensions, challenges, even conflicts.

A believable and vivid scenario is not only a powerful tool for breaking through resistance to promote active participation. Research indicates that when "isomorphic" connections are made, seemingly disparate elements can be linked to produce change (Gass, 1985). Thus, skillful linkage of the adventure experience to the workplace can foster real change back at work.

A skillful framing also positions the activity to speak to, support and advance the larger aims of a training. In the example above, Corporate Connection unfolded in a context where the client's overriding training aim was to promote a greater awareness of leadership tendencies and characteristics.

Suppose, instead, the client's aim had been to heighten awareness and appreciation of the benefits of interdepartmental cooperation. Material leading up to the activity might have included an exploration of the correlation between the Employee Satisfaction Index (ESI) and the Customer Satisfaction Index (CSI). When the group was divided into four teams, they might have been designated sales, service, parts and administrative. In defining the "customer connection," attention could have been called to the Customer–Supplier chain, along which work is not only handed off from department to department, but employees become both customer and supplier to one another.

In the debriefing, the accent would have been on interdependence: What benefits emerged from a unified and cooperative approach? What transpired to allow you to view each other as customers and suppliers to one another, and therefore to build an environment more focused on internal customers? In your own work, do you have more internal customers or external? What factors prevent this kind of cooperation at work? What would it take to create a similar level of interdependence in the workplace and view each other as real customers to one another?

Alternately, an intradepartmental focus might shift the design to speak of four production teams, each intent on continuous improvement. The gains from round to round would be explored through a lens of incremental and sustained improvement. Does your team feel successful? What factors contributed to success? Where were the barriers? How did communications flow between team members? How often did the team review strategy, and how effective was this process? What strengths did team members demonstrate in their collective approach to problem-solving? What weaknesses or areas for improvement?

Whatever the goals of a particular training, the use of appropriate language, images and concepts can capture people's attention and set their mental wheels spinning. Such details go a long way toward building a mood of engagement, expectation, even excitement.

It is not coincidental that this vital preliminary to an activity is called the briefing. The term, deliberately lifted by the adventure field from the military, implies excitement. It has a here-and-now orientation that is intended to galvanize attention and starts the process of building the momentum that will carry participants through all phases of the ELC.

Theoretical Underpinnings of I.M.M.E.R.S.I.O.N.

Time and again, adventure experiences have shown that once the imagination is engaged, concentration, participation and involvement—in a word, immersion—follow. Brain research strongly suggests that when people are thus interested and engaged, they shift into a state of "relaxed alertness" (Caine & Caine, 1991), the optimal state of mind for meaningful learning.

Before returning to this concept in greater depth, let's train an I.M.M.E.R.S.I.O.N. lens on the main theoretical work that undergirds the qualities of adventure learning. This is by no means a comprehensive survey; rather, it is a quick canvas to give a broad theoretical context to the adventure experience. (As W. Edwards Deming, the grandfather of quality management, used to say, "No theory, no learning.")

INTERACTIVE. In order for people to change, they need to be active participants in the process. Through goal-setting and opportunities for testing new behaviors and theories in real situations, people are able to grow and learn (Lewin, 1951).

Experiential learning not only opens the door to the range of abilities and strengths that participants bring to an activity. It requires them to use a variety of the seven intelligences identified by researchers (Gardner, 1990; Armstrong, 1994), among them linguistic, bodily, interpersonal and intrapersonal intelligences.

Adventure activities also draw them into a collaboration and reciprocity that requires a give and take with others (Noddings, 1992). It's easy to see this reciprocity in the dialogue, brainstorming and building of the sort of collective intelligence that fuels a "learning organization."

MEANINGFUL. Meaning happens at a very individual level. We can see the making of meaning happening—it's the moment you "get it," when pieces fit together and you exclaim, "Aha!" The search for meaning refers to making sense of our experience. Our brain is constantly searching for meaning—for a place to file experiences and connect new information with old. Absent meaning, experiences do not register because we have no place to mentally file them.

"At its core," write Caine and Caine, "the search for meaning is purpose and value driven." That is, in order for a new experience to make sense to us, it must have a purpose, it must have value. And for that to happen, we need to personally connect the information we are discovering to information we already have. Caine and Caine refer to this connection process as "active processing"—a consolidation and internalization of information in a way that is personally meaningful. This process, fueled by constant questioning, probing and searching for broad implications, must be a constant and integral part of the adventure activity.

MIRTHFUL. Norman Cousins examines the curative power of laughter in his description of laughter's role in his own recovery from a life-threatening illness (Cousins, 1979). Cousins cites more distant antecedents to this belief, noting Freud's fascination with humor as a reliever of tension. According to Cousins, laughter is one of the organism's intrinsic mechanisms for fighting stress and restoring the balance between body and mind required for good health. The laughter and fun in adventure experiences open us up to see the many meaningful connections between our work and this adventure.

EXPERIENTIAL. Several theorists have built upon a four-phase model that flows in a circle from activity to analysis, abstraction to application (Dewey, 1938; Kolb, 1984; Joplin, 1986). Fundamental to each of these models is the aspect of hands-on activities, followed by a metacognitive phase or a purposeful pause to think about the learning that has just taken place. The cycle, in other words, not only fosters participation, but encourages participants to step outside of the activity and look at both the experience and their roles in it.

The cycle also mirrors many of the corporate "quality cycles" spawned by the pioneering work of Deming, whose efforts in Japan after World War II would eventually revolutionize corporate America. Like those cycles, ELC emphasizes "continuous improvement" in both individual and group performance through the learning that comes from constant and close scrutiny.

Research into "peak experiences" also supports the power of immersion experiences. After interviewing people who had excelled in activities demanding intense challenges and involvement, Mihaly Csikszentmihayli coined the term "flow state" to describe the mental characteristics common to the experiences of individuals in his sample group (Csikszentmihayli, 1975). They included a merging of action and awareness; a centering of attention on a limited stimulus field; a loss of self-consciousness and transcendence of individuality. The design of many adventure programs includes opportunities for people to work towards and experience their own "peak experiences." Through careful and logical sequencing, the experience will often result in individuals and groups experiencing a flow state.

RISKY. Whether the risks involved in an adventure experience are perceived or actual, the activity is commonly tailored to evoke a stress response. That may sound odd, but according to Dr. Hans Selye, an appropriate set of challenging activities, accompanied by a positive attitude, promotes "good" stress, or "eustress" (Selye, 1978). Selye believes that much of the chronic negative stress, or "distress," of daily life results from a lack of enough appropriate challenge. Research by Dr. Sol Roy Rosenthal goes further, positing that risk activities simulate the release of norepinephrine, a brain chemical that affects the adrenals. Rosenthal draws a fascinating link between a lack of regular risk activities and the widespread incidence of depression.

SUPPORTIVE. "People discover that the best systemic insights don't get translated into action," writes Peter Senge, "when people don't trust one another and cannot build genuinely shared aspirations and mental models" (Senge, 1990).

The dialoguing and team learning popularized by Senge is also stressed by Stephen Covey, who speaks of a maturity continuum that moves from dependence to independence to interdependence. This last he defines as "the paradigm of *we*—*we* can do it; *we* can cooperate; *we* can combine our talents and abilities and create something greater together" (Covey, 1989). Adventure encourages groups to work and learn together, believing there is more power in the experience when multiple individuals contribute and develop collective learnings.

INTROSPECTIVE. The Experiential Learning Cycle supports research that shows there are different "ways of knowing" (Belenky et al., 1986). This literature, which concentrates on the process of learning, traces how a person initially relies on authority as the source of knowledge, then learns to listen to the inner voice and the voice of one's own experience to construct new knowledge. The ability to apply one's own reasoning powers, and a growing confidence in one's ability to develop ideas and reshape experience into an integrated whole, parallel the cyclic model of experiential learning.

OUT-OF-THE-BOX. "Because of the unknown and unfamiliar quality of the challenges," John Luckner and Reldan S. Nadler write about the experiential learning environment, "participants are put into a state of disequilibrium or disorder. They are stripped of their normal status, roles and defenses. Prior experience isn't as relevant in this environment. This creates a pure learning environment as the group has to self organize around the challenge."

That state of disequilibrium applies to and benefits the individual, as well as the group. "Only by venturing into the unknown do we enable new ideas to take shape," notes Margaret Wheatley (1992). Moments of meaning, according to Karl Pribram, are often preceded by periods of uncertainty and ambiguity, which he calls "active uncertainty," during which information and parts of the self are being rearranged, enlarged and reorganized (Pribram, 1987). This dovetails with the scientific theory of self-organization which demonstrates that states of disequilibrium are frequently followed by a spontaneous shift into a higher degree of orderliness (Prigogine & Stengers, 1984). The "unknown" aspect of adventure activities provide participants with an environment that encourages innovation and re-thinking of existing processes.

NATURAL. In their groundbreaking work on "meaningful learning," Geoffrey Caine and Renate Nummela Caine make a distinction between two potential emotional responses to a learning situation: "downshifting" and "relaxed alertness." We downshift when we are feeling threatened, when we believe the situation has no relevancy or connection for us. We are able to remain relaxed and alert when what we are learning is connected in a meaningful way to what we know and experience.

The distinction between downshifting and relaxed alertness is critical to understanding adventure learning. Caine and Caine define downshifting as a "psychophysiological response to perceived threat accompanied by a sense of helplessness and lack of self-efficacy. In addition, downshifting often accompanies fatigue." They found that people revert to old beliefs and behaviors when they are in a downshift mode, no matter what new information may be forthcoming. "Our responses become more automatic and limited," they note. "We are less able to access all that we know or see what is really there."

The term downshifting is used because physiologically, it utilizes the lower half of the brain. This lower brain is also responsible for the primitive behaviors associated with fight or flight. In a downshifted state, a person has difficulty absorbing and learning new material, and is obstructed from addressing and generating solutions to problems.

In a work context, downshifting happens when people cannot see meaningful connections between new behaviors, practices or structures and the work they do. Because they have not been able to make these critical connections, the employees downshift—typically reverting to a set of routines and behaviors that, though comfortably familiar, may be inappropriate when confronted by new circumstances. Because they do not understand the new opportunities, people procrastinate and avoid risk, ambiguity and uncertainty, all conditions essential to high-level thinking.

The converse of downshifting is "relaxed alertness," which Caine and Caine define as the state during which a person makes "maximum connections in the brain." To achieve this state, they say, "people need to feel safe and be deeply engaged." Toward that end, they identify the following conditions as critical: open-ended outcomes, which invite several possible solutions; maximized personal meaning; accommodation of individuals' styles and experiences; appropriate pacing that presents challenging tasks in manageable chunks; an emphasis on cooperation and creativity (Caine & Caine, 1997).

I.M.M.E.R.S.I.O.N. in an adventure experience promotes this highly desirable state. Indeed, adventure activities speak directly to those very goals: fostering open outcomes, maximizing personal meaning, appreciating individual contributions, optimizing challenges, promoting collaboration.

Field of Trust

At the heart of the Experiential Learning Cycle lie considerations of trust. While trust is not the only component required for effective group performance, it may well be the element most critical for developing not only a successful training experience, but a high-performance team, work group or organization.

It is not hard to envision trust as an invisible field, much like an electrical or magnetic field. Often when you enter a room, you can actually feel the intensity of the trust field enveloping a particular group. If the field of trust is weak, downshifting occurs. When the trust field is strong, relaxed alertness sets in, promoting open and creative thinking and interactions.

Trust, of course, is not an absolute state. It is a relative state that, like a wave, rises and crests and always has potential for becoming stronger, more pervasive, more influential. Teams, groups and organizations that have a desire to strengthen their performance benefit from an opportunity to experience what it feels like to create and perform within a trusting environment. Once people experience the dynamic quality of trust, the possibility emerges for recreating a trust-filled environment back in the workplace.

The Experiential Learning Cycle is designed to foster, nurture and strengthen an environment of trust. As the adventure consultant sets about building a learning community that is attuned to differing individual behavioral styles, accepting of consequences and supportive of behavioral change, trust evolves through an interactive learning process.

Often, the adventure consultant's behavior sets the tone by modeling the trust process. All along the way, he interacts and designs consciously and deliberately to build trust on many levels. This holds true from the consultant's first interactions with a new client, where the building of a collaborative partnership hinges on the forging of a strong trust, to the facilitator's parting message to a group.

In the training environment, every word, action and interaction must be viewed through the lens of building trust. Many adventure consultants favor exposing participants to ELC theory early in the training experience. This both provides participants with a conceptual framework and acknowledges that the adventure format may be unfamiliar and outside the normal comfort zone. By making the approach and process transparent, adventure consultants are striving to project themselves, their organizations and the industry as forthright and open. Additionally, most adventure consultants are more eager to share than mystify their particular brand of expertise.

This approach also stresses that all activities are doable and achievable, with multiple outcomes. The emphasis is on encouraging participants to relax, to "trust the process" (see box), to know that they always have the power to draw the line and say, "This is where I step aside." These messages are further reinforced by positive behavioral guidelines designed to allow for individual choice within a caring and accepting environment that challenges participants to grow. (See Chapters 5 and 6.)

Activities are then orchestrated that encourage active involvement by all members of the group. Thus engaged, concerns relative to trust within the group quickly begin to emerge. Almost immediately, participants make decisions about how much they are willing to risk to try an activity, how much they trust others to support their physical efforts, how much they trust the unfamiliar process, how much they trust speaking up, and so forth. Removed from their comfort zones, with their prescribed routines and behaviors, participants are now ready to engage, explore—and immerse in the adventure learning process.

Summary

Of the many paths that lead to knowledge, *doing* is the route that leaves the most vivid and enduring impression. The Experiential Learning Cycle that anchors adventure experiences engages participants in a dynamic process that moves cyclically from doing to reflection to generalization to transfer. This four-phase cycle, which heightens self- and group-awareness, appreciates that activity without reflection is just activity; reflection without generalization is isolated and nontransferable; generalization without transfer is not lasting; transfer without new experience is ephemeral. The learning experience can, and often does, begin at different phases of the cycle.

To heighten participants' immersion in the adventure experience, adventure purposefully seeks to involve the whole person—intellect, body, imagination, emotions—in the doing. Theoretical research indicates that when people are thus engaged, they shift into "relaxed alertness," the optimal state of mind for meaningful learning. The other I.M.M.E.R.S.I.O.N. qualities inherent to adventure learning are similarly girded by theoretical research.

Critical to the emergence and sustaining of these qualities is the development of a condition of trust. As in the work environment, so in an adventure milieu: the stronger the field of trust, the greater people's willingness to chance the sorts of risks that can produce new thinking and fresh outcomes.

"Trust the Process"

Even as adventure consultants encourage participants to "trust the process," they constantly must heed their own advice when they are in the roles of trainer and facilitator. That is because the adventure experience is unpredictable.

The voluntary nature of the activities leaves open how far a participant will go with an activity, and what that person's balking may mean for the dynamic of the group at large. The emergence of emotional issues often produces unexpected talking points and turns that can hijack a planned agenda. A trainer or facilitator's own demeanor can rub a group wrong or right, inhibiting or enhancing the building of trust.

Every adventure consultant knows the sinking sensation of feeling that a program is slipping off track. Results may be uneven. Participants may seem particularly anxious, inattentive or upset. The emerging issues may be so wide of the mark that the scheduled agenda may feel unrecoverable.

When this happens, adventure consultants tell each other: "Trust the process." The mantra is a reminder that adventure is organic, that learning is not always linear, that outcomes are not always certain, that renewal and discovery may come at any stage—that the course of change, in short, cannot be mapped.

During a training, the adventure consultant's internal journey parallels participants' progression through the phases of the Experiential Learning Cycle. During the experience phase, the consultant remains alert to such considerations as: How am I visible to the group and potentially vulnerable? How will I be judged? What will I expose about myself, both intentionally and inadvertently?

During the reflective stage, the consultant searches for any dissonance between the group's and his own interpretation of events, asking himself: Will others see it as I do? Will my perceptions be challenged? How will I respond? Should I step in and offer suggestions, or sit back and wait for the group to achieve its own discoveries, thereby risking that the group may falter? Wait a minute! Who am I to think that my perceptions are more valid than the group's?

The generalizing phase often feels particularly perilous as the adventure consultant wonders: What if I cannot see a learning to abstract from the activity? What if I offend somebody? What if my insights fail to engage the group? What if I make the wrong connection or offer a mistaken interpretation? What if that, in turn, affects the possibility of transfer to the next activity and, more importantly, back to the workplace?

The transference phase is especially critical as it reflects the willingness of the consultant to take the meaning of the generalizing phase and apply it directly to the ongoing training experience. Observations such as "I believe we need to further examine the meaning of leadership in this culture," and "I sense that more concrete and practical discussions on this topic should take place," help to bring the process full cycle.

When an adventure consultant subscribes personally to the ELC process of discovery, it mirrors, reinforces and strengthens appeals to clients to "trust the process."

5 The Full Value Contract

Full Value Contract \ˈful ˈval'yü ˈkän-trakt \n. **1:** A partnership agreement between adventure consultants and clients that establishes behavioral expectations and norms for the duration of an adventure training. **2:** A set of operating norms developed by a company, division or team that establishes behavioral guidelines in the workplace.

As is true with so many of life's experiences, to obtain full value from an adventure experience, a person must actively accord full value to the experience. That is the goal of the Full Value Contract (FVC), the second of the three foundational tools that undergird all Project Adventure work and together provide a seamless operating system within which each tool strengthens and reinforces the other two.

If the essence of an adventure consultant's work is to design and deliver learning opportunities that pave the way for behavioral change, the Full Value Contract and the Challenge by Choice philosophy (see Chapter 6) are designed to help participants maximize those opportunities. Where the Experiential Learning Cycle provides a means for effective processing of the learning that takes place, FVC and Challenge by Choice enhance the opportunities for meaningful learning by establishing behavioral norms that focus, emphasize and amplify the adventure experience and its attendant insights.

In clear and concrete terms, the Full Value Contract establishes behavioral guidelines that recognize and respect the skills, knowledge and strengths of each individual, and value and support the group as a whole. Participants are asked to make a conscious effort to pay attention to, and thereby value, themselves (microview), the group (macroview) and the learning experience itself (metaview).

All of this is more familiar than it may seem upon first encounter. Behavioral expectations, codes of conduct, team norms are all common features of the workplace. Employees learn quickly, for instance, whether meetings begin and end on time, if it is OK to state an opinion that differs from others', and how both positive and negative feedback will be given. As those examples suggest, the emphasis is often on what we don't rather than what we do.

The Full Value Contract accents the positive, rather than negative, behaviors. A concept widely embraced by adventure consultants, the FVC is presented in many forms today. When operating in the business community, PA consultants are partial to presenting the five tenets of the Full Value Contract in language derived from the work of Angeles Arrien, author of *The Four-Fold Way: Walking the Paths of the Warrior, Teacher, Healer and Visionary* (1993). In this presentation, the contract requests that participants:

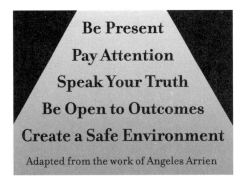

Be Present

Pay Attention

Speak Your Truth

Be Open to Outcomes

Create a Safe Environment

Adapted from the work of Angeles Arrien

This accent on the positive is not just so much "pixie dust," as one wary executive memorably put it. When attention is called to negative behaviors, it risks giving such conduct enhanced standing. If, for instance, a group is instructed, "No put-downs of other group members," that sets up a dynamic whereby everyone sits around waiting for the first inappropriate put-down to see what punishment the culprit will receive.

The Full Value Contract, by contrast, puts the focus on behaviors that emphasize mutual respect and make active support for group and individual efforts a priority. In some programs, the Full Value concept is offered as a general framework for groups to create their own set of Full Value tenets. The group effort that revolves around self-derived tenets can be powerful and meaningful. In other programs, participants are encouraged to commit to the five PA Full Value Contract norms for only the duration of the experience. Whatever the approach, once people operate within a positive learning community for even a limited time, they walk away with a powerful model for facilitating learning and effecting behavioral change in the workplace.

The Tenets of the Full Value Contract

Be Present. Participants are asked to make a commitment to being fully present during all activities. This refers to a mental, as well as physical, presence.

Capturing the attention of a corporate group during a training can be challenging. Often, participants are in attendance because they've been instructed to be there. They arrive thinking they'd rather be anyplace but. With their minds back in the office, their impulse may be to keep an eye on their watches, respond to beepers, make business calls during coffee breaks—in short, to try to conduct business from the training site.

This tenet acknowledges all of that. It implies, we know you have a business life elsewhere, we understand you have other priorities, we appreciate that you have weighty matters on your mind. But you're here. So, why not make the most of it.

Pay Attention. To avoid the pitfalls that can attend fragmented conversations and underdeveloped ideas, we ask that participants truly listen.

By that, we mean a level of receptivity that goes beyond hearing the words that are being spoken. At times, it means hearing the heartfelt meaning of a speaker's words. Sometimes, it means slowing down one's own thinking process to hear another person's full message before launching into a response or rebuttal. At other times, it means attending to your own internal monologue, that "second workshop" in your head.

This tenet works toward establishing respect for the group and the process. At the same time, it acknowledges that learning takes place at any number of levels, and that often, the most significant learning comes from within ourselves.

Speak Your Truth. This requests that participants share honestly, but with a spirit of integrity that steers clear of judgment or blame.

The sharing this aims to foster tries to get at the unspoken *it*. What *it* lives at the margins of the training and is having trouble surfacing in the mainstream of the experience? What *it* dwells just beneath the surface, creating tension? What *it* stands in the way of more productive communication? What *it* stands in the way of becoming a more effective learning community?

This tenet encourages participants to speak forthrightly, but respectfully. In groups where particular attention is paid to strengthening communication skills, such as the giving and receiving of feedback, this tenet is a potent reminder to participants that the truth they speak is *their* truth, not *the* truth.

Be Open to Outcomes. To reap the optimum benefits of an adventure experience, we ask participants to suspend judgment and be open to what unfolds.

Here, we aim to counter the "been there, done that" attitude business people often bring to trainings. Before they even enter the room, participants have often evaluated and judged the experience, based on their knowledge of or experience with adventure curricula. They also often come armed with assumptions about how others in the group will conduct themselves.

This tenet attempts to disrupt preconceptions and outfit participants with the eyes of a beginner. By relinquishing resistance, participants open themselves to potential learnings and outcomes. That includes the possibility that others in the group will show sides of themselves that they've never permitted themselves (or felt able) to share.

Create a Safe Environment. This establishes an expectation that it is everyone's responsibility to attend to the safety—both physical and emotional—of the learning community.

Beyond addressing the safety concerns people may have about some of the more challenging physical aspects of an adventure experience, it tackles head-on the fears and concerns people often bring to trainings about potential reprisals in the workplace. "If I really speak my mind, I'll have management all over me." "Whatever I say here will get back to the office before I do." "I know the score: praise in public, punish in private."

This tenet seeks to alleviate such concerns by emphasizing the confidential nature of the group's interactions. Participants are reassured that the adventure consultant will safeguard each person's input, and not breach anyone's confidentiality. Guidelines are also established that stress that once the training disbands, participants may speak only of their own participation; speaking of or for anyone else without that person's permission is not fully valuing and is discouraged.

As we encourage the learning process to unfold, there will be times when conflict arises. Implicit in this tenet is that the conflict will be managed with integrity and respect for personal dignity. This ensures a safe environment where team and personal learning can flourish.

So, Where's the Value?

This emphasis on establishing personal and interpersonal boundaries may initially seem superfluous, even a waste of time, especially for groups that are intact work teams (e.g., departments, groups of managers who meet weekly, executive boards). Such groups work together regularly, maybe even every day, and have their own expectations, guidelines and norms, whether implicit or explicit. So, why bother?

The reason is that in an adventure experience, comfortable assumptions about relationships and routines are disrupted. As people enter the experience, office roles and hierarchies may no longer be meaningful, and new roles are not yet clear. People's moods, assumptions and behaviors are no longer predictable.

The setting and props, by and large, are also unfamiliar. Even if a company has a regular training facility, it is not the workaday environment. In short, expectations for the day are often mixed, confused or uncertain. As a result, the dynamics of the group are much like those of any newly forming group. Some people are excited, eager, even elated by the prospect of encountering something new; others are uncertain, uncomfortable, even unhappy to have their routine disrupted.

The questions in people's minds have a variety of tones, but basically people want to know: How will I be treated? (Am I going to have to do something scary?) What is expected of me? (What's this booklet? Am I expected to read this now?) What am I allowed to do? (If this runs past 4:00, can I leave to take my kid to the dentist, as I'd planned?) What behavior is out of bounds? (Can I leave the room to make a phone call or go to the bathroom?) How honest can I be? (My manager said this is about building better communications, but if I really speak my mind, will I lose that promotion I'm in line for?) Why am I *really* here? (What's the hidden agenda?)

The FVC seeks to erase, or at least ease, those doubts and concerns by clarifying behavioral norms at the outset. It's common for adventure consultants to introduce the Full Value Contract near the beginning of a training, often after a brief icebreaker or warm-up activity. The sequence is designed to first give participants a quick sense of the adventure setting they are now in, then to provide them with some assurances about its parameters. Anywhere from 15 to 45 minutes is often set aside for discussion of the FVC, depending on when it is introduced or revisited in a program. This begins or continues the process of establishing parameters essential to the development of a trusting environment.

Whether the FVC is introduced quickly or at some length, initial responses tend to range widely from indifferent acceptance to voluntary but vague agreement to active interest and comprehension. As the training progresses and the FVC is revisited in light of the group's evolving experience, understanding tends to deepen both on an individual level and within the context of the group.

Establishing and then operating within a clearly constituted set of norms is often a unique experience for participants. While many companies say that employees are their greatest asset, the daily work environment frequently gives far greater attention (and, by inference, value) to the product than the people. In an adventure experience, the product recedes and people emerge as the primary focus.

That, in and of itself, can be valuable. Through the course of the experience, people become more attuned to their own behaviors, and to the ways in which they deal with others. They leave with a heightened awareness of themselves and their effect on others.

Often, groups come together solely for an annual off-site experience (e.g., managers from different geographies, salespeople from different regions, etc.). Since the members have little or no contact after they return to their respective work settings, their interpersonal relationships are no longer a focus once the group disbands. Hence, the formal application of the Full Value Contract ends for that group.

Even in such cases, the benefits of the FVC typically extend beyond the training. By the time people leave the supportive, trust-filled environment of an adventure experience, most have developed an understanding of the multiple layers of the Full Value Contract's tenets and an appreciation of their potential applications. For some people, the experience of confronting physical and emotional risks in an adventure setting produces an enduring personal awareness of what it means to "be open to outcomes" and "pay attention" to one's internal voice. Other people, excited by the levels of trust, honesty and sensitivity achieved during the adventure experience, feel galvanized to try to create a "safe environment" within their own departments so that colleagues will feel encouraged to "speak their truth."

But suppose the experience goes still further, and participants are able as a group to transfer some or all of these tenets back to the workplace? Imagine what it would mean for a business enterprise if its employees really *were* fully present. If they were truly focused on the business at hand. If they did not drain the energy from business meetings with a "been there, done that" attitude. If obstacles could be addressed forthrightly, without injury to others. If workers could count on each other to safeguard one another's well-being.

In other words, imagine if the workplace were a place where employees were continually receptive to learning and change. While some workplaces are, most are not. The Electro-Optics Division of EG&G discovered this need not be a fantasy. By developing their own set of operating norms, the division's employees realized a positive and enduring impact on their workplace.

Putting the Full Value Contract to Work

In 1993, the Salem, MA—based Electro-Optics Division of EG&G, a global technology company that provides complete systems, components and skills support services to government and industrial customers, approached Project Adventure with the aim of hosting a training for 20 group managers. Broadly, EG&G's aim was to strengthen teamwork skills. Specifically, EG&G wanted to identify behaviors that were impeding efficiency and effectiveness in the division, then develop a new set of norms that would improve the work environment.

The resulting design was a five-day program to be delivered over a two-month period, in three installments: two days, two days, one day. This time-elapse approach was PA's response to the client's request to build in time for dialogue, reflection and the building of relationships and commitments among the participants. Interestingly, the client had in essence requested a program that on a metalevel would follow the flow of the Experiential Learning Cycle: adventure experience followed by reflection and generalization, followed by transfer to the workplace, followed by a new adventure experience.

The design and program was so well received that the general manager decided to involve a greater number of people. The sequence was run four times to include almost 100 of the division's managers, support staff and contributors. That, in turn, had such a positive impact that eventually the entire Electro-Optics division was run through the program.

During the five-day training, the Full Value Contract was presented in some depth early in the first session. The contract was then reviewed at the start of the second session to remind people how they had agreed to be with each other during the course of the training. But in the ensuing discussions, it became evident that a refresher was not needed. Instead, we discovered, FVC roots had been spreading throughout the division and pushing through the crusty soil of resistance.

"It's definitely better than before," we heard again and again. Then, the skeptical follow-up, "But will it last?"

The employees' belief that they could positively alter and affect their work environment remained shallow. This suggested a need to transition out of PA's Full Value Contract and into a set of operating norms that the employees felt were their own. Toward that end, each group was charged during the second two-day session with developing its own set of operating norms. Participants were given two hours to address the following tasks as a team:

- List some of the qualities that represent how you would like your team to be.

- List some of the factors which might stand in the way of becoming the kind of team you envision.

- Develop a set of norms that will help you create the environment you desire to work within.

- Develop individual behavioral goals that will support the newly emerging work environment.

- In appreciation of EG&G's alliance with the natural world, identify a living "being" that represents the qualities that you want your team to embrace.

Before the end of the workshop, the groups had developed lists of preferred work-environment qualities (e.g., perseverance, honesty, support), obstacles (apathy, tight production schedules, cynicism), potential work norms (full team participation, overt solicitation of ideas from others, effective time management) and "beings" that were symbolically representative of the teams (Beaver, Wolf Pack, Dolphins).

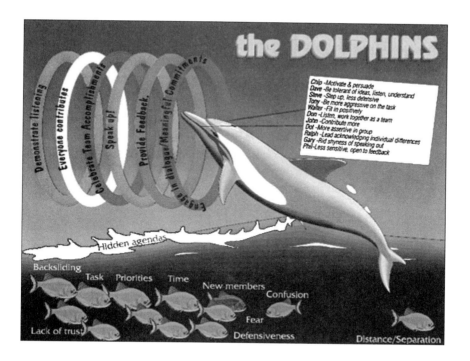

Though the training design had not included plans for further work on operating norms on the closing day, it proved to be central to the final session. To PA's surprise and delight—a good example of why adventure consultants strive to remain open to outcomes—each group returned with a completed presentation that included a "being" that symbolized their vision of what their own team looked like.

As we probed how these designs had come about, we checked to see if there had been competition. Yes, they admitted. But interestingly, they reported, the exercise had been more about the sharing of insights, with each group learning from the others. The true spirit of adventure and the attendant Full Value Contract had firmly taken root.

Or had it? Five years later, we checked back with EG&G and discovered that the attitudes of a true learning community still prevailed. Sue Michel of the human resources department told us that during a recent capital construction project, there had been less concern about which offices were going to be changed than where EG&G planned to place the "beings" that each team had constructed.

Moreover, when Product Platform Teams were recently created to improve Cycle Time, the teams requested a meeting to develop operating norms. The roughly half the members of these teams who had attended the trainings convinced the others of the value of taking time to develop norms up front before tackling a problem.

Additionally, Sue noted, by creating clear expectations of employees, the division had also created a basis for behavioral expectations to be a significant part of the performance review process. Furthermore, in subsequent internal trainings, EG&G's human resources department has maintained an adventure thrust that makes use of the Full Value Contract.

EG&G has concluded that in order for employees to give and receive full value in their work, there needs to be an agreement which addresses and establishes behavioral expectations.

The Three Roles Revisited

The Full Value Contract need not be an instrument used only to advance the goals of a training. PA consultants use it as a framework to inform and guide all interactions with a client.

Consultant. Application of the Full Value Contract begins with the first encounter with a potential client. It manifests in myriad ways. Availability. (We are present to hear your concerns.) Focused questioning. (We are paying attention.) Focused listening. (We are steering clear of preconceptions to remain open to outcomes.) Honest, clear assessments and responses. (We speak our truth.) Follow-up contact and correspondence that supplies answers to remaining questions and addresses concerns. (We are trustworthy; you can feel safe with us.)

In every communication and contact, attention is paid to co-creating a learning environment with the client. "We are learning from you," the consultant signals, "even as you are learning from us. Your input is critical to everything that follows."

Both sides of the interaction are crucial. The consultant brings the skills of the adventure specialist and the unclouded perspective of the outsider. The client brings specialized knowledge of her particular field and the intimate, up-close perceptions of the insider. "Together," the consultant conveys, "we can move toward achieving your goals."

Trainer. The trainer provides the lens through which a group views the Full Value Contract. From the first interaction with the group, the trainer strives to model what it means to value others. Any hint that the trainer feels superior to or disconnected from the people he is addressing risks undermining the contract.

Thus, the trainer approaches the group with all the respect and consideration that the contract implies. He mirrors through his words and actions the attentiveness, directness, honesty and commitment that he seeks from the group. Even as he encourages a deeper and more meaningful give and take, the trainer remains attuned to the group's (evolving) comfort level. Because he has responsibility for setting tone and mood and maintaining momentum, the trainer is attentive to the parameters and boundaries set by the group. Though he may nudge the group's boundaries with open-ended, broadly directed questions, his focus is primarily on keeping the training moving smoothly and meeting the goals of the planned agenda.

Facilitator. The facilitator, by contrast, is focused on exploring the many opportunities for inter- and intrapersonal growth, however and whenever those opportunities arise. While the facilitator respects that each group ultimately establishes its own boundaries, if those parameters seem to be getting fixed too quickly or too narrowly, the facilitator will attempt to nudge them outward. Simply invoking the contract draws people's attention to the shared responsibility of creating a safe learning environment.

Toward that end, the Full Value Contract can be a powerful ally. When a facilitator feels an individual or group is holding back more because of uncertainty or discomfort than considered restraint, she can use the contract's tenets to encourage fuller participation. Operating within the terms of the FVC herself, she may challenge the group at large and people individually with her personal observations and direct questions that call attention to issues or behaviors that have been overlooked or unaddressed.

Through such personal interventions, she becomes more than a detached observer. Her observations are judged accordingly, making her exposed and vulnerable. Thus, more even than the trainer, the facilitator mirrors to the group what it means to speak and act within the terms of the Full Value Contract. A group will detect if the facilitator's attention wanders, if she stops listening with an open mind and active curiosity, if she begins to speak guardedly. Any of those breaches of the FVC risks undermining the group's evolving trust. The facilitator is also on guard against her own preconceptions and any subtle manipulations that might guide the group toward validating those prejudgments.

Finally, like the trainer, the facilitator uses the FVC as a tool to maintain a safe environment. When participants do not attend adequately to physical safety or stray into conversation that could prove emotionally harmful (the more likely event), the facilitator uses the FVC to remind participants of other styles of sharing and interacting.

Summary

The Full Value Contract creates a context for learning. A community that openly supports learning, treats its members with respect, safeguards emotional and physical safety, and sets and monitors goals is a community that promotes optimal learning for all its constituent members.

The FVC creates a context for community. It establishes operating norms around which a community can grow and individuals can interact openly and honestly without inflicting unintended pain.

The FVC offers a context for interaction between consultant and client. It helps to quickly begin establishing the trust critical to that relationship. Then, it helps maintain that trust as the relationship evolves.

Finally, the FVC offers a model for operating within a set of clearly designated guidelines. The experience of identifying and working within a set of operating norms can be transferred back to the workplace.

The Five C's of Trust

Trust cannot be ordained, mandated or ordered up on a green requisition slip. Rather, it is built carefully, then must be nurtured and attended to constantly. While there is no recipe for trust, its component parts almost invariably include communication and cooperation, discretion and dependability, sensitivity and support, truthfulness and trustworthiness.

While the conditions of trust may be elusive, its radiating effects are not. When trust is in place, the following qualities permeate a workplace:

- **Caring.** Employees experience a true sense of people caring for and about each other. Individuals lend to that environment through expressions and actions, both spontaneous and considered, that demonstrate their care and concern for others.

- **Competence.** Employees observe and constantly strive to strengthen the skills, both interpersonal and technical, required to achieve the organization's mission. They work to develop a balance between the technical and interpersonal areas of their work life.

- **Common Purpose.** Employees have both an understanding of their shared commitments and a clear agreement to move in that direction.

- **Consistency.** Organizationally, policies and actions match the concepts and values that the company professes. Individually, employees strive to align their behavior and performance to support company policies.

- **Confidentiality.** The boundaries of each relationship are respected, with the terms of interaction understood. Where confidentiality is a condition of an interaction, privacy is safeguarded, without exception.

—Mark Murray

6 Challenge by Choice

Work. "I expect this on my desk by 5 p.m." versus "This is very important and your input would be greatly appreciated, but I have this unmoveable 5 p.m. deadline. Can you handle it, or should I find someone else?"

Play. "Let's go see the new Altman film" versus "Is there a movie you'd like to see? My own vote goes to the new Altman film."

Family. "Get upstairs and don't come back down until your room is clean" versus "The TV stays off until your room is clean. If you want to see your favorite show at 8, you might want to head upstairs now."

No matter what the age or circumstance, most people find a choice more appealing than a directive. Where an order stirs resistance and resentment, a choice invites cooperation, participation, responsibility. That seems so obvious that it's hard to imagine why virtually any endeavor would be "ordered up" rather than "offered."

Yet how often in the course of the day do we feel stripped of choice, either at work or at home? How often do we hear ourselves or others say: "Do I have a choice?" (sarcastic), "I feel like I have no choice" (frustrated), "No one asked my opinion about this" (ignored), "I had no choice" (forlorn, resigned).

Challenge by Choice, Project Adventure's cornerstone philosophy since its founding in 1971, positions voluntary participation at the center of all its programs and activities. During an adventure experience, participants are continually invited to determine, review and assess their own levels of involvement and engagement. Beyond honoring each participant's choices, the Challenge by Choice philosophy reminds participants to respect the choices made by others.

When a group embraces the principles of Challenge by Choice, it operates in an environment where each member has:

- The right to choose when and at what level to participate, physically, mentally, emotionally;

- The opportunity to back away from a challenge at any point with the knowledge that the opportunity to revisit it remains open;

- The chance to move outside one's comfort zone into unfamiliar territory within a supportive, caring and safety-conscious environment that attaches greater significance to the effort than to outcomes or performance;

- Heightened awareness and respect for other participants' ideas, needs, differences and choices.

On Change and Choice

Project Adventure's pioneering emphasis on self-defined participation reflects an appreciation for the centrality of choice in any change process. It recognizes and respects that for change of any kind—operational, structural, most particularly behavioral—to be positive and enduring, rather than begrudged and fleeting, an individual must have a sense of responsibility for and control over the evolving situation.

PA's philosophy evolved during the years when we worked primarily in the educational and therapeutic fields, where the focus is intensively on personal growth and change. Time and again, experience bore out that meaningful and lasting change cannot take root unless a person has a keen sense of investment, power and responsibility.

This holds no less true in the business arena. Experience has shown repeatedly that when involvement in a training is compelled rather than offered, there is a high risk that participants will lapse into a spectator mode that assumes decisions will be externally imposed and dictated, rather than internally initiated and driven. A passive posture of this kind reinforces feelings of insignificance, resentment, mistrust and indifference to outcomes—precisely the sort of attitudinal problems that may have convinced a company to seek external counsel in the first place.

Adventure academics and theorists have followed PA's lead to embrace the importance of voluntary participation. "Programs should operate under the axiom of 'challenge by choice,'" writes Michael Gass, an academician in the field. "When participants' power to decide for themselves is taken away by forcing their involvement, they are likely to attribute success or failure to the person who made them do it rather than to themselves . . . Programs are strongly advised to allow options for participants to pass and not coerce involvement" (Gass et al., 1992).

Project Adventure's commitment to choice supports our primary commitment to facilitating behavioral change. Whether training a group or coaching an individual, we know that for our work to be effective, participants must *choose* to commit to change. It is therefore imperative that we strive to create and maintain an environment that is receptive to choice, and by extension, change. Once that is achieved, the adventure consultant is well-positioned to guide and help manage any resulting changes as they unfold and mutate over time.

Choice as Concept

How does an adventure consultant foster a climate that is hospitable to that most threatening of life's conditions: change? And how does the consultant do it quickly, within the time constraints of a training?

As we saw with the Experiential Learning Cycle, learning tends to be most effective when there is active engagement in an initiative, followed by conscious reflection that sifts through the multiple layers of meaning to arrive at personal understanding. To help ensure that no group member gets in the way of another member's opportunity for learning, the Full Value Contract attends to the relationships within the group. Challenge by Choice attends to the individual, helping to encourage risk-taking that will promote personal growth and learning.

The Challenge by Choice philosophy emphasizes that every person maintains control over the degree of his immersion in each activity. At a deeper level, it signals that before a participant can internalize, or "own," any piece of what transpires, he must accept responsibility for his actions and nonactions. Whatever the outcome, however great the risk, when a conscious choice about one's role is missing, a participant is unlikely to accord significance to his input. Absent that sense of significance, a participant is unlikely to walk away with any meaning or insight that will effect sustained change.

As the adventure experience unfolds, participants discover that a commitment to "choice" has multiple levels of meaning. Initially, choice seems simply a matter of deciding how much or how little a person will participate in a proposed activity (microview). As the participants coalesce into a functioning group, they begin to sense new choices that involve interactions with others, and how those choices will impact the group's gestalt (macroview). A goal-setting process helps further clarify and reinforce the challenges individuals are willing to assume within the group context. Those who eventually extract personal meaning from the experience understand that "choice" is not time-limited to the training; those who take the insights home and make a personal commitment to change experience the deepest level of choice (metaview).

As an individual grasps and internalizes this deeper, more personal meaning of choice, he comes to appreciate the power of the Full Value Contract as a companion tool for change. "Being Present" can mean, for instance, being newly alert to what is unfolding within oneself. "Being Open to Outcomes" can be a springboard for receiving (sometimes difficult) information about oneself. "Paying Attention" may mean striving for enhanced awareness of one's inner voice. "Speaking Your Truth" may mean unearthing and addressing hidden aspects of yourself. "Creating a Safe Environment" may refer to paying closer attention to others' sensitivities or respecting one's own feelings as a person makes the choice to plumb still deeper.

Choice as Practice

At the outset of a training, adventure consultants introduce the concept of "choice" in order to address the most practical and important of considerations: personal ownership of the experience. How can I get these people to be fully present? How can I motivate this group to become actively engaged so that we can achieve the intended goals of the training?

A frontal attack on such concerns is particularly important in an adventure setting. Beyond the issues of control and vulnerability that routinely surface between business consultant and client, adventure specialists face an additional obstacle: the fear and resistance born of misconceptions about adventure activities.

Often when people enter an adventure setting for the first time, their heads are filled with frightening images conjured by media reports that have focused on dramatic and potentially dangerous escapades. A typical example was a 60 *Minutes* segment that showed people shouting, "Come on baby, you got it, you got it!" as a woman trembled atop a 50-foot "Pamper Pole" (an activity that involves climbing to the top of a telephone pole or tree, balancing on a small platform, and diving out to a trapeze suspended from cables), about to plunge into space on a belay system.

Such images are misleading and grossly misrepresentative. They do not make clear that such exercises represent the outer edge of the adventure experience. More damaging, they neither offer detail of the groundwork that has been laid to prepare a group for such a challenge, nor accentuate the safeguards that have been put in place to ensure a safe outcome. Moments of high drama also fail to make clear that in a well-run adventure experience, no one should ever ascend a Pamper Pole unless he or she chooses to.

As a direct result of such distorted images, people often approach an adventure training with a perception of physical risk that is far greater than any actual risk they will encounter. In reality, statistics show that there is a significantly greater risk of sustaining an injury while driving to work than while engaging in an adventure activity. Yet, it is not uncommon for participants to enter the training environment worrying: What will I be expected to do? What if I don't want to do it? Will I look like a chicken if I refuse?

The Challenge by Choice philosophy confronts and addresses these questions at the outset. As participants begin to test and exercise their choices, they discover that participation truly is voluntary. That, in turn, promotes "relaxed alertness," the optimal state for learning. It also enables participants to forget their fearful preconceptions and begin to trust the situation.

That trust is critical to the forging of any learning community. Challenge by Choice is a potent tool for cultivating a strong trust field. The "challenge" piece of the equation speaks to issues of risk, both emotional and physical; the "choice" piece speaks to issues of personal control. Taken as a whole, the Challenge by Choice philosophy surfaces and addresses two of the greatest barriers to effective consulting: fear and resistance.

On Embracing Uncertainty

"It's this simple. If I never try anything, I never learn anything. If I never take a risk, I stay right where I am. If I go right ahead and do it, that affects how much I continue wanting to do it. If I hold myself back, I trade appearances for the opportunity to find out what I am really like."

—*Hugh Prather, American author and poet*

Risk is both a central metaphor and a methodology of adventure learning. When an individual chooses to accept a challenge, he is agreeing to go beyond the safety of old boundaries and push into new territory, where he may encounter the unanticipated about his colleagues, his work situation, and most importantly, himself. Though people typically enter adventure trainings focused on the external risks posed by physical challenges, they often discover that the greater risks are the emotional ones that come from within.

The problem with risk is that it is—hmm, how best to say this?—risky. Any situation that presents an opportunity for learning, change and success also threatens the converse: losing face, derailment of the status quo, failure. The only demonstrated way to get around such fears and help people embrace uncertainty is to create an environment that explicitly supports all levels of engagement. Educational theorists have argued repeatedly through the decades that in group settings, people require a sense of safety and belonging to undertake the kinds of risk that allow for creativity, innovation and experimentation.

In practical terms, that means: fostering positive attitudes that encourage unfettered exploration; helping participants remain focused on self-selected goals and limiting distraction by competition or others' agendas; keeping the environment free of behaviors and attitudes that devalue the experience and make people feel self-conscious about their choices.

While participants are free to remove themselves from an activity, Challenge by Choice does not give them permission to check out mentally, leave the setting or engage in activities that could prove disruptive to others (e.g., making phone calls, doing other work). This is not simply a matter of basic courtesy. In an adventure setting, it is impossible to predict where an individual's sense of risk will come from. To safeguard the emotional and physical safety of all participants, a group remains alert to the fact that what feels perilous to one person may differ markedly from what feels risky to another. (See "Multiple Choices" box.)

When group members begin to feel concerned about, respectful of and responsible for each other's safety, they shift into that part of the trust terrain where substantive dialogue and enduring change become possible. A three-day training attended by nine managers from the Digital Equipment Corporation, an international computer hardware and software conglomerate, illustrates both that shift and the varying "risks" people can experience during the course of an adventure training.

Accepting the Challenge

As often happens in training situations, the managers arrived at the adventure site unclear about why they were there and what would be expected of them. After a PA trainer explained that the twofold purpose of the training was to explore individual leadership styles and to develop skills to work more effectively as a team, the group entered into convening exercises designed to help the group members start to know one another better and to break through restraints and inhibitions.

Within a few hours, the group members were throwing themselves into exercises unselfconsciously, laughing at their own awkward efforts without seeming embarrassment. All nine participants were sharing their ideas candidly, listening with respectful attention and attending to one another in ways that palpably valued the attempts, opinions and feelings of others in the group.

As an environment of caring and acceptance settled over the training, people began to give voice to issues that usually remain unspoken. What more could be done to enhance feelings of safety so that group members would feel emboldened to challenge themselves fully? How could they better learn from one another? How to heighten the emerging sense of support, so that people could give and receive feedback without feeling threatened? The group was plainly poised to benefit from a sequence of trust exercises.

The sequence progressed to a trust-fall activity, where participants were invited to climb onto a platform some five feet above the ground, then fall backwards into the arms of colleagues below. Phil Sardella, a manager in DEC's US Employment division, had volunteered to go first. He'd made the offer acutely aware that this kind of physical risk was difficult for him.

Now, as Phil stood on the platform, he was noticeably nervous. Several times, he moved into position to make the fall, heels poised over the edge of the platform, then balked, afraid to proceed. Each time, his colleagues responded with calls of support and encouragement.

"I want to do this," he called down, "but I'm not sure I can. I don't know what's stopping me." Again, he turned his back and placed his heels over the edge, preparing to fall.

Challenge by Choice. As Phil stood poised, the minutes ticking by, his colleagues could have continued their just-go-for-it cheers. But they seemed to understand that their well-intended encouragement was serving only to deepen Phil's distress and confusion. This time, they risked the discomfort of a potentially awkward silence, and a quiet attention developed.

It proved a respectful choice rather than an uncomfortable one. As the silence deepened, Phil was able to achieve precious moments of introspection to determine what he really wanted to do. At the same time, Phil's peers felt they could see the world through his eyes and appreciate his struggle. How many times had each of them brushed up against the tough reality that a desire to do something might not be enough?

Several minutes passed, then an associate, Pat Coxen, asked gently, "Phil, what do you need from us right now?"

After a lengthy pause, Phil responded, "I need to know that you will really catch me." He paused again. "And I need to know it's okay if I don't fall." Challenge by Choice. The risk Phil had just taken was apparent to everyone. How often does a colleague give voice to the anxiety that arises from being torn between wanting to stay safe and wanting to take a risk? How often does a person give voice to the need for peer approval? How often does a colleague let such vulnerability show?

"Phil," a colleague answered, "you need to know that if you choose to do this, you will be doing it for you. You won't be doing it for me or for us. There are no judgments made here about you, whether you fall or not. I want you to know that."

With statements echoing that sentiment, the group erected a safety net that would catch Phil, no matter what choice he made. These expressions of support not only reinforced the Full Value Contract, but reminded Phil that the most important goals were those he chose for himself.

Once again, Phil moved into the falling position. He started to lean back, bellowed, "I trust! I trust! I trust! Oh, God, I trust!" then let go, continuing that cry until he was safely nestled in his colleagues' arms.

The exuberance that followed Phil's flight was shared by everyone. The fall itself seemed the least of it. Phil's willingness to entrust his vulnerability to his colleagues had been far more meaningful. As is so often the case in an adventure experience, the emotional risks proved more daunting and meaningful than the physical ones.

Group members understood that the celebration was as much theirs as Phil's. Had they not created an atmosphere of trust, encouragement and empathy to support Phil's effort, he probably would never have allowed himself to fall.

The experience had a marked effect on the remaining two days of the training. With the group now operating deep within trust territory, people were more willing to share parts of themselves that they had never thought to bring to the office. They began to discover new ways to support and to challenge one another as both leaders and as members of a team.

That's not to say that every moment was easy. Group cohesion and a safe environment are not permanent conditions; their maintenance is no less challenging than their creation. Time and again during the remaining two days, the sense of solidarity was tested, particularly in the activities designed to highlight participants' leadership skills and challenge their ability to function effectively as a team.

When each manager was given the opportunity to lead the team through a low ropes course activity, power tussles emerged. As individuals vied to wrest control of the activity and push the group toward achieving specific objectives more swiftly, the same people who just 24 hours earlier had responded with such sensitivity to Phil's fears now resorted to competitive, defensive and sarcastic behaviors.

Again, Challenge by Choice became a powerful tool to help the group learn from its own behavior. The facilitator reminded the group that Challenge by Choice meant not only a personal choice about giving and receiving feedback, but also a heightened awareness and respect for each other's (and one's own) discomfort during that process. Then discussion was guided toward helping them look openly and honestly at what had transpired.

The managers agreed that while it was important that they be able to give honest feedback to employees, it was no less important that such directness be proffered in a way that would enable the message to be heard. They then revisited some of their recent interactions, and brainstormed how they might have handled the situation more effectively.

They emerged from this exercise with a stronger understanding of the linkage between confrontation and trust, and the unanticipated outcomes of feedback. They recognized that building trust was both a continuous task and imperative, if they wanted themselves and employees to feel able to risk honest feedback without fear of repercussion or injury.

All of this deepened the group's trust. People felt emboldened to share their ideas and feelings even more freely. By the time the nine managers left the training, they had a hard-earned appreciation for the role environment plays in enabling people to break out of familiar habits and take risks. They voiced a determination to continue building on this trust back in the workplace.

Apparently, they succeeded. Three months after the training, one of the managers, Pat Coxen, reported, "Everything we do with each other has greatly improved since we came back to work from the workshop... The communication between the group, both positive and negative, is more free and constructive...We are able to say what is there on our minds without fear of reprisals. This only happened because we were able to take risks and build trust."

Like many of the others who attended that training, Pat also indicated that she had mined meaning from the experience that might affect some of her future personal choices. "I came away," she said, "feeling that I could be anything I wanted to be."

On Choice and Resistance

"The hardest part of consulting is coping successfully with resistance from the client."

—*Peter Block*, Flawless Consulting

The DEC managers' experience demonstrates how an adventure experience can build and fuel on itself. As trust deepened, participants grew more willing to push further on all fronts: emotionally, physically, intellectually. As in any learning community, each person's willingness to push the boundaries of personal discovery was shaped to some degree by peer influences. In this case, individuals benefited from the collective strength, enthusiasm and openness of the community.

Some corporate groups arrive at trainings even more ready than the DEC managers to plunge into the experience. Happy to be in an environment where they expect to experience something fresh and thought-provoking, they are open to outsiders' input, curious about what they might learn, and willing to immerse themselves in whatever unfolds. For such groups, "choice" skips quickly from the first level of meaning to those deeper levels where inter- and intrapersonal understanding is enriched and lasting change becomes possible.

The converse is also true: a group can arrive with a strong contingent of naysayers in tow. In such a community, individuals can be dragged down by the collective resistance, wariness and restraint. Skepticism or lack of enthusiasm from even a single member can kill the excitement for everyone.

For consultants in general, and adventure consultants in particular, such resistance is not uncommon upon first encounter with a corporate audience. If just one or two people have invited the consultants in, it is understandable that others may experience these so-called "experts" as unwelcome intruders, imposed from on high. Whether spoken or unspoken, the attitude is often: Who do these guys think they are to come in here and try to solve our problems? Don't we know our business and work associates better than anyone else? If *we* can't make this better, then how can *they*? Who says there's a problem, anyway?

Peter Block, a consulting theoretician, identifies 14 common faces of resistance. Some of the most common strategies involve timing excuses (the client wants to go ahead with training but the *timing* isn't right), demands for more detail (the client wants detailed design thoughts), moralizing (the client feels superior, certain that he know what's best for "those people"), flight into health (as the training nears, the problem miraculously evaporates) and intellectualizing (the client uses clever rationalizations to avoid confronting the problem).

That last one is perhaps the most common face of resistance when PA's adventure consultants encounter a training audience for the first time. "That's all very nice," goes the standard refrain, "but we have no choice about being here." In other words, take your cornerstone principles and . . .

Block points out that vulnerability and control issues are usually at the root of resistant behaviors. As a result, consultants must strive to present recommendations, ideas, design thoughts and interventions in a way that doesn't exacerbate their fear or heighten those feelings.

PA's preferred strategy is to try to build in choice from the very start. Clients are encouraged to make attendance in adventure programs optional. When the suggestion is ignored, we often experience heightened resistance in the subsequent training. To allay fears and reduce anxieties, we seek access to the participants long before the training, both to get their input during the needs assessment phase and to answer concerns and questions they might have about the pending training. We also encourage the principal decision makers to share with participants their vision and purpose for the training.

Ultimately, however, we can only present choices, not make decisions. "I still have no choice about being here," goes the refrain of resistance. "If I don't show up, it goes down in the big book." (In some companies, eligibility for bonuses can be withdrawn if an employee fails to attend a required program.)

How to combat such persistent resistance? In addition to developing a thick skin, adventure consultants have several techniques that work on lowering the volume of the naysaying choir. The most obvious is a roster of activities so absorbing that participants eventually forget to resist. Opening sequences of convening exercises, for instance, tend to pull people in with challenges that are interesting and unthreatening, and score high on the mirth scale.

Seduction apart, the aim remains for people to come around and choose to participate. When the choice is conscious, a deeper commitment and more enduring results follow. While some hold-outs cannot be budged, the more typical course is for resistance to melt when hold-outs see their colleagues immersed in an activity or involved in a meaningful exchange and their own right to "choose" honored.

The strongest antidote to resistance is to create an environment where people believe that whatever degree of participation they choose is acceptable.

As Stephen Covey puts it in his bestseller, *The 7 Habits of Highly Effective People*, each person has *"responsibility*—'response-ability'—the ability to choose your response."

Resistance is a choice, too. Moreover, resistance need not be an obstacle or barrier. When it's well-handled, it can emerge as a useful, even powerful, vehicle for helping a group to confront workplace attitudes and behaviors that they might otherwise avoid or overlook.

Resistance as a Learning Opportunity

During a three-day Kodak training that focused on teaching coaching skills to approximately 16 team leaders and managers in Rochester, NY, participants requested some work on coaching difficult people. In particular, the participants said, they needed practice dealing with resistant behaviors in one-on-one situations.

Since 1996, Project Adventure has had an ongoing and ever-deepening relationship with Eastman Kodak, a company that devotes considerable attention to enhancing employees' understanding of the company's core values. With Chairman and CEO George Fisher at the helm, all employees are required to receive at least 40 hours annually of development as documented in an employee development plan. Given this strong emphasis on education, Kodak employees tend to enter training situations with the trusting assumption that something helpful or useful will emerge.

So, Steve Butler, the PA consultant running this particular training, knew that he could count on the group to be cooperative and candid in a discussion of real work situations involving resistance. But Steve sensed that such an approach might yield a cognitive understanding of dilemmas and potential solutions that would be temporary, rather than enduring.

To really bring the situation to life, he felt, the group members needed to confront real resistance that would compel them to utilize the coaching skills they'd just been learning. To further complicate Steve's choices in designing an appropriate activity, the group had been debating whether or not a coach needed to have knowledge and skills superior to the "coachee" to be a successful coach. Steve had argued that expertise was not essential, but sensed the group was not convinced. He wanted participants to see for themselves that a person could coach effectively, particularly where it related to interpersonal skills issues, even when not armed with expertise.

He chose for the activity basic three-ball juggling, then framed the experience as a skill development plan for the team. "Your business unit," he explained, "needs each person to acquire these new skills and be able to demonstrate them to the rest of the group in public." He said everyone would have to demonstrate their juggling skills in 24 hours.

After ascertaining that everyone could throw and catch a ball, Steve observed, "You already have the necessary individual skills. Now, you have to integrate them."

He gave 10 minutes of instruction that broke the juggling down into three practice steps, then produced enough balls so that half the group members could practice at any one time. "I ask that team members be responsible for coaching each other and developing the skills of everyone," he said. "I expect to see 100% of you juggling by this time tomorrow." Steve provided 15 minutes of practice, then moved on to other activities.

As the day unfolded, people picked up the balls during coffee breaks and lunch. Some people demonstrated little skill at first, but great enthusiasm and eagerness to master the skills; several asked if they could take the balls with them overnight. (Yes!) Others tried the juggling once or twice, then gave up, apparently convinced they could not succeed. One or two people chose not to try at all.

During the course of the day, all of the participants engaged in coaching someone else, with varying degrees of intensity and effort. Some people were better at coaching than learning the skills themselves.

Only one man displayed resistance to the entire process. Initially, Bob's resistance was passive. As time went on, his resistance became overt. "I'm not going to bother to learn this, since juggling has no relevance to the work I do," he said. "It's a waste of time." Steve responded by acknowledging Bob's feelings, offering this point of view: "While I appreciate that you don't see a direct connection to work, the exercise is intended to look at how you might coach others on a task when you don't have the expertise. I still think there might be value to try coaching someone, but the choice is up to you."

The next morning when Steve began the day with a check-in question, "Any thoughts, ideas, learnings from yesterday you want to discuss?," people wanted to discuss their juggling efforts. Some spoke of their developing facility with the three balls; others spoke of their frustrated learning curve. As he listened, Steven pondered how to nudge their observations toward a greater awareness of how adept some of the weakest jugglers were at coaching others.

Then Bob asserted again, "This exercise is a waste of time."

Here was one of those unpredictable moments that highlights the unique potential of adventure learning. As Steve shifted from trainer to facilitator mode, he sensed that tackling Bob's challenge head-on augured one of two possibilities. The response, if open, could push the group's understanding of resistance to a new level, offering valuable information that was directly transferable back to the workplace. If the response was closed or hostile, Steve risked alienating not only Bob, but the entire group.

Challenge by Choice. Steve chose to take the risk.

"Bob," Steve asked, "have you ever encountered resistance at work from people who feel they are being asked to do something that is a waste of time?"

"It's commonplace," Bob said. Several people nodded in agreement.

"What would you do to coach someone like that?" Steve pursued.

Bob offered several suggestions. Then Steve asked, "How could we coach you to help you see the value in the juggling process? The juggling itself is not the point here. But I want you and the rest of the team to understand how better to coach in difficult one-on-one situations."

Challenge by Choice. Bob could have chosen any number of defensive postures. Indifference. Incomprehension. Incredulity. Instead, he stepped up to the plate and helped make the experience a home run. Openly and without being defensive, Bob likened his earlier resistance to behaviors he'd seen at work, then analyzed aloud how his feelings of resistance had impacted his participation in the training.

"To be an effective manager and coach at work," he admitted, "I'm going to need to get over some of my ideas about what's valuable and what's not."

Challenge by Choice. The combination of Steve's willingness to risk vulnerability and Bob's willingness to risk honesty had produced an outcome of far greater value than the activity had initially suggested. Everyone, Steve included, went home feeling better equipped to handle resistance issues.

Summary

For change to be meaningful and enduring, it must be preceded by conscious choice. Challenge by Choice is a philosophy that encourages individuals to take responsibility for and exercise control over their own learning and behavioral changes.

Challenge by Choice operates from the premise that interpersonal and intrapersonal gains are most forthcoming when people choose and commit to challenges that they have identified for themselves. The conditions fostered in a Challenge by Choice environment help to create the sense of safety that encourages people to venture risk, while at the same time respecting that individuals know best their own limits and challenges.

As the Full Value Contract attends to the relationships within a group, Challenge by Choice addresses the individual, helping to encourage intellectual, physical and emotional risk-taking that will promote personal growth and learning. At the same time, the Challenge by Choice spirit supports and strengthens the trust critical to the building of an effective learning community.

Creating Multiple Choices

Challenge by Choice is all well and good, but when activities are viewed by participants as "either/or," as in you do either this or nothing at all, many quickly become *non*participants. One way that adventure consultants prod participants to accept the challenge at some level is to offer a menu of choices within each activity.

This is particularly true for the kinds of adventure challenges on high ropes courses that inspire sweaty palms, dry mouths and "I can't do it" responses. Though high ropes course elements account for only a small percentage of the adventure curriculum, they loom disproportionately large in people's minds.

So, let's use a high ropes challenge, "Multivine Traverse," to see how choice can be created within an activity. In a standard application with a focus on individual challenge, this activity challenges a participant to traverse a distance of roughly 30 feet on a single, tensioned foot cable with a series of multiline ropes suspended from an overhead cable, positioned just beyond an average-sized person's reach. Usually, a person referred to as a Belayer stands on the ground below, attached to the other end of the Climber's rope, providing a "bottom belay" to arrest the Climber's fall, should he slip.

In this standard model, two individuals are actively involved, with the focus on the climbing and traversing aspect of the activity. Creating choices can involve more people and shift the emphasis of the challenge. Let's broaden the use of the element to a team context, and consider the same activity using a five-role model.

The five roles break down this way. In addition to the Climber, who is attached to a belay (safety) rope, there is the Primary Belayer, who serves as the Climber's primary back-up safety person. A Back-up Belayer buttresses the Primary Belayer's efforts. The Spotter has primary responsibility for aiding the Climber onto the element and monitoring the system of belay ropes. The Process Observer keeps an eye on the entire performance, intervening only if he sees something potentially dangerous evolving.

Within this team of five, only one person leaves the ground. Yet, the roles create choices for individuals to pick and choose their level of challenge—raising the chances of actively involving more people. An out-of-shape employee afraid of heights, for instance, may find the idea of traversing the "cable" petrifying, yet accept that risk. An administrative assistant may find her challenge by being the Primary Belayer, with responsibility for the physical safety of her manager; breaking through the organization's hierarchical boundaries may enhance her feelings of empowerment. An athletic leader, by contrast, may find dangling from ropes fun but not challenging and instead, may find his "edge" in placing himself in a back-up role—a position he rarely assumes at work.

Whatever the choices, there are opportunities for varying levels of engagement. A person who chooses to be the Climber could feel very involved ("Yikes, that's me up there!") or very passive ("No big deal. The rope will catch me, and that part is up to them."). A person who opts to be the Process Observer could feel most responsible ("It's up to me to spot potential safety issues.") or least responsible ("I'm not touching any of the ropes."). The challenge is there. The question is how each participant chooses to view it.

ASSESSMENT

CUSTOMIZATION

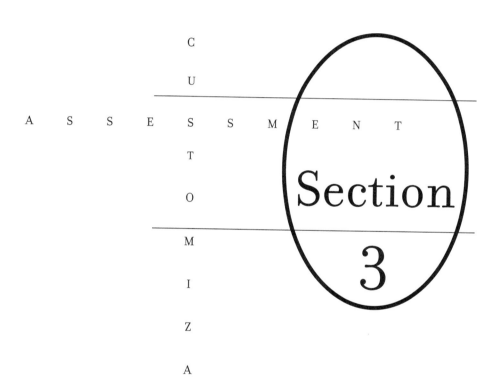

Section

3

CHALLENGE #3

Pie Pieces

A program design needs to contain different components, provide a consistent connection to the goals and the workplace, and create a complete experience for the participants.

If the circle below represents a day of training, **drawing only three lines** divide the circle into eight sections.

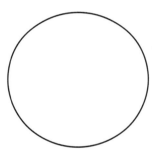

Volume, Volume, Volume

As adventure consultants, we always need to know what contents are present in our toolkit. This problem asks you to measure precisely the contents of your personal toolkit since it holds exactly four gallons.

You have **only** two containers available. One holds **exactly three gallons**, the other holds **exactly five gallons**. There are **no other props or materials available** to assist you in creating a solution.

Using only the two containers, how can you measure **exactly four gallons** of liquid, not a drop more or less?

In today's challenging business environment, generic solutions no longer suffice. Companies require personalized attention to diagnose and address very specific constellations of problems and challenges. Adventure consulting offers a highly effective method for identifying needs and designing customized programs that achieve enduring results.

The key to this approach lies in adventure's capacity for cultivating and sustaining strong partnerships between client and consultant. The collaborative aspects come into play right at the outset, during the assessment of a company's needs, and continue to build and strengthen through the design and delivery phases.

During the needs assessment, the emphasis is on pooling information and perspectives to clarify and sharpen the client's particular needs. Through a constant give and take between client and consultant, goals come into focus, needs and resources are aligned and mutual understanding is achieved.

The back-and-forth exchange continues through the design phase, when an architectural blueprint for the customized learning experience is produced. The ensuing adventure design, which revolves around the Experiential Learning Cycle, focuses on presenting a sequence of adventure activities that cumulatively illustrate, ignite and reinforce the client's desired message.

To engage and speak to the broadest possible spectrum of learning styles, an adventure design strives to integrate exercises that will variously engage mind and body, emotions and spirit. Often, a corporate design also includes traditional training devices such as learning instruments, theoretical models or content pieces more attuned to business audiences.

For adventure consultants, what stamps the needs assessment and design phases of the consulting process as "adventure" is not the inclusion of particular exercises or activities (though some of these can be unusual, indeed!). Rather, it is the highly interactive nature of the client–consultant exchange. At all points in the consulting process, an effort is made to imbue the proceedings with the I.M.M.E.R.S.I.O.N. qualities particular to adventure learning.

Thus, adventure learning is not just a training tool. It's a way of interacting with people that is employed in the service of developing effective client and partnering relationships. The qualities and tenets of adventure learning inform every aspect of the consulting relationship.

7 Assessing Needs, Managing Expectations

A s with any type of consulting, the road to the successful design and delivery of a corporate adventure experience begins with a careful assessment of the client's needs. What are the client's concerns? What issues does he want to address? What does he hope to achieve during the training? Do the client's wants match his greatest needs? Are the client's goals realistic, given budgets, time constraints and the individual personalities involved? What would the desired outcomes look like when transferred back to the workplace?

Though easy to ask, such questions are rarely easy to answer. Gathering, interpreting and evaluating information is never a straightforward process. Diagnosing a set of problems and needs accurately, clearly and diplomatically can be tricky. Gaining a clear-eyed view of the potential obstacles and conflicts that could impede an effective intervention can be trickier still.

Because humans are neither omniscient nor omnipresent, any individual's perception of a problem or need is inherently shaped and limited by the lens through which she views the situation. Given that, how many stakeholders' views need to be sought to obtain a "full" view of the problem? Whose perspectives are most reflective of the "real" situation? Whose views speak to team issues, and whose speak more to personal issues?

The first round of answers is provided by the client (the key stakeholder), who presents the consultant with an internal assessment of the needs and problems requiring attention. To further identify those problems and isolate those needs, the consultant then probes deeper, sometimes conducting this next phase of the needs assessment independently of the key stakeholder.

Whether the resulting investigation affirms the client's perceived assessment or yields different conclusions, the consultant and client have in effect created their own visions of the situation. When the time comes for the consultant to put forward his design recommendations, it can be an anxious moment for client and consultant alike. (Will the design approach produce the outcomes the client views as critical? Will the consultant's ideas be accepted, considered or discounted?)

PA consultants view needs assessment in much the same light as they see adventure activities. It's only a beginning, not an end in itself. Instead, it's part of a fluid process that inextricably links inquiry, design and delivery, with each of those phases informing, illuminating and igniting the others, in much the same way that the four phases of the Experiential Learning Cycle fuel and feed off of each other. Moreover, like any adventure activity, it benefits from the I.M.M.E.R.S.I.O.N. qualities that are the hallmark of adventure learning: interactive, meaningful, mirthful, experiential, risky, supportive, introspective, out-of-the-box and natural.

Approached this way, needs assessment becomes an adventure activity unto itself, where the emphasis is on achieving a shared vision constructed through a constant give and take of information. Optimally, the assessment is not a one-time event. Instead, like the Experiential Learning Cycle, it's a continuous loop that benefits from information added at each step of the consulting experience as the process cycles through design, delivery, post-delivery and then often on to a new collaboration. The close collaboration that the adventure consultant establishes with the client during the inquiry phase then builds and persists through the design and implementation phases.

An Adventure Approach to Assessing Needs

From this adventure perspective, the primary purpose of a needs assessment is to reach a consensual understanding between client and consultant of needs, goals and desired outcomes. The needs must be understood in context and sharply defined; the goals must be clearly articulated and attainable; the desired outcomes should be observable and realistic. The road to achieving such clarity is neither smooth nor clearly marked.

As any consultant knows, the needs assessment process must bridge several gaps between vision and reality. First, there is the potential gap between the client's vision of the need/problem, and the reality that is experienced by others in the company. Second, there is the potential gap between a client's vision of what he hopes to achieve and the reality of what is attainable, given the constraints of time, budget and human nature. Finally, there is the potential gap between the consultant's vision of what sort of intervention she might want to stage and what is feasible, given the client's mindset and parameters.

To close such gaps, adventure consulting favors a collaborative approach. The aim is to establish a close collaboration built on mutual respect between client and consultant during the needs assessment process that will remain active throughout the design and delivery phases. This approach is informed by the following convictions:

- The best relationship between client and consultant is a partnership.
- The client, not the consultant, is the expert in their business.
- Multiple perspectives enhance, clarify and amplify the picture.
- Needs assessment is a two-way street that builds information and trust.
- Adventure activities are a valuable tool for assessing needs.
- Optimal results hinge on clear goals and realistic expectations.

The Partnership

From the very first contact with a potential client, Project Adventure's consultants seek to forge an interactive dynamic that makes learning and the exchange of information constant and reciprocal. This reflects the dual convictions that all parts of the consulting process should be entered into by choice, and that collaboration enhances the effort.

Many of the diagnostic tools for the inquiry phase are familiar. Interviews, questionnaires, attitude surveys, focus group discussions, employee and customer satisfaction surveys, and assessment centers are all employed.

Less familiar may be the consultant's constant attention to unspoken messages, mood and client affect. This approach draws upon processing skills that have been researched and validated by behavioral scientists, then practiced and honed by PA during our work in educational and therapeutic settings. It strives to keep questions open-ended and statements nonjudgmental; to share the consultant's reading of verbal and nonverbal cues; to explore areas of potential conflict or concern openly as they emerge; to share perceptions and nonconfidential information at every turn; to be open, unmysterious and accessible.

The "Expert" Conundrum

In traditional consulting practices, the consultant often draws a distinction between the "presenting problem" (the client's assessment) and the "underlying problem" (the consultant's assessment). This bit of trade lingo is telling. Wittingly or not, it implies that the consultant's diagnosis is "right," and the client's flawed.

After conducting an independent assessment, the consultant then fashions recommendations around his diagnosis. While this sequence is often highly effective, it has several potential drawbacks. First, the new diagnosis may not resonate with the client. But having already invested the time and effort, the consultant is now highly motivated to convince the client to accept his view of the problem. If he fails to achieve that buy-in, he risks having his ideas and design proposal discarded, and his "expertise" and credibility questioned. This sequence also limits opportunities for mutual brainstorming. Finally, it risks creating an Us (consultant) versus Them (client) mentality that can breed resentment and tussles for control during the design and delivery phases.

The adventure thrust is to forge a We (collaboration) that emphasizes the synergistic benefits of sharing information, impressions and insights. Whether working solely with a client or coordinating with other consultants to produce a multiple-function training, the adventure consultant seeks to foster a climate where the many stakeholders will perceive a benefit in pooling information and perspectives.

The adventure consultant neither regards himself as the "expert," nor wants the client to regard him that way. From the start, the consultant conveys that the "ultimate" expert is the client, who is intimately acquainted with the company's problems and challenges. The consultant's job is to offer a more detailed perspective and to provide learning experiences that will enhance the client's ability to maximize, leverage and harness the company's strengths, competencies and expertise.

Multiple Perspectives

Assessments of a company's problems and needs vary widely, depending on the lens through which the situation is viewed. Any such appraisal is highly subjective. There is no right and no wrong, only perceptions.

Hence, it is imprudent for a consultant to accept at face value the assessment offered by any one person. Often, such a view is offered either by a top-level executive or a human resources manager, neither of whom usually works directly with the constellation of people (and problems) that will be addressed during delivery. At best, such a vision may not fully reflect the reality experienced by the people around whom the training is to be designed; at worst, it may grossly misrepresent employees' perceptions (particularly if that decision-maker is perceived as integral to the problem).

To narrow this gap between vision and reality, the adventure consultant openly and actively seeks the input of as many people as time, resources and access permit, from the CEO to managers to line personnel who will be involved in the training. As he gathers information, he attempts to listen neutrally, affixing no more or less importance to any one person's view. He stresses confidentiality, so that people may speak without fear of reprisal.

As he seeks a 360-degree view of a company, the consultant does not accumulate, hoard and leverage information in order to enhance his standing, make him seem "in the know" or buttress his resulting recommendations. He recognizes that while his role as outsider may give him access to information (often related to "hand" and "heart" issues) that the company's executives and internal consultants may be unable to tap, only an insider (with a firm grasp of the "head" issues) can put that information into a perspective that appreciates the larger context of the whole company.

Without breaching confidentiality, the adventure consultant gathers and shares, gathers and shares, constantly feeding information back to the client so that this insider can expand upon the findings with further reflections and insights. Through this continual give and take, client and consultant together watch the picture sharpen and finally come into clear focus.

Though the client often wants the consultant to only reach down into the ranks to obtain the sort of candid feedback that may be inaccessible to top management, the adventure consultant strives to reach upward, as well. Critical to the success of any design is a clear understanding of what messages senior management will or won't support after the consultant's departure. To spend time on a program that is not in alignment with both the company's values and the top executive's personal outlook is a waste of the client's time and money.

Two-Way Street

From the very first encounter with a client, the adventure consultant begins cultivating the invisible field of trust imperative to building a successful learning community. By presenting himself as open and accessible, the consultant aims to convey, "I do not presume to think that I can 'solve' your problems; rather, by sharing information, we can learn from one another."

Approached this way, an interview, whether conducted one-on-one or in a group, can be a two-way tool for gathering and disseminating information. Aware that an interview subject's discomfort with a stranger or the very idea of the consulting process can stand in the way of an uninhibited exchange, the adventure consultant attends to establishing an atmosphere that encourages questions, comments and the voicing of concerns about any aspect of the unfolding process.

Sometimes, this requires addressing media-generated conceptions about adventure activities. By inviting interviewees to ask questions, the consultant creates an opportunity to demystify and allay concerns about experiential learning. "No," he makes plain, "you will not be 'required' to bounce off cliffs, leap from tall buildings, plunge into roiling rapids."

Even more than those who utilize other consulting techniques, adventure consultants must be alert to the possibility that one of the "needs" presented by a client is a need to gain information about and comfort with the consulting process and its tools. Any resistance that can be overcome prior to delivery leaves more time and energy during the training to focus directly on achieving the client's program goals and desired outcomes.

Adventure Tools

It is often helpful during the needs assessment phase to engage the client in an adventure activity. A brief immersion experience can serve a variety of purposes, from engaging interest and building excitement, to easing anxiety and planting some new conceptions about the range and scope of adventure learning.

Most important, it enables the client and consultant to connect in the manner unique to adventure learning. For the client, the immediate impact may be one of those "aha" moments that suddenly makes an elusive point or dynamic refreshingly clear. Short-term, the client samples the sense of connection and trust fostered by an adventure experience. Long-term, it enlarges the client's understanding of the contours and potentialities of adventure learning.

This is no less important when working in tandem with other consultants. Interestingly, despite the rapidly more widespread use of adventure consulting, some of the most rigid pre- and misconceptions about adventure learning are held by fellow consultants. When collaborating, adventure consultants often find it worth taking the time to engage other vendors in an adventure activity, so that all of the involved consultants can proceed with an enhanced appreciation of each other's skills and maximize each other's offerings.

The adventure consultant, in other words, uses adventure learning as a tool in developing client and partner relationships. Adventure is not just a training tool. It's a way of interacting with people during all phases of the consulting process and at all levels of corporate life.

Managing Expectations

Successful design and delivery hinge on well-defined goals and realistic expectations. That makes the bottom line for needs assessment clear: client and consultant must achieve a mutual understanding of goals and desired outcomes.

One way to gain such clarity is to press the client to define, up-front, how success will be measured. Often, clients rely exclusively on "smile sheets" that are handed out at the end of a training to gauge participants' opinion of what just transpired. That's fine if the goal is to boost morale with a novel experience that enhances and celebrates team spirit. When the goals are more far-reaching, the smile-sheet approach is usually inadequate because it allows no space for hindsight, perspective or assessment of commitments to action. It fails, in short, to assess whether the client's stated goals and desired outcomes have been achieved.

The adventure consultant wants to know how the client intends to measure behavioral change. What will that change look like three or six months from now in terms of both performance and production? If a client says she wants to "build trust" or "build better teamwork," what will that look like and sound like in the workplace? How will it be measured or benchmarked? What skills will be stronger? What practices will no longer be present? What behaviors will have diminished and what will have replaced them? What new operating norms will be in place?

When a client is able to articulate goals, desired outcomes and plans for evaluation up-front, there are a variety of advantages. The client is then able to see if the time and resources committed to the venture are adequate. It creates an alignment of expectation between the client and consultant. And it mitigates against the consultant's over-promising and under-delivering.

An assessment and articulation of the adventure consultant's needs is essential, as well, if the succeeding phases are to go smoothly. If, for instance, the consultant feels it essential that he have access to the CEO prior to the design phase, he must make this clear to the client. He must address practical and operational concerns, particularly when working cross-culturally across time zones and international borders. Differences of values must be reconciled; ethical considerations must be resolved.

Different Needs, Different Outcomes

No single example captures the variety of purposes an interactive needs assessment can serve. So, instead of following a single process from beginning to end, here is a selection of snapshots from three different appraisals. They illustrate variously how a collaborative needs assessment can:

- Sharpen goals
- Redefine needs
- Achieve consensus

Sharpening Goals

The Office of Solid Waste within the Environmental Protection Agency was trying to figure out how best to respond to a mandate from the federal government to "create a government that works better and costs less." Specifically, OSW was under pressure to reduce its management staff, decentralize decision-making and promote the formation and use of teams to improve efficiency and communication.

The five groups targeted to attend a two-day training aimed at these problems were the senior management team (who ran OSW), the office managers (who managed office logistics) and three branch teams: International, the Permits and State Program Division (PSPD) and Industrial Waste/Special Waste. These teams varied in size from six to 16 people.

As part of the needs assessment process, Project Adventure consultants spent a day on-site at the OSW offices in Washington, DC, conducting group and individual interviews, administering team questionnaires and sampling OSW's culture. During the five 45-minute meetings with representatives from each of the five teams, it became apparent through a mix of dialogue and adventure activity that though the teams shared some issues, their needs, concerns and levels of cohesion were quite different.

· The senior management team, which didn't indicate major internal problems, was eager to cooperate and quite willing to share their impressions of team issues and dynamics. Primarily, they wanted to learn about adventure techniques and hear about the other teams' concerns. Another team, by contrast, was initially reserved and skeptical about adventure training. After the members engaged in an activity and loosened up, they became more candid, indicating that they felt a lack of power, resented being at the beck and call of other teams and lacked a sense of group cohesion.

The other three teams also had distinct problems. One team focused on interpersonal issues, speaking about a lack of trust and candor among team members, and discomfort with their supervisor's role and style. The members of another team, which had recently experienced a high level of turnover, were tense and fearful about OSW's reorganization and did not feel they operated well as a team. The third team, comprising two groups which had recently been merged into a single unit, seemed to be in the most fragile state. Still in the dark as to who their new manager would be and how they were to combine operations, both groups were resistant to the merger. Tension was high, morale was low and there was wide skepticism that any training could help heal their divisions.

Some of the most telling information emerged through brief adventure activities. An initiative involving ropes and circles, for instance, gradually narrows the "playing" space until all members of a group are compelled to share a space the size of a hula hoop. The "aha!" that unleashes creative solutions comes when someone recognizes that to fit a group of people into a small circular loop and

meet the activity's parameters, it isn't necessary for everyone's body to be completely inside the hoop; just their feet will do very nicely.

Watching individual team members respond to this type of challenge can shed light on a group's dynamic. Who eagerly complied with the solution? Who resisted—and why? Was it discomfort with shifting into a new paradigm? Or was it personal resistance to the team member who suggested the solution?

By synthesizing the information offered both verbally and behaviorally, the adventure consultants uncovered issues that would impinge directly on design and delivery. Among them: the teams had very different concerns and issues; the issues were variously structural, interpersonal and hierarchical; the levels of interest in the training were all over the map.

The consultants' observation was that the design would have to accommodate and address five distinct sets of needs during the training. The client stakeholders at OSW agreed. The upshot was a design that began and ended with the larger OSW group comprising five separate teams. Built as a *circuit* design, the five teams were able to experience a variety of initiatives in rotation, with each of those initiatives customized to address each team's specific needs. The group were brought together for opening and closing activities and discussion.

Redefining Needs

A particularly tricky challenge was presented by a company that specializes in intellectual software. For the third year running, PA had been invited to deliver an annual "team-building" program. During the needs assessment process, a vice president named Steve told the adventure consultants that as a result of divisional downsizing half of the employees who would participate in the two-day team-building program would soon be fired, laid off or relocated elsewhere in the company.

"Why," the consultants asked, "do you want to do team-building exercises with a group of people who will soon be removed from the team?"

Steve responded that if the group went off-site and developed a greater sense of cohesion and trust, its members would be better prepared to handle the bad news. By enhancing team trust, he believed, people would feel more comfortable talking with colleagues about their feelings of anger and disappointment, and more inclined to seek help. Steve also hoped that, for those who were to be relocated, the company's commitment to addressing trust and teamwork issues would make them feel better about staying with the organization.

Ordinarily, an effort would have been made to speak to many more people. But in this case, further information was unlikely to clarify training objectives or benefit the design process. Instead, the immediate need was to reconcile the client's desire for team-building training with PA's own reservations about such an approach serving the company's needs.

One distinct possibility was that the client was going forward with its annual event simply because the company could not find a comfortable way to cancel it. That posed an ethical conundrum: how could PA, which premises its work on building an atmosphere of trust, enter in good faith into a situation where half the participants would be misled by the proceedings?

The consulting solution was to suggest that the focus be shifted away from team-building and toward skill-building around team issues. The proposed skill-building design would, among other things, augment the participants' understanding of the relationship of trust to productive teamwork; enhance skills for giving and receiving feedback; strengthen communication skills; and help individuals to better capitalize on resources and turn limitations into opportunities. The client agreed that this approach would create more lasting take-aways for both constituencies to be served by the training: those who would stay on with the company, and those who would be let go.

Though this training, early in PA's corporate work, produced a satisfactory outcome, experience now points in another direction. Presented with the same scenario today, the likely recommendation would be for the client to wait until after the restructuring, then develop a fresh team-development opportunity that might explore team strengths, development opportunities, team maintenance behaviors and desired operating norms under the new reorganization.

Aligning Expectations

In working with BMW South Africa, the challenge was to design a program for the 25 field consultants who service the country's 90 dealerships in the areas of sales, after-market service, business management and technical support. The company wanted to address three key areas over the course of a two-week training: behavioral skills, team-building, and leadership and consulting strategies.

BMW had recently reconfigured its "Dealer Support" program, shifting away from a structure with a clear functional emphasis to create five cross-functional teams. Interviews with field consultants made it clear that the reorganization had left them confused about which "team" they regarded as their "primary" unit. Was it the functional groups, the new cross-functional regional teams or the collective field force?

Clarification was essential to team identification and development. It therefore would be central to any training design. But further probing unveiled further confusion. The reorganization had been developed and implemented by the former Sales and Marketing Director (SMD) in conjunction with the new Managing Director. The new SMD's views on this new structure were not well understood, nor was it clear whether he fully supported the field training initiative.

In pressing for clarification, the adventure consultants solicited input from, shared evolving information with and strove to maintain the commitment of many people. The key players were Beverley Whitehead, the human resources manager responsible for the training; the managers of the field consultants; the SMD; and Flip Diedericks, a consultant from Stratcon, a locally based organizational development consulting firm with whom PA was partnering. By the time we entered the design phase, we had clarified the managers' views of which team should be considered "primary" under the reorganization, and confirmed that the new SMD supported the training initiative.

The need for a clear alignment of expectations did not stop there. The process, already complicated by the large number of stakeholders, was further complicated by the logistics of dealing with a company based so far away. After an initial meeting in the US, Beverly, Flip and the PA consultants would not be meeting again until the delivery phase. During the remainder of the needs assessment and design phases, the parties would have to navigate three time zones spanning a 10-hour time difference and a 10,175-mile divide. Expectations were carved out up-front to help make smooth navigation of these various divides possible.

Consideration also had to be given to cultural and corporate differences. The consultants were particularly attentive to the nuances and connotations of verbal and body language; sensitive to differing assumptions about seniority and rank; flexible about the way the inclusive, process-oriented adventure tools would be applied in this stratified, achievement-oriented environment. They also actively solicited input from their BMW partners on how best to navigate the multiethnic, multilingual training audience, whose members came from a variety of sociopolitical and educational backgrounds.

Failure to acknowledge and address these various differences up-front would have invited frustrating project delays, role confusion, control issues and communication obstacles. Failure to align the expectations of the various stakeholders about how business would be conducted across time zones and borders would have invited needless confusion. Failure to align expectations about the messages that would be conveyed and supported during the training about team identification would have courted fragmentation and thwarted the building of the shared vision critical to any successful intervention. Instead, the needs assessment addressed all of those issues by: gaining the active sponsorship, commitment and involvement of managers; establishing lines of communication and review among all key stakeholders for the design process; achieving a mutual understanding of each others' expertise; linking the development needs of the trainees to content, theory and activity.

Summary

A successful consulting intervention begins with a skillful needs assessment. The adventure approach favors an interactive dynamic that engages the client and consultant in a partnership that is mutually supportive and synergistic. By working collaboratively, the client and consultant make effective use of each other's abilities, perceptions and information, while cutting down on misunderstanding and divergence of purpose.

The reciprocal approach employed during needs assessment adheres to the same values supported in the training environment by the Experiential Learning Cycle, the Full Value Contract and Challenge by Choice. Thus, adventure learning is introduced at the outset of the consulting relationship and informs all the phases that follow.

Throughout the needs assessment process, adventure tools are specifically employed to: build a partnership with the client; make best use of the client's expertise; develop a picture that features multiple perspectives; open pathways for the transmission and reception of information and trust; align expectations about goals and desired outcomes.

The needs assessment then continues throughout the consulting experience, mirroring the remaining phases of the Experiential Learning Cycle.

As the information is gathered, the learnings and extrapolations become grist, first for the training design, then for delivery, and eventually for transfer back to the workplace. At each of those stages, the needs assessment continues in an unending attempt to further identify, clarify and address the client's needs.

Bringing the Consultant Into Focus

In the last decade, the consulting field has exploded. The range of options can be as baffling as it is exciting. When it comes to adventure consulting, in particular, how do you know which vendor to choose? The following questions can serve as a guide for making that choice:

- What are the history and track record of the adventure consulting organization?
- How wide-ranging is their experience? Who are their clients? Are references available?
- What is their experience partnering with clients? Have they ever been part of a design that involved other external consultants?
- What are their underlying philosophies and underpinnings? Are they in sync with our own culture and values?
- Are they accessible? Are they responsive?
- What adventure and traditional tools are in their toolkit? Does the range of tools suggest a design flexibility?
- What are their portable capabilities?
- Do you want a custom-tailored design or an off-the-shelf product that can be used internally many times?
- Do they have experience working with groups with mixed physical abilities?
- What is their staff capacity to deliver multiple sessions at multiple venues?
- What is their safety record? (See Risk Management Appendix.)
- What is our chemistry with them? Do they feel like people we can talk to and trust?

Bringing the Client Into Focus

In the competitive world of consulting, it is common for business clients to invite a variety of consultants, both adventure and traditional, to bid on a contract. Typically, this requires that the consultant submit a detailed proposal, with no guarantee that the invested time and costs will be remunerated. Consultants might want to consider the following questions before deciding whether to enter into a bidding process. Most of these issues deserve consideration even when a contract is offered flat-out.

- Is there valuable learning involved, whether we get the contract or not?
- Will we potentially be developing an intervention or creating a training opportunity that could be used in the future, irrespective of this contract?
- Is it likely that the client has already chosen a vendor and is just going through the standard protocol of inviting bids?
- Are we an appropriate match with this client? Is there anything about the practices of this client that might contradict our own values or practices?
- Who will we be expected to work with, and is it likely we can form a comfortable partnership?
- Should we request a preliminary meeting with the client, even if time and other costs are at our own expense?
- Would a phone conversation be enough to further assess both the nature of the bid and the levelness of the playing field?
- Are we likely to achieve consensus with the client on goals and expectations, or is there cause to worry that a shared vision will not emerge?
- Do we have something of value to offer, or would another consulting approach be better suited to this particular set of needs?
- Might our time be better invested elsewhere?

The Art of Design

8

"The essence of design is helping to create an emotional connection to an intellectual problem or idea."

—*Rodney Napier*, Do It . . . And Understand!

Program design is the critical link between the vision and realization of a client's goals. Like an architectural blueprint, a design lays out the contours of the client's new structure, which may be a groundbreaking creation or an addition to an existing structure. Either way, the design must address, accommodate and juggle multiple considerations.

First and foremost, like an architectural blueprint, an adventure design must rest upon a firm foundation and be structurally sound. It must respond to the specific needs and desired outcomes of the client. And it must work within the client's parameters on several fronts, including stated goals, program length, site location, budget, group size, participant-to-staff ratios and content specifications.

Furthermore, the design challenges of a half-day or full-day program are quite different from a multi-day or circuit effort (see Appendix I). A site that has an existing ropes course or a space for portable outdoor activities offers different design opportunities than a site that restricts activities to the indoors. Where outdoor opportunities exist, some clients want high challenge course experiences, some want low, some want to steer clear of challenge courses altogether.

No matter what the variables, architects of behavioral change must remain alert to the reality that it is the client, not the consultant, who will live with the results of the training. For that reason, PA consultants strive throughout the design phase to build upon the client–consultant partnership initiated during the needs assessment, imbuing the process with I.M.M.E.R.S.I.O.N. qualities to further engage the client's interest.

When clients are truly open to outcomes, not tied to them, close collaborations, almost without exception, yield designs that are sharply focused, finely detailed and highly innovative. As a result, they are also satisfyingly memorable.

A Blueprint for Designing

Though adventure designs vary dramatically, the process by which the consultant and client get to that design is fairly uniform. The first step, of course, is the needs assessment. It is through this process of gathering and sifting information that the client's agenda becomes clear. Often, the client will prove to have primary and secondary goals.

During the design phase, these broad goals are honed, ever-sharpening the focus to produce clarity of purpose. Throughout this refining process, a careful eye is kept on the client's parameters. If, for instance, goals and time boundaries are not congruent, the resulting design may have a fragmented focus that will dilute the impact of the training and leave participants without a memorable message.

Early in the design process, the adventure consultant seeks to identify or create a theoretical framework that will support the client's goals. Sometimes, an explanation of the experiential learning model underlying the design is all that is required. Often, however, additional theoretical references are sought to help create the metaview that will overlay the design and inform the selection of adventure activities. Sometimes, a client will request the integration of a specific content piece, or "deliverable" (e.g., a leadership inventory, a behavioral profile, a problem-solving model).

A big-picture outline, or macroview, is then sketched to map out the design's flow, which will include a mix of content pieces and adventure activities. Considerations include: Which content pieces require that the group function as a single unit? How often will the large group be broken apart into smaller units? If the group is subdivided into smaller teams, is it appropriate to reconvene as a large group and if so, when? After breaks, how will attention be refocused?

A more detailed outline, or microview, of each day's events is then developed. While some designs need only a loose plan, other designs require minute-by-minute scripting. It is at this point that the adventure consultant begins to select and customize specific adventure activities around the program's content, drawing from an extensive toolbox that includes both a wide array of adventure activities and more traditional consulting tools, including inventories, models and media components. The deeper the adventure consultant's knowledge of the client's goals, staff and product, the greater his ability to tailor initiatives and create metaphorical frameworks that will make each component of the design meaningful and memorable for participants.

As the specific tools and activities are selected, an eye is always kept on the sequence of presentations. Does it build logically and systematically, taking advantage of what preceded and pointing toward what will follow? Is the overall message cogent and coherent? What are the contingency plans if there is inclement weather, if a keynote speaker alters his arrival time, if a group fails to respond, if the materials don't arrive on time, if twice or half of the anticipated number of participants show up?

In close, collaborative efforts, much of the thought process is shared with the client for further elaboration, editing and refinement. Why? Often the ongoing needs assessment process, as well as unanticipated developments, present new variables that dictate changes in the design. An anticipated site with outdoor facilities may fall through, forcing the consultant back to the drawing table to design an indoor training. The CEO may suddenly decide that he wants to deliver a speech during the post-lunch module. And so on.

Before turning to an actual design, a few caveats. As mentioned earlier, adventure designs range from half-day to multi-day models. Some designs use a "circuit" approach to manage large participant numbers; others keep the participants together throughout without ever subdividing the group. The customized design described here, a one-day program, was selected because it affords the opportunity to reconstruct both the flow of a design and its component activities without overwhelming newcomers to the process with detail. A multi-day design, of course, would have greater latitude, a wider focus and many more components.

Finally, though an adventure design, like an architectural blueprint, attempts to anticipate and address the client's every need, consideration and

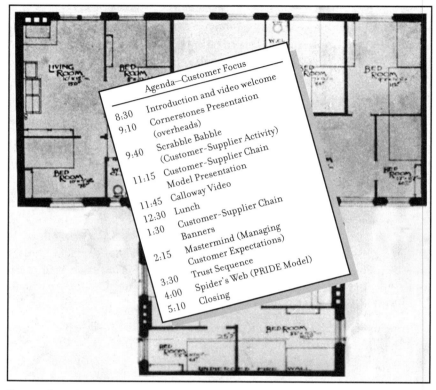

Agenda—Customer Focus

8:30   Introduction and video welcome
9:10   Cornerstones Presentation
      (overheads)
9:40   Scrabble Babble
      (Customer-Supplier Activity)
11:15   Customer-Supplier Chain
      Model Presentation
11:45   Calloway Video
12:30   Lunch
1:30   Customer-Supplier Chain
      Banners
2:15   Mastermind (Managing
      Customer Expectations)
3:30   Trust Sequence
4:00   Spider's Web (PRIDE Model)
5:10   Closing

Blueprint: Design by Jacob Riis. Courtesy of the Museum of the City of New York.

problem, it's only a plan. As during construction, so during delivery: unpredictabilities arise, human priorities clash—flexibility is essential.

A One-Day Design

In an effort to strengthen company-wide commitment to "customer focus," BMW North America approached Project Adventure to help design and deliver a one-day program that would enhance the internal staff's understanding and appreciation of customer satisfaction and service.

Entering the design phase, PA consultants had a high level of familiarity with many of the customer issues particular to BMW. Four months earlier, we had partnered with BMW to launch "Premier Care," a five-day program delivered to BMW retail center owners around the country that focused on customer-related issues, among them enhancing understanding of the importance of customer and employee satisfaction, anticipating customer demands and working effectively with the manufacturer to achieve maximum support in customer service.

During the program, the retailers had suggested that BMW's internal staff could similarly benefit from some work on customer relations. (This suggestion reinforced a top management idea that an all-employee training would be timely and valuable.) Eventually, they settled on a one-day "Customer Focus Training" for the roughly 950 internal staffers at BMW's headquarters, Vehicle Preparation Centers, financial centers and warehouses in four regions.

The needs assessment uncovered that BMW's internal staff had a varied understanding of "customer"; moreover, their concept was often at odds with the retailers'. Because internal staffers often had minimal or no contact with external customers, many employees perceived little connection between their work and the ultimate satisfaction of the end user (i.e., the BMW owner). In some instances, internal employees felt divorced from the company's bottom line. BMW's upper management wanted to send the message that the retailer's ability to serve customers hinged directly on the information, material and services provided by BMW's internal staff.

Coming into the design, then, the overarching goal was to make clear to internal staffers that they, too, had customers, and that provision of outstanding service to those *internal* customers directly affected the retailer's ability to provide outstanding service to BMW's *external* customers. Secondarily, there would be an accent on the positive benefits of effective cross-functioning teamwork.

Further collaborative honing by BMW managers and PA consultants resulted in the identification of five specific training objectives:

- To introduce a new way of thinking in which everyone sees that *each* employee is both a supplier and a customer;
- To create a company-wide understanding that building positive relationships between customers and suppliers is critical to the success of the overall franchise;
- To create a shared understanding that different employees have different customers;

- To create a supportive environment wherein participants feel comfortable identifying and discussing who their customers are, what needs those customers have and how best to serve them;
- To begin building an enhanced team sense within departments, within regions and across regions that reflects this new understanding that "customer focus" has both an internal and a retail component.

The desired outcomes clarified, PA consultants began to identify various theoretical models that could overlay the design. We found ourselves drawn to the "customer–supplier chain theory," which envisions employees as part of a continuous chain where all links are both suppliers and customers. After investigating several models, we received permission from Organizational Dynamics Inc. to adapt aspects of its customer–supplier chain curriculum. In particular, we chose a tool which addresses the challenges of aligning customer needs with supplier capabilities. Its acronym, PRIDE, stands for Product, Relationship, Integrity, Delivery, Expense.

Logistical considerations revolved chiefly around the fact that we would be delivering the one-day training at a variety of locations around the country to roughly 60 people at a time. That meant that whatever we developed would have to be adaptable to each venue; materials would have to be portable, shippable and durable for reuse; an internal PA team would have to be assembled so that the delivery would be consistent as we took the program from site to site. It also meant developing a design that would permit the cross-functional scheduling of groups, so that no department would have to shut down on a training day. Finally, BMW wanted to contain the training within normal business hours.

As mentioned earlier, design and needs assessment are an integrated and fluid process. Initially, we approached the design with plans to integrate outdoor elements. But as BMW's meeting planners identified each of the venues and we inspected the various facilities, it became clear that we would need to work with an all-indoor model in order to keep the 16 trainings consistent.

The design that was ultimately co-delivered by BMW and PA looked like this:

8:30 BMW Introduction

The day opens with introductions of the half-dozen members of the joint BMW and PA training staff, and a videotaped message from BMW President

Vic Doolan that outlines the day's three themes: Customer Focus, the Customer–Supplier Chain, Teamwork.

8:45 Large Group Introduction Activities

To set the tone, "Categories" was used, a nonthreatening activity well-suited to groups where people are meeting each other for the first time. Categories are called out, and people group themselves accordingly for brief conversation. Some categories are totally unrelated to the day's work ahead, e.g., "Group yourselves according to your preferred morning beverage" (tea lovers, coffee drinkers, etc.), and provoke quick moments of shared amusement. ("I'm a latte person." "Me, too! Tall, Grande or Venti?")

Other categories are crafted to introduce participants to some of the language that will be used throughout the day. "Divide yourselves according to the number of customers you believe you serve daily." "Divide yourselves into ratings, on a scale of 1–10, according to how satisfied you are with your suppliers."

While a trainer provides the directing statement, it is up to the participants to further define and interpret the category, so all of this is attended by a lot of good-natured shouting and waving that loosens up the group. ("Orange juice drinkers over here!") It also happens very quickly, with people having only a minute or two of chit-chat before the next grouping is called. By the end of the activity, the mingling has begun to create the supportive environment that is crucial for enhancing a greater team sense. And, people have had an opportunity to connect with the majority of participants.

9:10 Cornerstone Presentations

A PA trainer introduces participants to the Full Value Contract and Challenge by Choice (see Chapters 5 and 6). To present the Full Value concept, the group is subdivided into five groups and assembled around five flip charts, where participants are asked to brainstorm and bullet ideas about what each of the five FVC tenets means to them in their work environment. When the group is reassembled, each group reports back its ideas. Participants are encouraged to seek further clarification and add additional thoughts. Ultimately, a group commitment is sought to operate throughout the remainder of the day within the tenets, as the group has interpreted them. The framework within which participants will be expected to engage with one another becomes clearer as these cornerstones are introduced.

After Challenge by Choice is introduced, risk release forms are distributed. The purpose of the Medical Information and Release of Liability portions are explained, and time is allowed for participant questions (see Appendix III).

9:40 Customer–Supplier Activity

To begin focusing participants' attention on the customer–supplier relationship, the design opens with "Scrabble Babble," an initiative that stimulates without overtaxing, compels people to begin working with each other, and has a light tone that helps to continue the convening process. It also begins to introduce the concept that *each* employee can potentially be both a supplier and a customer, while also illuminating the benefits of cross-functioning.

The generic rules of Scrabble Babble are simple. Take a stack of cards, each with an individual letter on it, and form words. Words can be either freestanding or connected Scrabble-style. No letters can be reused. The objective is to form as many words as possible within a 10-minute period.

For this audience, stacks of cards are placed at 10 locations around the room, and a metaphorical framework is provided. "Everyone in this room belongs to one company," says a trainer. "The 10 stacks represent the company's distribution centers where you are free to go to procure resources. A customer is requesting that you form as many words as possible, using up all of the letters available. The customer wants you to understand that his key concern is volume."

Set to the task, the participants spontaneously form groups, with clusters of people gravitating to different stacks around the room. Most people move to the stacks closest to the tables where they've been seated.

As the program rolled out over the months, facilitators worked from the participants' responses to guide the debrief. Among the avenues pursued: What was the customer–supplier chain in this activity, and which role(s) did you play? As a customer, did you always receive what you needed from your suppliers? As a supplier, did you feel the resources (letters, people, etc.) were used to maximum effect? How did the teams each determine how the letters would be used? Was there discussion between groups about how resources were being allocated? Did you develop an efficient and effective process? Did you strive to make as many words as possible, or did you aim for the larger words that have greater value in the Scrabble paradigm? Did that serve the customer's needs? Did you experience anything that was similar to situations at work? What would you do differently?

10:10 Customer–Supplier Definitions

The "Customer–Supplier Chain" concept is introduced, using a series of overheads and other visual aids (an approach that often engages those people whose learning style does not take readily to hands-on activity). Definition is given to the theory's five key components (customer, supplier, inputs, outputs, added value). Then we look at the theory's main precepts: everyone is both a customer and a supplier; knowing your role at any given moment helps you improve the customer–supplier relationship; the hand-off of work from supplier to customer creates the chain; each time an employee "touches" the process, he adds value.

These concepts and definitions, presented in a straightforward manner, are further reinforced by a booklet of materials that participants are encouraged to consult throughout the day, make notes in and take home. The definitions are also posted around the room for easy reference. This presentation is purposefully kept brief. After all, Project Adventure's own purpose is to *show*, not tell, why this chain is so critical.

10:15 Break

10:30 Customer–Supplier Activity

To enhance participants' sense of being part of a chain, the next activity is "Pipeline," an adventure initiative that involves the transfer of items across a designated distance, in a limited amount of time, within a restrictive set of guidelines.

The group is divided into four subgroups, then dispatched for the next 45 minutes to different rooms, each with an assigned trainer. Generically, the challenge calls for transporting a variety of round objects to a container and dropping them in. The hitch is that the objects can only be touched by and carried in plastic chutes, each of which is about a foot long. It is up to the participants, each of whom is given one chute, to figure out how to bridge the chutes to create an effective conduit for the rolling objects.

For the BMW group, the activity is tailored this way. Each group is given five BMW golf balls and five marbles and told that these represent deliverables (e.g., products, services, information). "The goal is to transport these deliverables to that container over there," the trainers explain. "Your management of the materials [chutes] can add value to the chain of delivery. Each time a golf ball or marble is dropped into the can, that represents a satisfied customer."

Simple, right? "Well, the customer has a few expectations that will challenge your ability to maneuver." The objects can't stop, roll backwards, drop or be touched by a person. (In other words, the balls must have a continuous forward motion, and participants are not permitted to stop the ball in order to better control the transfer from one piece of piping to the next.)

"Any infraction of the rules is considered a glitch in the customer–supplier chain and will require service recovery." To wit: participants must return to the starting area and begin again. Once an object reaches the can, however, it may remain there.

This highly engaging, highly energetic exercise tends to bust through any lingering resistance as people race around, struggling to catch a transferred ball, pass it along to the next person, strategize a particularly challenging curve or obstacle, or best position themselves for the next pass off.

The debriefing of the activity focuses participants on how they (as customers) received the items from those ahead of them in the chain, and how they (as suppliers) delivered the items to the next person in the chain. People are able to see vividly how they affected the chain, in terms of both the direct pass-off from one person to the next, and the successful functioning of the overall franchise.

11:15 Customer–Supplier Chain Model

To shift understanding and appreciation of the customer–supplier chain from the general to the specific, participants are given 11 x 17 sheets of paper, pens and markers. Using the terminology of the customer–supplier chain theory discussed earlier, trainers ask them to create a series of five-link chains, each with themselves at the center of the chain. Each chain should include: (1) who supplies them (supplier); (2) what value was added as the work passed to them (input); (3) what they did (value added); (4) what value they added before passing it on (output); (5) who they then supplied with this work (customer).

To ensure understanding, a trainer presents a detailed example of a customer–supplier chain process that occurred during the development of the program between BMW, Project Adventure and the selected venue. As participants identify and diagram several of their own customer–supplier relationships, the trainer reiterates that they need to pinpoint the value they personally add to the process. The point here is for participants to specify whom they directly provide services to and receive services from. The exercise creates a shared understanding that different employees have different customers and that "customer focus" has both an internal and a retail component.

11:45 Calloway Video

This video, featuring motivational speaker Joe Calloway addressing a BMW group, was originally prepared for BMW's "Premier Care" training. In the clip excerpted for this audience, Calloway vividly recounts good and bad customer service experiences, many of them personal and instantly recognizable to participants. Because the footage focuses on external customer relationships, the participants are asked to regard the video as a tool for reflecting on internal customer relations.

For the debriefing, a trainer uses flip charts to record participants' reactions to the various good and bad scenarios discussed in the video. Participants are asked to think about their "worst" experience as a customer, and to describe how they felt when their needs weren't met. They are also asked to identify their "best" experience as a customer and the attendant feelings. The group is then asked to use lunch to reflect on and discuss some of their own best and worst internal experiences, and to be prepared to share those stories in the afternoon.

12:30 Lunch

1:30 Check-In on Calloway Video

Participants are invited to share "wow!" stories about internal customer satisfaction. A facilitator then leads a discussion that invites participants to identify common threads between those stories and strategies for best serving the wide-ranging needs of customers.

1:50 Customer–Supplier Chain Banners

Returning to the last hands-on activity before lunch, the building of personal customer–supplier chains, participants are asked to look at their 11 x 17 sheets of paper and select one of their diagrammed customer–supplier chains. Each participant is handed five car-shaped cards and asked to transfer that customer–supplier relationship to the cards, and connect the "cars" with brass clips. Participants then post these chains on the wall, having to choose from among several categories where to hang their chain: National/HQ, Region, Factory, Retailer, Owner, Staff, Co-worker, Pre-Customer.

As participants roam around the room, examining the 60 posted chains, they are no doubt struck by the vast array of customer–supplier connections internal to BMW operations. During the ensuing debriefing, the questions include: How many of you are the sole provider of the service you described as your added value? Is the customer internal or external to BMW? As a supplier, how many of you "wow" your customers on a regular basis? As a customer, how often are you "wowed"? Is there any relationship between the responses to those last two questions? In three years' time, how many of you will be providing the same service or product that you are providing today?

Echoing a theme in the Calloway video, the facilitator concludes with the thought: "The only enduring aspect of your work will be the relationships you create."

2:15 Managing Customer Expectations Activity

To shift the focus within the customer–supplier chain to the challenge of managing customer expectations, a trainer introduces "Mastermind," an adventure initiative which generically involves a variety of conceptually oriented activities that must be solved within a limited time.

After dividing the group into small teams, the trainer explains, "You are all part of one company. The different teams represent BMW's headquarters, regions, departments and so forth. Each team is responsible for solving its own tasks and meeting the expectations of an internal customer."

Each team is then given a medley of adventure brain teasers of varying degrees of difficulty, ranging from relatively simple paper and pencil exercises to more complicated deductive reasoning challenges and mathematical puzzles. Though each team is given all the resources required to solve each of the Mastermind challenges, time will prove short, with the various tasks making competing claims on each team's time.

During the debriefing, the facilitator's questions link the activity to issues related to the management of customers' expectations and continue to underscore the importance of building positive relationships between customers and suppliers. Among the directions a facilitator might take the group: Did teams stick to themselves (they are, after all, responsible for solving their own challenges and meeting customer expectations) or choose to share people and resources with other teams (they are all part of one company)? Did the teams go it alone, or organize and develop a plan? Did customers and suppliers come into alignment? What resulted from that alignment or nonalignment? Is it similar to or different from work? Were customers' expectations satisfied? Exceeded?

3:15 Break

3:30 Trust Sequence

This sequence of activities is cumulative, with each piece enhancing awareness of a different aspect of the customer–supplier relationship. Among the concepts stressed is the need for trust, for keeping commitments, for not agreeing to requests that cannot be met, for negotiating an acceptable commitment when saying "no" is not acceptable. Sequentially, the trust sequence provides a beneficial segue into the initiative that will follow this activity (one that requires lifting and spotting).

The group is redivided into the four subgroups that were created for the morning's Pipeline activity. Each subgroup returns to its respective breakout room, where the same assigned trainer introduces the PRIDE concept (Product, Relationship, Integrity, Delivery, Expense) to initiate a discussion of trust in customer–supplier relationships. Among the issues explored: Product/Service (Is it what my customer needs?), Relationship (Is there trust? Have we discussed how we'll work together?), Integrity (Can I provide what my customer needs? If I can't, what will I do?), Delivery (Do I see that the product/service arrives in timely and usable fashion?), Expense (Is the product affordable? Does the customer believe it has good value?).

After establishing the value and importance of trust in the customer–supplier chain, trainers explain and demonstrate the "Two-Person Fall," a trust-building exercise that calls upon a person to blindly fall backwards into another person's arms. After participants are instructed how to fall and catch properly, they pair off and try out both the role of customer (faller) and supplier (catcher).

Though the task seems simple, a successful fall requires split-second timing, mutual communication and trust. Customers must convey their needs and expectations clearly ("Are you ready to catch me?" "Can you step a foot closer?"). Catchers must similarly assess and convey their needs and capabilities ("I need you to pull in your elbows." "I'm here and ready").

For some, the skills and trust levels are high from the start. For others, it requires several false starts, often with people moving into a falling position, then taking a step just as they start to tilt into the fall. After several different attempts, most pairs feel comfortable enough to execute a fall.

The debriefing includes a look at what was required to establish trust. Did behaviors match words? How did customers (fallers) gauge suppliers' (catchers) proficiency? How hard was it to rebuild trust after a failed effort? Were customer's needs and supplier's capabilities in alignment?

Often, this activity dramatizes the common business attitude that people feel more comfortable in the role of supplier (catcher) than customer (faller) because they perceive themselves as having more "control" over a situation. This can precipitate a thoughtful discussion about the seeming contradiction between the relative comfort of the supplier role and the high levels of stress associated with being expected to meet someone else's needs, schedules, etc.

4:00 Spider's Web

Remaining in the breakout rooms, the small groups are next introduced to the "Spider's Web," an adventure initiative that requires each subgroup to get though a fabricated "web" without touching any of the component ropes. The effort requires careful planning and organization because each time a member passes through a web opening, it is closed and cannot be reused.

To frame the challenge and up the ante, a trainer tells participants, "The web represents a customer–supplier model. Each touch of the web represents a setback for the end customer, and indicates a problem in some input or output in the chain." In order to revisit and rectify the problem, a parameter is given that half of the participants who have successfully completed their passage must return to the starting side of the web and repeat the exercise.

The web is one of the adventure field's most popular low-element rope course activities. It's visually intriguing, intellectually stimulating, physically challenging. It's also an activity that often stirs up conflict within a group. As people jockey to strategize the group's passage, group needs sometimes preempt those of the individual, unless a person (customer) thinks to speak up and make his needs known.

"George, you're big. You'll need to go last and help with all the lifting." (Never mind that George has a bad back.)

"Donna, since you're small, we're going to pass you through that highest opening." (Never mind that Donna is afraid of heights.)

During the debriefing, such behaviors are explored through the customer–supplier lens. Did people identify and voice their needs as they performed the supplier and customer functions? Did the customer who was afraid of heights, for instance, state that she would prefer to be passed through a low opening in the web? Did the supplier with the bad back make clear that he was incapable of single-handedly lifting a customer through the web? Did the group establish a trusting environment that enabled people to articulate their needs without fear of embarrassment? Did customers have their expectations met? Were they "wowed"?

The debrief is structured around the PRIDE model, which is referenced on a flip chart in each room. So participants are also asked: Were suppliers of Products attentive to meeting customer needs? Was there Integrity in meeting customer needs (e.g., were touches called or did people hide them?). And so forth.

The subgroups are then asked to reflect on the day's activities and answer the following: What were the most meaningful and significant learning points you learned or relearned today? What is the biggest challenge you'll face in implementing the PRIDE concept? What is one commitment you are willing to make to enhance your effectiveness at serving (and "wowing"!) customers during the coming month? Ditto, the one commitment you're willing to make to be a more engaged and productive customer?

After a discussion, the subgroup is asked to bullet three key team learnings to share with the larger group when it reconvenes for the closing. As people re-enter the general session room, they are given evaluation sheets and asked to assess the training program.

5:10 Closing

Each subgroup presents its key learnings and supplies any additional thoughts that might be useful to the group at large. Closing comments include a reiteration of the importance of making a personal commitment to carry the learnings of the training into the workplace. To encourage participants to remember what they've explored during the day, T-shirts are distributed with a colorful spider's web graphic, and participants are encouraged to take home and consult the booklets they've had on hand throughout the day to jot notes in and consult for reviewing concepts.

Key Takeaways

Until this training, many BMW staffers had neither viewed their co-workers as customers nor understood how their performance directly impacts the satisfaction of external customers. They also hadn't been aware of how and where work tasks flowed after their hand-off of a product or service to the next person in the chain.

Through the day's activities, BMW's internal staff gained an awareness of and appreciation for the critical importance of understanding and managing customer expectations, including those of superiors. The immediate impact of the training was indicated by the comments on the evaluation forms. Asked "What key learnings or insights did you take away from today?," the following sentiments were expressed repeatedly:

"The customer is our reason for being."

"My customers are anyone I produce product for."

"Our concept of satisfying the customer is not necessarily theirs; communication is important."

"We should not only strive to satisfy the customer, but also to 'wow' them."

"Learning to work together increases customer satisfaction."

"Team is there to help, share ideas, help in problem-solving."

While such comments are heartening, they are not altogether convincing when they are made while still immersed in the adventure environment. So it was encouraging to hear feedback a few months later that internal staffers were acting on what they'd learned during the training. To avoid delays, misunderstandings, missed deadlines and other problems, we were told, people were taking time to ask questions to clarify customer needs and to map strategies to meet them. Skills that had been showcased and practiced during the training were being applied to improve response to customers, both internally and externally.

Our follow-up affirmed that the five objectives we'd addressed in the design had been met. More internal staffers were now seeing themselves as both customer and supplier, and appreciating the centrality of those roles to BMW's overall success. There was enhanced respect among employees about who served whom in the chain. For individual staffers, there was the greater pride and commitment that come from seeing how their daily interactions and responsibilities ripple through the company, affecting both internal and external customers. Finally, there were the stirrings of an enhanced sense of team both within and between departments.

Summary

The customized adventure design process, which evolves directly out of the needs assessment, refines and sharpens a client's goals. As desired outcomes are clarified, they are set against the client's specific content requests and training parameters to arrive at a realistic big-picture agenda. All of this requires a constant give-and-take between client and consultant, a process that the adventure consultant seeks to imbue with the I.M.M.E.R.S.I.O.N. qualities particular to adventure learning.

The detailed design that results is firmly grounded in the time-tested educational tenets of the Experiential Learning Cycle. While some client situations require a meticulously detailed design of framed activities, briefing connections and clear linkages back to the workplace, other client situations benefit from a less scripted, more free-flowing approach. Typically, designs for corporate audiences integrate one or more business theories, inventories or models of learning. As specific activities are identified to bring certain issues and behaviors into focus, a careful eye is kept on the evolving sequence to make sure that the initiatives build on one another to produce a cumulative impact.

Attention is also paid to logistical considerations to ensure maximum smoothness in the day's flow of events. Contingencies are built into the design to accommodate such uncontrollable situations as weather and flight schedules. As for the unpredictable quirks of human nature, flexibility is a constant watchword in the design vocabulary.

9 The Adventure Toolbox

A good design, of course, is only half the challenge. Ultimately, success lies in the details of that blueprint's specific elements. Each segment of the microdesign must grab and hold participant interest if the consultant hopes to construct and sustain a learning community.

For this part of the design process, the adventure consultant requires state-of-the-art consulting tools and materials that variously stimulate all of the learning receptors: body and mind, emotions and spirit.

Corporate clients often approach their first adventure experience with a limited and limiting understanding of the contents of the adventure toolbox. Working from media images, they assume that the selection of activities includes mostly physical challenges, most of which require an outdoors backdrop and involve ropes courses laced across the high branches of trees.

In fact, a higher percentage of activities in most adventure programs is done low to the ground or at ground level. Moreover, physical activity is only one of four possible points of entry to an adventure experience. The other three portals, which can provide just as vivid and memorable a learning experience, involve cognitive, creative and introspective challenges.

These four portals appreciate and make use of the range of learning styles common to any gathering of people. By utilizing activities that cut across the various styles of learning, all participants have the opportunity to operate from positions of both comfort and discomfort, leadership and followership, safety and risk.

Broadly, the toolbox contents used to conceptualize, create and customize adventure activities include the following raw materials and techniques:

- *Physical:* games, high and low ropes elements, rigorous initiatives, expressive movement
- *Cognitive:* metaphors, writing exercises, question-and-answer formats, deductive reasoning problems, brainstorming puzzles, video
- *Creative:* dramatization, music, poetry, drawing, clay, role-playing, imaginative play
- *Introspective:* guided imagery, reflection, meditation, discussion, select readings, journals

Though hardly comprehensive, the list of materials hints at the variety of tools the adventure consultant must have on hand to customize activities that will engage both those who conceptualize abstractly and those who strategize concretely; those who intuit their way to a response and those who employ reason; those who like to leap in and "do" and those who prefer to sit back and reflect. And those tendencies only hint at the wide range of learning and behavioral styles identified by such respected diagnostic tools as David Kolb's Learning Style Inventory, Carlson's Dimensions of Leadership Profile and Personal Profile System (DiSC), Haye McBer's Managerial Style Questionnaire, and Bernice McCarthy and Suzanne Sander's Leadership Behavior Inventory.

A state-of-the-art adventure toolbox, by the way, boasts a healthy array of familiar content tools. This part of the inventory includes, but is not limited to, problem-solving and leadership models, organizational climate and influence strategy exercises, behavioral and learning style inventories, personality and management style indicators and team development, and total quality management models.

Alongside such diagnostic and theoretical tools are an array of familiar props that aim to engage those whose learning style may be less responsive to adventure's more playful props (ropes, fleece balls, giant puzzle pieces, wooden blocks, plastic chutes). This more conventional inventory includes overheads, preprinted posters and charts, flip charts, manuals, cards and customized videos.

Itemization of the toolbox's specific activities (e.g., "Look Up/Look Down," "Traffic Jam," "Toxic Waste") would have little meaning to anyone not in the adventure field. Even those tools whose names are now familiar to you (e.g., "Scrabble Babble," "Group Juggle," "Corporate Connection") have a breadth of applications that no list can begin to accommodate.

Most importantly, a list would miss a point that should by now be evident: adventure learning is a process, not an isolated exercise or activity. Any given activity may create diversion, fun, engagement. But for meaningful learning and transfer back to the workplace to occur, the activity must be effectively framed, presented and debriefed.

One Toolbox, Three Approaches

There are three ways to utilize the adventure toolbox. The approach most widely used by adventure consultants is to regard the toolbox contents as fixed and immutable. A design undertaken in this manner involves the judicious cutting and pasting of standard activities that fall, broadly, into the following categories: convening and tone-setting exercises, problem-solving and transfer initiatives, transition and closure activities.

The second approach involves taking familiar activities, then customizing a framing or metaphor to suit a particular audience. Imagination can be a powerful force for drawing people into an adventure activity. The fantasy need be neither wild nor exotic to seduce. Indeed, with corporate audiences, the more believable and vivid the scenario, the more engaged participants become.

"When these connections are motivating and relevant to the client," notes adventure theorist M.A. Gass, "the transfer of learning is usually enhanced" (Gass, 1995).

This was the approach employed to design the Atwell car repair activity described in Chapter 2. The Atwell drama was a tailored version of "Mastermind," the activity put to entirely different use in Chapter 8's customer–supplier focus training. The special customization requirements of the Atwell example included adapting Mastermind to accommodate scheduling conflicts and creating a metaphor vivid enough to pique and sustain audience interest over several hours. (This was particularly important since time would not be set for participants to work specifically on the medley of challenges.)

Gass stresses that when working with metaphor, "facilitators should not underestimate the importance of properly comprehending the client's reality." He further warns: "Truly effective framing requires much more than merely placing labels or images from the client's environment onto adventure experiences" (Gass, 1995).

The Atwell experience bore that out. To make that playful scenario significant for the BMW dealers and relevant to the workplace, it was imperative to vividly summon the dealership environment, with its attendant pressures and conflicting demands. Before that could happen, PA's consultants had to become familiar with the dealership owner's work landscape. In addition to the information gathered during needs assessment for that particular program, PA consultants had previously visited several dealerships and been immersed in the details of daily operations, thus observing first-hand the client–dealer relationships.

The final approach to the adventure toolbox is to regard its contents as a starting point, with none of the implements and their applications fixed. It may involve reconceptualizing an existing tool to achieve a new and different application. It may involve blending state-of-the-art adventure methodologies with traditional consulting tools and client data to create an activity that reinforces learnings from other parts of a training. Or it may involve creating whole new initiatives.

Such was the case with the auto exercises described in Chapter 3, where the client was eager to integrate the company's product into the adventure design. In that instance, two existing adventure activities, "Keypunch" and "Minefield," were reconceptualized, and whole new initiatives were created to make use of the BMW product in a different way to provoke challenge and excitement.

For adventure consultants, there is nothing quite so challenging or electrifying as enlarging upon the contents of the adventure toolbox. It not only deepens the program base, but challenges creativity and broadens expertise.

New design initiatives, of course, can be risky. As the R&D leader in the adventure field, Project Adventure not only feels a responsibility to test its new hardware products, but strives to test-run new initiatives as well. In the case of the tarmac exercises, for example, the joint design team of PA and BMW staff tested the activities on more than one occasion, actively soliciting input from people outside the design group, including a risk manager, pro drivers and actual clients. The feedback produced changes in the design. In an adventure context, the behavior of participants is unpredictable enough without having to worry whether or not an activity will work as theorized.

All three uses of the toolbox are available to the adventure consultant as she shifts among her three sets of responsibility as consultant, facilitator and trainer. A trainer might decide, for example, that a judicious cutting and pasting of a tried-and-true activity is the best way to address the emerging (and perhaps unanticipated) needs of a particular group. Alternately, during a two-day training, a facilitator might choose to reframe an activity planned for the second day around a new metaphor to further illuminate points that emerged during the first day's activities and discussion. A full reconceptualization of an existing tool is usually the domain of the consultant, since such highly customized work is typically, but not exclusively, a direct outgrowth of the needs assessment process and requires careful planning, testing and piloting.

To illustrate the ins and outs of the microdesign process, let's take the second approach and look at how two existing activities can be customized to produce multiple applications and learnings. These examples highlight one of the greatest assets of the activities in the adventure toolbox: often only small variations are required to meet the needs of a specific audience.

A Bit About Twelve Bits

"Twelve Bits" is an initiative favored by adventure trainers for several reasons. It's easily portable. It explores the cognitive dimension of adventure by presenting a deductive reasoning challenge. And it is so versatile that any one of several subtle alterations—how the challenge is framed, how its content is presented, how the debrief is conducted—can serve a variety of purposes and produce dramatically different results.

The generic rules of this activity are simple. Twelve strips of paper, each containing a clue or bit of information, are distributed among the members of a group. "Among you, there exists all the information required to solve the problem," the group is told. "Moreover, the problem itself is stated somewhere within the clues."

The only restriction is stated at the top of each strip: "Although you may tell your group what is on this slip, you may not show it to anyone else to read." In other words, while each group member is free to tell others what is on her strip, she may not show it to anyone else. As a result, the group is blocked from laying out the 12 clues so that they can all be seen at once.

What group members don't know is that the information a member communicates may be an interpretation of the clue, rather than the actual clue. Let's say your slip states: "You read Chapter 9 after completing Chapter 8." When the group begins pooling information to create a sequence for the activities described in the clues, you report, "My clue says we've got to read Chapter 9 right after Chapter 8." In fact, the clue is far more vague, and leaves open the option to read Chapter 9 after Chapter 10 or 12.

The most traditional application of Twelve Bits is within the context of team development. Told only that they have 25–30 minutes to solve the puzzle, group members are compelled to find a way to work together effectively to share the information on their slips of paper, pool their reasoning talents and fashion a strategy for identifying the solution.

When the activity is used this way, the debriefing focus might take the following directions: How did the team set about solving this problem? Did a plan and process get defined and followed? How did team members communicate with one another? How did the team handle disagreements over deductive reasoning? What paradigms did the team get locked into? How effectively did people listen? Was all of the information shared? Who emerged as a leader? How did others feel about that? Did the leadership shift, and at what point?

The beauty of Twelve Bits is that, with subtle adjustments, it can also be used to work on or showcase any of the four other main thematic drivers: *leadership, customer focus, learning organizations, values*. Moreover, the content of the 12 strips can be tailored to reinforce the vocabulary, concepts and learnings from other parts of the day's training.

Take, for instance, a version customized for a five-day management workshop for a group of franchise owners and managers, in part focused on delineating *leadership* from management skills and issues, and better understanding the different leadership focuses people employ. On Day One of the training, each participant filled out a Carlson Dimensions of Leadership Profile, which delineates four distinct lenses through which leaders see, interpret and respond to situations: character, accomplishment, analysis, interaction.

After the Profile was completed, self-scored and briefly discussed, a customized Twelve Bits activity reinforced the inventory's four "Focuses of Attention" through clues that utilized the Profile's language and concepts. The strips, which challenged the group to answer the question, "In what sequence did Dennis's group study the Focuses of Attention," included such statements as:

- "Of all the leadership Focuses of Attention explored, Rod resonated to Accomplishment most."
- "The extent to which a person focuses on internal characteristics of a leader (Character) in comparison with the external environment the person affects (Accomplishment) is important to understand."
- "Phil's group learned about Character before they studied Accomplishment."
- "Each principal resonated to a different Focus most. They arranged their itinerary so they would study and interpret the Focus they resonated to most—last."

As the group set about solving the cognitive challenge, traces of each leadership focus emerged, as did identifiable differences between those who attempted to manage the situation and those who were inclined to lead. The debriefing explored those behaviors, and what it felt like to be on the receiving end of each focus of attention.

A different leadership variation, designed for the Quality Improvement Facilitation training, involving team leaders and managers, made use of the Twelve Bits exercise to practice and strengthen the skills needed to run a meeting effectively. In each group, a "leader" was designated to facilitate the process and manage the flow of information.

The debriefing questions focused on the leader's style of facilitation and the effectiveness of that approach. The leaders critiqued their own performance, then others shared their observations and offered feedback on how it felt to be facilitated in a particular manner. That, in turn, precipitated discussion of the various effects of the different leadership styles on different types of employees, how difficult it is to give a leader feedback when an employee feels mismanaged, and so forth.

When reconfigured slightly for a group of mid-level supervisors who were working on strengthening their coaching skills, Twelve Bits proved even more challenging. In this version, the "leaders" were asked to switch groups midway through the activity, offering participants a direct contrast of leadership styles—and a true-to-life recreation of what happens when a team's manager is switched mid-project. In the debriefing, participants explored how the leaders responded to the new groups, how the groups responded to them, how long it took to recover and regain momentum, and so forth.

For a training at Ohio-based Progressive Insurance that had a strong emphasis on company values, the language of the clues reinforced both the company's five core *values* (Aspiration, Excellence, Integrity, Golden Rule, Profit) and the message the company wanted to convey about the importance of these values. The clues, which directed participants toward solving the deductive problem statements, also reinforced the training's main message. To wit: "The core values are the principles upon which company leaders and managers strive to base their behavior and decisions," and "It was clear from the training that the core values support the corporate vision."

During the debriefing, questions focused on the values demonstrated during the activity. Did participants' behavior model the company's values? Did people complete the exercise by adhering to the guidelines? Did people both listen and disagree respectfully? How did the group balance its interest in being the first to solve the problem (Profit) with its interest in involving all group members (Golden Rule)?

Twelve Bits can also be an effective tool for illuminating *customer focus* problems and issues when it is included in the medley of problem-solving activities presented in a "Mastermind" initiative. Such was the case with the BMW Atwell example, where participants had to deal on an ad hoc basis throughout the day with the various brainteasers.

During the debrief, the focus was on how the various groups juggled competing demands. How did they divvy up the tasks to make most effective use of their time? If they failed to meet the customer's expectations, how did they handle the resulting disappointment or irritation? Did they make excuses or become proactive in trying to remedy the damage? Did they blow off the exercise altogether? If so, why, and what did this say about where customer concerns lay in their list of priorities?

A similar approach was taken during a three-day training with a corporation that was working on building a *learning organization*. In that instance, the language of the clues highlighted the component disciplines for building learning organization, as discussed in Senge's *Fifth Discipline*: Systems Thinking, Personal Mastery, Mental Models, Team Learning, Building a Shared Vision.

This version of Twelve Bits was overlaid on a tightly packed schedule. Midway through the first day, participants were each handed a clue and told, "Figure out the problem and solve it by the end of the program." Here, there were no designated teams, no designated periods for working on the problem, no designated leaders, no designated anything!

On Day Three, the debriefing focused on how the group set about imposing order on chaos. The linkages back to the workplace concerned how to develop mastery of the disciplines required for a true learning organization. Did individuals have a vision in mind as they tackled the problem? Was this vision conveyed to others to create a shared vision of how to accomplish the task? As individuals realized their own reasoning errors along the way, did they share that information with the other group so that team learning could take place?

Web of Intrigue

If Twelve Bits is one of the more popular cognitive adventure tools, "Spider's Web" is a front-runner for honors as the most often adapted physical challenge in the adventure toolbox. Like Twelve Bits, it is portable, versatile and engaging. Spider's Web offers a combination of cognitive, emotional and physical challenge that strikes a near-perfect balance between mind, body, emotions and spirit.

As mentioned in Chapter 8, the generic rules for Spider's Web involve a small group of about 10–15 people navigating their way from one side of a prefabricated web (constructed of bungee rope, string, nylon cord or the like) to the other, without ever touching the web material or using an opening more than once. If someone touches the web, that wakes the spider, who will send everyone scurrying back to the start.

Like Twelve Bits, the Spider's Web can be customized to punch up learnings from more traditional consulting tools, and it can be enlisted in the service of any of the management themes dominant in today's business climate. In Chapter 8, we saw the web employed in the service of customer–supplier chain theory to train a lens on *customer focus.*

A shift in the debriefing focus can similarly offer a vivid and powerful lesson in values. At the individual level, did people admit to touches or hide them? Did witnesses collude (to help the team win) or did they call attention to the touches (and risk being perceived as a whistleblower)? How was this interaction handled by the person who called the touch? How was it received by the person who caused the infraction?

At the group level, how did the other members of the team respond? Was greater frustration directed at the person who touched the web or the person who called attention to it, and thereby forced the group to abide by the rules and forfeit precious time? Did the team distinguish between "degrees" of infraction? Were they more likely to admit to a touch when it involved someone trying to pass through the web, as opposed to someone who was lending a helping hand? What did the team's reaction say about what its members truly value?

Most commonly, the Spider's Web is used in the service of *team development*. Typically, at the start of the activity, groups realize that to be successful, some planning and organization is necessary. Confusion and conflict arise when the initial solution doesn't work as anticipated and adjustment is required.

How the group handles (or mishandles) such setbacks is often illuminating. During the debriefing, as the members of the group reflect on their individual and collective performance, people typically start identifying behaviors that focus on task completion without regard to the needs or feelings of the group's members. This leads to the question of what the team's behavior suggested was more important: a focus on the task and outcome, or a focus on the people and process?

Even when used in a team context, the web is versatile, not static. Sometimes after a lively debriefing, the group and trainer together will choose to repeat the initiative, this time with more stringent or limiting rules in place. (Example: Once a person chooses an opening no one else may pass through it and if there is a touch, the whole group needs to start over.) Often, a group won't complete the web on this second attempt, but improvements in the team dynamic and process will leave them feeling that they have had a success.

For a half-day training at Nintendo of America Inc. in Redmond, Washington, the 11th of a succession of trainings that had varied in length from half-days to three days, PA trainers used the Spider's Web for the penultimate activity. This time, it was used to call attention one last time to the specific workplace behaviors that group members had first identified as critical, then committed to, over the five-month course of the 11 trainings.

Toward this end, trainers tacked to the web the "commitment cards" that participants had written during an exercise earlier in the day. Each card featured a person's description of a specific behavior that he or she pledged to implement in the workplace.

Now, as a trainer laid out the rules, the web was presented as a metaphorical representation of the many barriers that stand in the way of creating a healthy organization. Passage through the web symbolized successful movement of the team members towards their collectively desired work environment. To reinforce the components identified by the group as critical to a healthy workplace, it was stipulated that before a person could pass through an opening, he had to remove one of the hanging commitment cards and read it aloud to the group.

"The card may not reflect your own personal commitment," the trainer explained, "but it represents one made by a valuable member of your team. By sharing these, the entire department will benefit by knowing the personal goals that exist throughout the department."

Had this been a "typical" training (if there is such a thing!), the exercise might have involved a 1:10 ratio of 4 trainers to 40 participants. That would have allowed for four webs, with each group having an autonomous experience with the web. In this instance, however, the training involved 125 people, five trainers and a very tight schedule.

That made for an interesting microdesign challenge: how to involve so many people and keep them engaged, while at the same time maintaining safety for everyone involved? With only five trainers on hand, safety considerations limited the activity to five webs. (Though participants are trained to spot each other during physical challenges, PA protocol calls for a trainer to closely monitor safety issues whenever an activity involves people leaving the ground level.)

The solution was to arrange the five webs in a star-like shape so that participants on each of the teams would migrate from outward posts to a common space in the center. Rules were modified so the openings could be used twice before closing (therefore accommodating the larger individual teams). Finally, it was stipulated that once people passed through a web into the center space, they could help and support the efforts of any of the teams.

That last rule required a paradigm shift from thinking in terms of teams to strategizing in terms of the collective organization. As we saw with "Group Juggling" (Chapter 2) and "Corporate Connection" (Chapter 4), such paradigm shifts are critical to the expansive patterns of thinking that fuel a learning organization.

This version of the exercise, therefore, had values and learning organization components, though the focus was on team development. The earlier customer focus version touched on values and team issues. The values-focused debriefing had a distinct overlay of team issues.

And therein lies the greatest beauty of the Spider's Web. The very nature of the web's challenge interconnects the major themes that dominate and drive modern corporate life. Once viewed as linear and hierarchical, organizations today function based upon a web of relationships.

Summary

The success of any adventure design lies in the details of the microdesign. These are the specific elements that draw participants into the adventure environment, then sustain their interest. These elements may be standardized, customized or wholly new creations and may be employed in any one of those forms by the adventure consultant in each of his roles as consultant, trainer and facilitator.

The adventure toolbox is well-equipped to address the wide variety of learning styles that are typically represented in any assembled group. Activities unique to adventure, involving imaginative initiatives, ropes courses, playful props and so forth, may particularly appeal to people who favor a let-me-get-in-there-and-give-it-a-try approach to learning. The analytic discussion often triggered by presentation of the foundational tools may best engage those who prefer a reflective or cerebral approach. Multiple-choice inventories, leadership profiles and so on may best speak to people who favor an analytic style. None of these tools, however, is intended to stand alone. Instead, the aim is to use these richly varied tools to engage all of each participant's learning receptors: body, mind, emotions and spirit.

The sophisticated adventure design features a sequence of highly customized activities that successively illustrate, illuminate and reinforce a client's main messages. To customize or create such activities, the adventure consultant draws on a rich variety of tools that include both familiar diagnostic instruments and initiatives unique to the adventure setting. Cumulatively, they present physical, cognitive, creative and introspective challenges that awaken curiosity, ignite excitement and stimulate fresh thinking.

DELIVERY

AND

TRANSFER

Section

4

Word Puzzle #2

> Spell the longest word possible by tracing one line from one letter to an adjacent letter moving up, down, horizontally or diagonally.

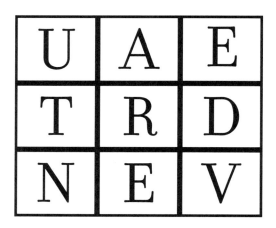

Bringing Learning to the Surface

Consultants always face the challenge of how to bring new learning to a group's attention. In this activity, bringing the "cap" to the surface represents successfully creating a new learning.

> For this activity, you will need **two props**, a narrow top bottle and a plastic pen top.
> Place the **empty** bottle on a flat surface. Drop the pen cap into the bottle and check to be sure the cap can move freely. Without touching the bottle, without poking anything inside the bottle to "hook" the cap, without altering the bottle in any way, **get the cap out of the bottle.**

Each time an adventure consultant convenes a group, he or she sets in motion a powerful dynamic that holds potential for significant and enduring behavioral change. It is a formidable prospect that no responsible adventure consultant takes lightly. As he sees it, his role is to help create the sort of environment and circumstance that will enable participants to respond to the unfolding events with maximum alertness, openness and interest, and minimal defensiveness, indifference and fear.

The leadership aspect of this experience has four chief components: Presence, Discernment, Actions and Intuition. While some aspects of these leadership components are readily apparent to participants, other aspects are as unapparent as the events they are tracking: the drama and patterns that are unfolding invisibly beneath the surface. All along the way, the adventure consultant strives to model the behaviors he seeks from participants, constantly sensitive to the impact of his own demeanor, actions and words on the group. While intuition and discernment help him assess what's transpired and make adjustments accordingly, he knows that it's his actions (his attention to physical and emotional safety, his way of connecting ideas and activities, the manner in which he stands back or intervenes, etc.) that speak most loudly to participants.

No matter how prepared and practiced an adventure consultant may be, the best measure of his skill is how he handles the unpredictable. Whether it's the irritating absence of a needed prop or the startling presence of an emotional exchange, the adventure consultant sees the values in these unexpected turnings and seeks ways to tap such moments to further illuminate the learning goals of the training.

The adventure consultant's greatest challenge is to help participants bring the adventure home to the work environment. If behavioral change is the goal of adventure consulting, then time and space must be provided to let the ideas and learnings set in and take hold. The adventure consultant's role may end at training's close—or it may be the beginning of a change process that will extend into other vital areas of the corporation's life. Either way, the adventure consultant seeks to ease the transition back to the workplace, with its transfer of ideas, hopes, symbols and goals.

10 The Leadership Adventure

"I knew at that moment of awakening that what I had been seeking to reflect in my work could be expressed in terms of three gifts: the gift of discernment, the gift of presence, and the gift of heart. Within them lie the blend of the rational and the intuitive, the integration of the body, mind, emotions and spirit; and the courage to act according to one's beliefs, convictions, knowledge, and feelings."

—Daryl Funches, Three Gifts of the Organization
Development Practitioner, 1989

The moment of awakening—what a powerful image. It implies both the discovery of new ideas and information, and the rediscovery of old learnings and understandings. It implies the growth that comes from taking external knowledge and perspectives, and internally transforming them into insight and wisdom. It implies the changes that result when that new awareness is applied to existing patterns and behaviors.

I.M.M.E.R.S.I.O.N. experiences are full of moments of awakening for participants and adventure consultants alike. Each time an adventure consultant convenes a group, he sets in motion a powerful dynamic that holds potential for significant moments, even turning points, in the participants' lives. The moments, which range from small *ahas* to momentous new insights, are variously deliberate and unexpected, immediate and delayed, whimsical and profound. They alternately engage the body and mind, the spirit and emotions, the rational and intuitive self. However they emerge, these moments are what give the I.M.M.E.R.S.I.O.N. experience its impact, both immediate and long-term.

The primary goal of the adventure consultant is to create, nurture and maintain an environment that encourages these moments to evolve. At every turn, the emphasis is on making learning accessible, engaging and appealing. The array of adventure initiatives is only the springboard to the meaningful learning that comes when people achieve "relaxed alertness," the state defined by Caine and Caine as "low threat and high challenge" and identified as a prerequisite to behavioral change. For the adventure consultant, the challenge is to create and sustain an environment that keeps participants' dueling perceptions of vulnerability and productive challenge in balance physically, intellectually and emotionally.

At the same time that adventure consultants cultivate an environment that encourages relaxed alertness, they also seek to engage participants at a deep level of absorption, described as "flow" by Mihalyi Csikszentmihalyi, a psychology professor at the University of Chicago. Csikszentmihalyi, who has studied what makes experiences enjoyable for people, identifies several variables as enhancing a person's sense of enjoyment and engagement in an activity. They include having a sense of completion; being able to concentrate on the task; providing clear goals and immediate feedback; being removed from the worries and frustrations of everyday life; feeling a sense of control over the actions; losing a sense of oneself; feeling an alteration in one's sense of time, so that hours can seem like minutes or vice versa.

In a state of flow, Csikszentmihalyi writes, "There is no excess psychic energy left over to process any information but what the activity offers. All the attention is concentrated on the relevant stimuli." A flow experience provides "a sense of discovery, a creative feeling of transporting the person into a new reality." At the same time, it pushes the person to higher levels of performance, and leads to previously untapped states of consciousness. "In short," Csikszentmihalyi contends, "it transform[s] the self by making it more complex"(Csikszentmihalyi, 1991).

Adventure consultants guide participants toward this highly desirable state by presenting an intriguing variety of activities that alternately engage mind, body and imagination. The activities do not unfold, however, in a vacuum. Only with artful, spirited and thoughtful direction do these activities begin to assume a meaning that transcends the context and personalizes the experience. Therein lies the leadership challenge for the adventure consultant.

When a training is underway, there are aspects of the adventure consultant's leadership that are readily observable and transparent (his presentation, personal style, humor, skill at making interventions). Other aspects of his guiding

Four Attributes of Adventure Consultants

influence are sensed and interpreted by participants (his ability to discern, sense of timing, openness, accessibility, acceptance of ideas and people, ability to probe and make connections). Some aspects are apparent only to fellow practitioners (the ability to make spontaneous changes in the agenda, the internal thinking that produces the right question or change of subject at the right time, the evaluation that influences when to guide and when to step back).

Throughout the adventure experience, the consultant's leadership manifests in three areas: presence, discernment and action. Overlaying all three areas is the adventure consultant's intuition. While the following discussion addresses each leadership aspect separately, during a training they are as inextricably interwoven as the threads of a Spider's Web.

The Consultant's Presence

An adventure consultant appreciates that his leadership presence radiates from the very first moment of encounter. He knows that his presence will be the integrative factor for all that follows. Given the short time he will be with a group, everything—*everything*—he does has significance.

Much of what he projects, of course, is intrinsic to his personhood and largely unalterable. But the consultant's presence also has a skillful overlay that speaks less to the *what* of the experience than the *way* it is offered. These attributes focus on creating an empowering environment that fuels on authenticity, courage and support, sustained by engagement, valuing behaviors and empathy.

This leadership approach empowers the environment, not the participants. Rather than try to give power to others (it is not the adventure consultant's to give), this leadership presence strives to create an environment where people become aware of, claim (or reclaim) and finally own their personal power. It is an approach that helps participants realize that dependence is the absence of power and interdependence is the balanced use of power. While this approach is particularly forceful during team development work, virtually all consulting work involves an undercurrent of power issues: Who has it, who doesn't? Who gives permission, who withholds it? Do I want it, or don't I?

When the focus is on empowering the environment, attention is paid not only to the emergent needs of the group and its individual members, but to the emergence of ideas—especially those that do not fit into the planned agenda. In one memorable moment, a group came up with a novel plan for navigating the Spider's Web that would accommodate a nervous participant's need to remain at ground level. (Specifically, the group brainstormed the idea of actually lifting the web, placing it horizontal to the floor and lowering a hole in the web directly over the person who was standing stationary. The person then stepped out of the hole, thus never leaving the ground.) When the plan succeeded, three other people who had opted out of the exercise for fitness reasons rejoined the activity. Had the consultant been more locked into a particular plan than supportive and responsive to the group's own needs and ideas, that creative solution would not have unfolded.

How does an adventure consultant set about creating an empowering environment? Her own behavior and qualities must mirror what she seeks in others. One of the most critical of those attributes is authenticity. According to Webster's, to be authentic means to be "worthy of acceptance or belief," "true to one's own personality, spirit or character." The adventure consultant must be all of those things if she hopes to establish an environment where people will be willing to take physical, intellectual and emotional risks, and do so in front of the very people they will have to work with tomorrow back at the office.

An authentic consultant acts with honesty and openness. That does not mean boldly and heedlessly speaking what's on one's mind at every turn. (That would fly in the face of the Full Value Contract.) But it does mean being alert, aware and reflective. It means approaching the experience with candor and frankness, risking vulnerability. If trust lies at the heart of the Experiential Learning Cycle, the building of that trust begins with the consultant's ability to convey her authenticity.

By modeling her willingness to risk candor and vulnerability, the adventure consultant helps to create the sort of safe environment where it becomes possible to give expression to difficult truths and emotions without fear of diminishing one's esteem with colleagues. Members of the group see that forthrightness and vulnerability come from a place of strength, not weakness; they also see the positive shift in their own response to the consultant. All of this lends to participants' willingness to venture into difficult terrain themselves.

So does the consultant's courage. By courage, we mean recognizing risk and choosing to brave it, mindful of the possible consequences. Such moments are likely to present themselves throughout a training if the consultant is behaving in an authentic manner. He may challenge assumptions, introduce an uncomfortable observation, confront behavior that is counter to the goals of the program.

When, for instance, an adventure consultant seeks to raise dialogue to a new level by offering an observation, particularly one with an emotional component, he risks alienating the group or having the observation fall flat. When the latter occurs, the consultant may wind up feeling uncomfortable and vulnerable. If he then acknowledges that discomfort or admits to an error in judgment, he lets a humanness show that makes him more appealing, approachable and dimensional.

His behavior invites trust. It says, "I'm not just asking you to put yourself on the line; I'm putting myself on the line, too." When a participant senses courage on the part of the adventure consultant, it becomes possible to internalize the message: "This is a place where I can search for challenge, risk new behaviors and discover more about myself and others."

In addition to authenticity and courage, the adventure leadership presence conveys unconditional and sustained support. That support manifests in ways both large and small. It means being attentive so that the adventure consultant will know the right moment to ask a meaningful question, encourage a participant to venture a bigger physical or emotional risk, make an observation. The supportive leader wields recognition, not evaluation, as a means of encouragement. He takes time to affirm individual achievements as well as group successes. He also makes time to acknowledge and air discomforts and disappointments, helping participants to appreciate that learning highs often result from experiential lows.

If authenticity, courage and support help to cultivate an empowering environment, engagement, valuing and empathy help to sustain it. Engagement is the thread that connects the consultant to the participants, keeping him in a state of constant alert as he gathers, assimilates and relays information. It is an unflagging attunement that picks up on the murmured comments and body language, as well as the ideas that are deliberately shared. It is a radar that often prompts participants to remark, "I was surprised you heard that" or "I didn't know you'd noticed that little rule violation."

Engagement is what enables the skilled adventure consultant to recall a detail from an earlier activity or debrief that now may seem relevant. It is also what invites participants' engagement. It is part of a positive reinforcing loop whereby consultant engagement reinforces group engagement reinforces consultant engagement.

Ditto, the valuing behaviors the consultant strives to model. Throughout the experience, the adventure consultant remains self-aware of his words and actions, and their impact. Words, tone, actions all communicate to participants how much their input is (or isn't) being valued. He is also alert to the messages each participant is receiving from others in the group, and encourages participants to speak openly and honestly about those moments. There are few, if any, neutral exchanges in a training experience. Everybody has blind spots in interactions with others. By helping participants to give voice to instances where they feel undervalued, participants become more aware of behaviors that may be provoking a similar response in the workplace.

In our daily lives, we often find that our emotions, more than our actions, need permission for expression. In our work lives, this is even more the case. When the leader is empathetic, permission is granted implicitly. Not only do participants then feel safe to express their feelings, but they feel as if they have an ally in the process. "It's as if you know what I'm thinking" is a refrain familiar to empathetic adventure consultants.

To help participants feel safe with him and to model the sort of behavior that will create a safe learning community, the adventure leader strives to be open and encouraging, sensitive and trusting. The empathetic leader tries to convey not only compassion and understanding, but receptivity and sensitivity to others' feelings and ideas. He is attuned to when a person's silence is introspective and should be respected, and when it stems from a fear to speak up and requires a tactful intervention.

Often, the empathetic presence expresses itself emotively. The consultant understands that in order to encourage participants to give expression to their feelings, he may have to give of himself in the same manner. His emotional presence must be transparently accessible and it must be sustained. At all times, he must be a full partner in the proceedings and not shift into a detached mode.

Empathy tends to be most observable at the moment when the expression of real emotion occurs. Often, such expression makes others in the group uncomfortable. The consultant's understanding, confident and comforting response "allows" the moment, and helps the individual and group see that they may be on the threshold of a powerful and meaningful moment. A simple question like "Do you want to further explore this issue?" reminds participants that the choice is theirs, not his, to make.

If this all sounds a bit too touchy-feely, be assured that this emphasis on empowering is not an attempt to turn a business workshop into an encounter session. The presence of empathy and emotion does not mean the absence of thoughtfulness and reason. Rather, they are preconditions for establishing the kind of environment wherein people feel safe to address personal and group work issues candidly without fear of reprisal.

The Consultant's Discernment

Like everyone else in the room, the consultant has a second workshop taking place in her head, one that is separate, evaluative and mostly unshared. This mental workshop can be a place of great, indeed greatest, learning. For the adventure consultant, it is at this workshop that she observes emerging patterns, brings to the surface assumptions about the experience, questions motives, draws conclusions, attends to her own affect.

Discernment is the act of fully attending to this workshop. Where participants may perceive the training as a series of discrete activities, the adventure consultant regards the unfolding experience as a single learning event with multiple components. She monitors emerging behaviors, searches for patterns, seeks to make connections. Failure to attend to these silent messages can harm a group's building cohesion.

A key aspect of discernment is the ability to recognize the emergence of patterns. In the experiential part of the activity, the consultant may come to see that the group approaches each challenge with enthusiasm, but emerges disappointed from the experience because they pressed for a solution too quickly, rather than letting the activity unfold. Or, in the debriefing phase of activities, the consultant may discern that not only do the same voices dominate, but that it is a sense of resignation on the part of other team members that allows this to happen.

Key to acting effectively on these observations is the consultant's ability to assess his own inferences when he sees such patterns emerging and be aware of which inferences stem truly from what is unfolding, and which inferences may stem from his own belief systems and entrenched assumptions. He must, in other words, be both aware of his own inner drama and capable of carving some distance from it as particular behaviors push his internal buttons.

Take, for instance, when a participant voices sharp disagreement with various points of the Full Value Contract. Coming right at the outset of a training, a consultant might conclude, "This participant is very resistant to this entire learning process. He thinks it's just so much fluff in a world that needs quick action, tough direction and meaningful consequences. I'm going to find myself in a constant struggle with him as we progress through these three days." Discernment requires that after the consultant mentally acknowledges that he has reached those inferences, he then remain attuned both to how the participant is actually responding to activities as the workshop progresses, and how he himself is responding to the participant.

If the consultant clings to his initial inference, his subsequent (potentially resentful) response may impact not only the individual participant, but the entire group. Quickly, a reinforcing loop is established that can bind everyone into misguided assumptions. Fortunately, there are tools available that can help a consultant maintain a clear-eyed view of the situation (see GRABBS box).

A consultant must be attuned not only to his own inferences, but to the emotional signals he is sending as well. A defensive response to that same participant could mitigate against subsequent messages about openness and trust. A stoic countenance, on the other hand, though intended to mask both approval and disapproval, may wrongly create an impression that the consultant is emotionally detached. Visible or not, participants will sense and react to the consultant's emotional response.

The Consultant's Action

The adventure consultant is an active participant in every aspect of the learning community. While his role during the course of a training varies between high and low levels of visibility, interaction and intervention, his actions are always felt. This aspect of leadership involves monitoring, storytelling, connecting, educating, intervening, questioning and adjusting. Though they will be described here as distinct functions, the adventure consultant uses each of these skills fluidly and interchangeably to influence the group's and his own understanding of what is transpiring.

The most basic function of leadership is monitoring. Maintaining a safe, trusting environment is a responsibility that requires constant attention. The consultant is the gatekeeper who monitors and maintains the various important boundaries that must be honored. He keeps an eye on the time to make sure that the training remains true to its scheduled agenda. He monitors the rules spelled out at the start of an activity. He shares with participants the monitoring of physical and emotional safety. He takes the lead to establish the parameters for safe play, anticipate situations that will require intervention and maintain an environment where risk feels challenging, but not threatening.

Of course, it may be that infringements of time or rules are just what participants need. How they navigate those infractions among themselves may prove one of the greatest opportunities for learning. The experienced leader knows that meaningful and enduring change is more likely when a group claims authorship for its own learning. Knowing how and when to intervene is more than a necessary skill, it is an art for adventure consultants. The prerequisite stage to intervening is monitoring.

As a safe environment is created, the leader can begin storytelling. Creating an engaging, yet realistic, scenario for the program and its activities helps to invite participants into the experience. The consultant strives to engage, excite and intrigue by modeling a fun-loving attitude that invites people to let down their guard and enter unself-consciously into imaginative play. She sets the tone, manages the pace, senses the rhythm. The storyteller provides the backdrop that allows the participants to bring the experiences to life.

The leader injects energy when it's low, calms and soothes when it's disturbed, invites reflection and observation when energy and focus are drifting, challenges when it feels ready to overlook a problem or difficult issue. A leader adapts to the changing dynamics and energy of the group, always seeking to maintain a flow experience where people feel actively engaged and involved with the experience.

The connecting function builds off the metaphors and scenarios. The adventure consultant explores every activity, debrief, presentation and interaction for insights that may relate to programmatic goals and workplace transference. While adventure experiences often provide unfamiliar contexts so that people can participate without reserve or judgment, the adventure consultant strives to connect the experience back to the "real world."

As she shifts the focus away from the adventure activity, the consultant directs the group's attention to the process that has just unfolded. She offers observations of her own and helps the group seek out pieces of that process—learnings, ideas, patterns, behaviors, feelings—that mirror workplace issues and dynamics. She guides participants toward making connections of both an individual and group nature, so that the experience can be seen as having a direct relationship to experiences that occur in a workplace environment.

Closely linked to connecting is educating. The consultant provides information that is intended to enhance the effectiveness of participants' interactions. In this role, the consultant seeks to help the group make meaning from the experience without stripping participants of the important ability to learn for themselves. The educator knows when to let the group struggle, and when to offer observations that will ease or direct the dialogue. The consultant applies the theoretical knowledge to the experience at hand, bringing abstract concepts to light in the context of the adventure experience.

This role requires a high level of interpersonal skills, including a clear ability to articulate concepts that often seem fuzzy to others. The consultant must both model and be able to educate participants about effective ways to listen, provide feedback, confront one another and solve problems with others.

Proficiency requires working knowledge of a wide variety of theoretical models (e.g., problem-solving, feedback, communication, leadership, etc.), as well as experience and intuition.

Another critical yet sometimes difficult function is intervening. Interventions can become necessary at any time and may be needed to address many types of issues and problems. Typically an intervention is needed if the group's energy is stuck or off target. The adventure consultant must be able to diagnose the nature of the obstruction quickly, then know which approach is most likely to prove effective. When working with a group's energy, it is important to know whether to be direct, diversionary or redirecting.

A direct response attempts to identify and work with the cause of the obstruction. Rather than fight the stalled energy, it accepts and works with it. This strategy involves observations that are largely intuitive: "I sense that you are upset. Can you tell me what's bothering you?" "I sense a lack of respect here. What are others feeling?" Though the intent is to honor what is unfolding and use it to reignite the group's energy, there is a risk that participants may perceive such questions as confrontational, further intensifying the feeling of being stuck. How the consultant influences and guides the situation can further escalate it, thus testing the leader's courage.

Alternately, the consultant may perceive that a group is stalled because it is too wrapped up in a particular problem. An enlarged context may provide the diversion from the immediate logjam that enables the group to proceed. "How does this issue relate to what you experience at work?" "Let's see how large a list of possibilities we can come up with." By enlarging the psychological space, the consultant distances participants from the source of frustration, unleashing their thoughts to roam more freely.

At times, a wholescale redirection may be required to move a group off a point. Humor and lightness can be effective. By changing the tone with a quick dose of fun, participants may relax, regain their balance and remember that there is more than one way to regard a situation. Another technique is to blend directness and diversionary stratagems. "I hear your frustration. Can you hold onto that thought and we'll come back to it after we complete this topic?"

When considering an intervention, there is a fine line between "doing something" at the moment it's needed and waiting to explore the situation in a reflective discussion. Sometimes the best intervention is doing nothing: logging the interaction, the infraction, the behavior, the comment, then bringing it to the attention of the group or individual at a later moment when their full attention can be focused on evaluating the significance of the event. Effective interventions can be direct (taking a time out and asking for clarification, stopping someone if they are talking too long, pausing the action to capture a teachable moment) or inconspicuous (asking a question, allowing an extended silence).

A final critical aspect to intervening is knowing when to keep the attention on an idea, feeling or concept, and when to move on. As debriefs unfold, many groups raise so many ideas that they collide into one another. If they are not focused and directed, the learning will become too fragmented to prove meaningful and enduring. When energies threaten to splinter, the consultant must hold the focus, pulling participants back to a common place.

John: (to Sarah) "You interrupted me while I was talking."

Sarah: (looking concerned) "I'm—"

Hal: (the team manager) "Our team is famous for interrupting each other."

Bill: "Yeah, but it's not unusual for the members of teams that have to multi-task to interrupt and speak over each other."

Gwen: "Is that what we do? Multi-task? I've never heard that word before, but it makes sense."

This exchange by the members of a work team is typical of the multiple directions a conversation can take off in during a debriefing. It is up to the consultant to provide the focus. She must be sensitive to the fact that John and Sarah may feel uncomfortable cutting off their own manager to finish their exchange, and must find a way to tap this opportunity for a meaningful exchange. Respectfully, she will interject and encourage John and Sarah to continue. During the interplay, the consultant will be listening for the meaning behind the words, and their application to the workplace.

"So, this is not really about interrupting," she may suggest, after hearing out John and Sarah. "It's about being a member of a team where you feel you can't have your voice heard without yelling and don't receive a response to your opinions. What viewpoint do others have on this observation?"

Questioning, as this example shows, can be a useful intervention tool. While there are many circumstances in which telling or stating is not only appropriate but important, the approach favored by adventure leaders is effective questioning. It is a technique that encourages participants to determine their own learning.

An adept questioner functions much like a whirlpool, harnessing the energy that is swirling on the surface and pulling it below the surface to plumb for deeper meaning. He knows how to maintain a neutral, nonjudgmental demeanor. He knows to ask questions rather than make statements.

Once the energy is harnessed, he must then be an adept listener. That means not only hearing the meaning behind the flood of words that often pulls the group's focus in several directions at once, but reading the clues revealed by body language. Master listening involves all of the senses, including the intuitive sense. Even the best questions can lose their impact if effective listening doesn't follow the inquiry.

Lastly, a leader must be able on a moment's notice to recalibrate the planned agenda, the briefing of an activity or the next question in a debrief, based on what is happening or has just happened. Adjusting is a function that complements a leader's assessing skills. Once a leader has assessed the dynamics in the group, she must make decisions about what to do. In many cases, the planned agenda flows smoothly and readjustments are minor.

But most leaders have experienced that jarring moment when a training suddenly seemed poised to veer off course due to an unexpected comment, action or behavior. At that moment, the consultant must be able to pull the goals of the training into alignment with group and individual needs. It does not necessarily mean abandoning the goals or caving in to the whims of the group. What it does mean is constantly interpreting the data one gathers, then making conscious decisions about an appropriate response.

The Consultant's Intuition

Many adventure leaders can describe a day, sometimes a moment, when they felt as though they suddenly "knew" that they had achieved a deeper level of understanding as a leader. What they are speaking of is intuition, a hyper-aware understanding that goes beyond knowledge, skill and experience and affects how one perceives and responds.

Intuition is impossible to measure, difficult to describe. Some people experience it as an "inner voice" that provides sage advice. Others have a "gut reaction" that grabs one's attention with a distinct physical sensation. Sometimes it presents itself as a strong "feeling" that indicates how to guide the moment.

However it manifests, intuition permeates virtually all aspects of the seasoned adventure consultant's performance. It complements rational, conscious decision-making by synthesizing the knowledge, experience and observation that happens just beneath the level of awareness, then sending up a flash of insight. Those impulses provide another valuable sensor to guide decisions, behaviors and comments. When intuition is applied effectively to observational, interpretive and analytic skills, the adventure consultant's greatest artistry emerges.

Intuition informs presence by helping to bring the consultant's particular style into closer alignment with the needs of the group. While a leader cannot alter his personality, intuition helps inform when the moment might best be served by a question, a respectful silence, a supportive observation, a polite intervention.

Intuition enhances discernment by heightening awareness. An adventure consultant relies on all his collected knowledge, skill and experience to create his own understanding of a situation. Intuition helps to sift that information and to mediate when various indicators may send up conflicting signals.

Intuition guides our actions in a situation by providing options. Often, it directs actions, manifesting as an impulsive decision. Only later, after the choice has worked out just as the consultant had (for unknown reasons) anticipated, does he realize that intuition was at play.

Those consultants who know how to trust and work with intuition are usually the ones who know how to lead people most effectively to and through the moments of awakening to make an adventure experience impactful and its learnings enduring.

Summary

As an adventure consultant leads a group through an adventure experience, he relies on presence, discernment and action to build and maintain a trusting learning community. Each of those three components is informed by a fourth aspect of leadership, intuition.

The consultant's presence affects all that will follow. Everything he does, says and projects has significance. In an adventure learning community, where the accent is on empowering the environment rather than the individuals, the consultant seeks to project and model authenticity, courage and support, engagement, valuing behaviors and empathy. More than anything the consultant says, his demeanor and example sets the tone.

The consultant's discernment is attuned to observing emerging patterns, bringing assumptions about the experience to the surface, questioning motives and drawing conclusions. At every turn, the adventure consultant keeps a careful eye on his affect, monitoring how his own performance and inferences are impacting the group.

Though the consultant's involvement ranges from visible, active intervention to more subtle and passive observation, his actions exert influence on the group dynamic at every moment. To help the group cohere and function as a learning community, he relies on a range of skills, including monitoring, storytelling, connecting, educating, intervening, questioning and adjusting.

The experienced adventure consultant also relies on a honed intuitive ability to read and guide a group. When properly attended to, intuition provides an invaluable sensor that further enhances observational, interpretive and analytic skills.

The GRABBS Assessment Tool

Only by understanding the dynamics of a group can a leader adjust an activity or alter an agenda effectively. This series of questions provides a systematic approach for examining what is happening within a group and assessing the emerging needs.

Goals. What are the goals and objectives of the team? Do team members know, understand and feel a commitment to the goals? Are individuals' goals aligned with those of the team?

Readiness. What skills and abilities does the team have? Is the team employing those skills effectively? What is the team's level of motivation? Are people engaged and involved, or resistant and apathetic? Why?

Affect. What is the feeling within the group? What behaviors are observable? Do behaviors diverge from statements? What is unspoken? What expectations and assumptions are at play? What is the level of empathy? Trust? Support?

Behavior. How is the group acting? Are they restive? Agreeable? Disruptive? Resistant? Cooperative? Are participants more self-involved or group-oriented? Are there any interactions that are affecting the group either positively or negatively?

Body. How tired are the group members? What kind of physical stress, if any, are they experiencing? Can people maintain concentration, or are they easily distracted? Are people physically uncomfortable? What do they need to re-engage in the task?

Stage. Which developmental stage is the group at? What about the individuals? What stage does the group think it's at? Are the behaviors consistent with the consultant's assessment?

11 Navigating the Unexpected

The dissection of adventure into I.M.M.E.R.S.I.O.N. qualities and leadership components helps to illuminate the many considerations that go into the building of a sturdy learning community. But it does not capture the excitement of the adventure challenge as experienced by the consultant. As we guide others through the adventure labyrinth, shifting fluidly between the roles of consultant, facilitator and trainer, and drawing on the attributes of presence, discernment, influence and intuition all along the way, the word that most aptly describes the unfolding drama is this: unpredictable.

That is because, for all the assessing and designing, planning and preparing, it is impossible to predict, much less know, exactly how a given group of people will react to the experience. It is this unknown factor that adventure consultants count on and draw on to keep our energy levels up, our imaginations lively, our work fresh.

Unpredictability promises that each training situation will be for the adventure consultant much like what it is for the client: dynamic. Mind-opening. Fun with a serious agenda, where each adventure activity holds up a mirror to reflect back information about personal styles, modes of interaction, options, choices, potential.

Like a reporter who aims to produce an insightful story, the adventure consultant who hopes to deliver a meaningful experience must attend constantly to the five W's: *Who* is doing what? *What* is happening right now? *Where* do we go from here? *When* should we move on to the next level of exploration? And most importantly *Why* am I doing what I'm doing?

Lest there be any confusion, we should make clear that unpredictability does not mean out of control, just as the presence of risk does not mean an absence of safety. While the unfamiliar adventure environment tends to breed more unfamiliar twists and turns than the ordinary course of a business day, *no* situation, adventure or otherwise, is totally predictable. Ordinarily, we shrink or erase the unexpected by overlooking or downplaying it, ignoring it or pretending it didn't happen.

Adventure consultants, by contrast, celebrate the unpredictable by striving to confront and embrace it. For our clients, we understand that the unexpected can be an invaluable building block for meaningful learning. For ourselves, it mitigates against downshifting and compels us to remain alert, aware, engaged in the learning process from beginning to end.

We never know where the wildcard element lies in wait. It may emerge from the personal reaction of an individual or the dynamic of an entire group. It may stem from profound safety issues that could be either emotional or physical in nature. Or it may arise from seemingly petty logistical considerations. And even if everything goes smoothly, there is still no predicting what will stick and have enduring impact.

In the following examples, we look at some specific unpredictable situations encountered by PA consultants. In each instance, we invited the adventure consultant who dealt with the situation to tell his or her own story. We should caution that though the challenges represented in these examples aptly reflect the kinds of unpredictable hurdles that can arise during a training, these particular examples are more dramatic than the norm.

In roughly 80% of our trainings, the unpredictable moments neither disrupt nor alter the overall agenda, achievement of goals or desired learning outcomes. The more memorable 20%, however, demand immediate redesign efforts, improvisation or ingenuity to achieve the stated goals, reach desired results and, often, produce additional learning outcomes. In our experience, it's on-the-spot challenges like these that help the good adventure consultant to grow into an excellent one.

Client: Plant of a Large Manufacturer of Hardware Computer Products

Project Adventure Consultant: Steve Butler

Program Goal: Strengthening interpersonal skills with an emphasis on improving product quality in the units on the assembly line; achieving more effectiveness by tapping others' expertise; enhancing communication on the production line to ensure quality, safety and consistency.

Program Parameters: 22 groups, 70 to 100 people per session, with six to eight PA consultants at each four-hour workshop.

The Challenge:

What do you do when a group exhibits high resistance to a program and refuses to participate?

The Situation and Intervention:

Our introduction and opening remarks to the group of almost 100 people had been greeted with a passive silence. Our repeated request that people move to a "play" area in another part of the room had been met with resistance. Now, as we faced listless milling and a refusal to move in response to our instructions for the first activity, I began to feel a vague sense of panic. *We're here, we're being paid—no one is doing anything!*

Tapping on my experience in less dire circumstances, I decided, *Start small, create some positive energy.* I asked those people closest to me if they would participate in an activity. "What is it?" someone said warily.

If I try to explain it, they'll think it sounds too weird and pull the Challenge by Choice card for all the wrong reasons. "How about if you let me explain it and you agree to just try it," I said neutrally. "I think you'll find it fun and safe. If you don't like it, you can stop. But will you at least just try this one activity, and if you like it, we can try another." This is more coaxing and cajoling than I'm used to, but I was certain they would enjoy it if we got going—and let's face it, I was feeling pressure to deliver.

This was Challenge by Choice on a minute-to-minute basis. At any moment, someone might back out, making everyone else self-conscious and demolishing the tiny spark of interest I'd ignited. After assembling about a dozen people, I chose a quick and easy Convening exercise. They responded unenthusiastically, but it was okay. *Keep it short. Just keep moving, build on the energy.*

Now what? Others were watching, and this group looked ready to bolt. "Want to try another activity?" I asked. "We're going to be here a few hours anyway." Quickly, I moved into another short convening activity, one that thankfully generated a little laughter, tweaking new interest from some of the spectators. "Please feel free to join us," I called out, and enlisted the other PA trainers to fill newcomers in on the rules.

For the next 10 to 15 minutes, I just kept dipping into my toolbox and coming out with one short activity after another. Very slowly, I could sense, the group was beginning to relax and have some fun. In spite of themselves, they were gradually shifting out of the downshift mode and into the more open mindset of relaxed alertness. *If I can just get these people immersed, they'll begin making some real choices.*

After perhaps 45 minutes, we'd grown to some 60 people, a little better than half the group. Determined to make one more effort to enlarge the participants' circle, I asked people to go find a partner from the outside group and return quickly to the circle. *Perhaps an invitation from a colleague will be harder to refuse.* In some cases it worked, drawing new people in. Others still refused. A few participants, made self-conscious by a balker, dropped out. Now, we had about 80 people.

After one more large group activity, we broke into smaller groups to begin the planned agenda. By that point, momentum was established, and those who had opted in remained with us through the remainder of the training.

Reflections:

Challenge by Choice was an obstacle in this program. It's the only time I can recall feeling that people were really going to use it as a way out. Keeping the activities short, accessible and nonthreatening helped to build credibility. By initially coaxing a few to give I.M.M.E.R.S.I.O.N. a try, it created an opportunity for the majority to take the same plunge. Key to overcoming the resistance was a willingness to change the planned agenda and be spontaneous. People have to trust in the process and in the consultant before they can fully participate. Also, it was critical that we honored Challenge by Choice even as we struggled to overcome the inertia. Had our ploy been less invitational and more directive, I think our efforts would have backfired. We relied on the power of I.M.M.E.R.S.I.O.N. and it worked.

Given that strained beginning, it may seem surprising that the next situation involved the same company and same workshop. But it was a different day, a different group, and by now, PA consultants had adjusted to work more effectively with the client.

The Challenge:

What do you do when a group exhibits such high energy that they outpace the planned agenda?

The Situation and Intervention:

The large group had been broken into subgroups of roughly 15 people each to do "Group Juggling" and its sequel, "Warp Speed" (see Appendix II). My group had finished both activities with great efficiency, cheered their own efforts with great brio and identified many useful observations about teamwork during the debrief. Plainly, this was a high-energy, high-performance group, and I wanted to take advantage of that.

Suddenly, an idea for a daring—perhaps even daunting—variation on Group Juggling popped into my head. *Don't you dare*, cautioned the adult in me. *I dare you*, sang the kid. "Do you feel ready to try an additional challenge using the same skills you've just practiced?" I asked. When they assented immediately, I felt obligated to warn, "This involves a higher level of risk. Are you sure?" Again, they gave enthusiastic assent.

The group had already practiced and demonstrated proficiency throwing balls and objects. Now, I went over to my equipment bag and returned with a dozen raw eggs (no, I don't always carry raw eggs in my bag—they were intended for an activity planned for later in the day). They looked at the eggs, then looked at me with expressions that said: "Are you serious! Are you crazy? Are you seriously crazy?" Calmly, I said, "Juggle as many eggs as you feel comfortable attempting."

The group reviewed their commitment to try something more risky, and slowly achieved consensus to go for it. They approached the challenge with considerable caution and revised their "juggling" technique to accommodate the higher level of risk and a slight rule adjustment I'd made to preclude their relying on the solution they'd achieved earlier. After practicing with one egg, the group moved to juggling multiple eggs. The result was a successful process, with no broken eggs.

During the debrief, the group discussed how they approached risk back at work, and how they responded to uncertain or unknown demands. They recognized that sometimes they underestimated their skills and didn't push themselves to the fullest. They resolved to push still harder in the day's remaining exercises.

Reflections:

For the client, again, choice was key. Though they didn't know exactly what they were opting into, they still had debated and decided to challenge themselves. That conscious process of deciding and choosing was essential to overcoming uncertainty and fear. For myself, the spontaneous (ahem, impetuous) decision to introduce raw eggs was true to the creative spirit of adventure. It enabled me to adjust the challenge to meet the group's abilities. And it reminded me that a spark of imagination can make something new of something old. Behold! "Group Juggling" + raw eggs = "Eggspediency." It, too, is now a standard in the PA toolbox.

Client: Prominent Producer of Computer Software and Games

Project Adventure Consultant: Moe Carrick

Program Goals: Explore expectations for becoming a "healthy" organization; clarify the communication channels that must be opened to achieve this; strengthen cooperation, trust, responsibility and functionality within and between subgroups of the Information Services (I/S) department.

Program Parameters: Participation included a total of 115 employees from the I/S department, including the leadership team of 30 managers; the 30 managers attend an initial three-day training followed by a half-day follow-up; the rest of the department, divided into four groups, each attends a two-day training, followed first by a half-day follow-up for the subgroup, then a second half-day follow-up with the entire department.

The Challenge:

What do you do when the training schedule and the group's mood are impacted by external variables such as the weather, travel glitches or uncomfortable accommodations?

The Situation and Intervention:

I arrived at the training site, some three hours from our client's Seattle headquarters, the evening before the second of the four trainings was to get underway. A bad snowstorm was brewing. When I awoke early the next morning to discover four feet of snow on the ground, I tried to contact the client and warn that the mountain passes might be closed. Too late. Group 2 was already on a bus en route. Shortly after that, I received a message that the bus had turned back and concluded that the training was off. But a few hours later, I received another call that they'd found an accessible mountain pass and would arrive within two hours.

By the time the bus pulled up at 11:30 a.m., this was not a happy group of campers. Not only had they just spent five hours on the bus, but many of them had traveled one to two hours by car to meet the bus. I kept the greeting short and quickly sent everyone to lunch.

While they ate, I worked quickly with my co-trainer to alter the training plan. Already we had lost a half-day. Though we obviously couldn't deliver precisely the same workshop that the other groups received, we wanted the learning outcomes to be similar. Our first move was to gather information from the human resources director and attending manager about the group's mood and frame of mind.

I launched the afternoon by asking participants to write a headline that captured their bus ride experience, then to post them around the room. That helped open a discussion that allowed people to give voice to their anger about the ride and their feelings that the company had put them at risk on the road. Most, however, said they felt welcomed, well-fed and ready to move on. The rest of the afternoon proceeded smoothly.

As we broke for the evening, there was some tension about whether they would be able to go home the next day. The prediction was for another storm. And the prediction was right. Two more feet of snow blanketed the training site that night. Though we publicly minimized the snow and proceeded as planned the next morning, my colleague and I had two concerns: Should we send this group home early? And should we allow the next group, scheduled to arrive the next day, to come?

At noon, we conferred with our client partners, Donna and Kyle, then called Seattle to speak with Stanley, the head of the I/S department. A lot of hemming and hawing ensued. Stanley didn't want to make a call about the weather from Seattle. Donna and Kyle didn't want to antagonize Stanley. I didn't want to usurp an authority I didn't feel was rightfully mine. In the end, Stanley determined that he would send the next busload as planned, and the on-site team would make the call about when the current training group would head for home.

In the spirit of Challenge by Choice, I urged that the matter be put to the group. Later that afternoon, Kyle asked the group whether they wanted to try to get home that evening, or stay another night and wait out the weather. After much discussion, it seemed the group favored staying the extra night. Stanley finalized the decision, worked the details out with the conference center and signed off on the plan.

Kyle and I then took this back to the group and reiterated all the good reasons for staying put: people would be able to drive home in daylight, feelings of risk would be minimized, a half-day of missed training could be recovered. Kyle also tried to make the delay more palatable by renting videos, cross-country skis and snowshoes for that evening. The day ended on a high note, with trust and open communication running high.

Reflections:

Rather than fuming about the weather and feeling that it had derailed our plans, we worked with the elements and discovered a mighty ally. Better than any of our planned adventure activities, the weather served to hold up a mirror to the group's problem-solving process and helped them to bond into a more cohesive unit.

That was Day 1. Day 2 brought an entirely different challenge.

The Challenge:

What do you do when a group is distracted or preoccupied by issues back at the office?

The Situation and Intervention:

As I went to my room late that same evening, I bumped into a participant who appeared very angry. Probing a bit, I learned that Sally had heard about an e-mail from Stanley that suggested the group had "voted" to stay over. Contrary to there having been a vote, Sally insisted, she had been "made to stay" the night. Moreover, the e-mail had not conveyed the seriousness of the weather conditions and the safety issues at stake.

"Did you see the e-mail?" I asked.

"No, I just heard about it," she answered.

At breakfast the next morning, most members of the group seemed wound up by the by-now infamous e-mail message from Stanley. Like Sally, they were miffed by the suggestion that they had participated in a "vote" that deliberately kept them from returning to work. Stanley, in turn, was taking the grumblings so personally that he did not want to participate in the workshop. He felt that the group did not appreciate his efforts to solicit their input, reach a consensual decision and make their stay more enjoyable.

Before we got underway with the day's workshop activities, I spent some time with Kyle, helping him to put the complaints and feedback into perspective. I noted that the day before, the group had spent time with a traditional communications tool called the Ladder of Inference, which is a common mental pathway of assumptions we make, often leading to misguided conclusions. By making our ladders of inference more visible to others, we not only become more aware of our own reasoning, we also make it more available for others to understand and question. I first helped him walk down his own Ladder of Inference in this case, then encouraged him to take a risk and be authentic by sharing his perspective with the group.

At the end of the half-day session, we had a brief activity scheduled that would speak to personal commitments. Instead, it turned into a dramatic session with key learnings that struck like lightning bolts! First the group groused about the "unfair e-mail" and the implication that they had "voted" to stay away from work.

"Has anyone actually seen the e-mail?" I asked. "Has anyone spoken directly to Stanley?"

The answer to both questions was no. After revisiting the Ladder of Inference concept, I asked the group to consider checking out Stanley's e-mail message and intent before arriving at their conclusions. Kyle then stepped forward and modeled the concept by walking down his own Ladder of Inference. He verbalized that he felt it was unfair of the group to conclude that management had "decided" for them to stay the extra night, that they gave no credit for their input being solicited and that he felt misunderstood.

Kyle's willingness to risk vulnerability opened up a valuable discussion that brought to life the content of the Ladder of Inference tool. Why did the group assume that Kyle had a particular intent to represent management? What did they assume was Stanley's intent when he went out his way to arrange for cross-country skis, snowshoes and videos for the group? Why was their assumption so negative? How could they now check out the facts and ascertain his actual intent?

Reflections:

Once again, real-life issues brought the content of the training agenda to life. By confronting the strains and anxieties head-on, rather than ignoring them and proceeding with the planned agenda, the group got a far more meaningful lesson in the power of Ladders of Inference.

The learning didn't end there. As Group 2 was preparing to leave, Group 3 arrived. The newcomers seemed angry, grumbling that the existing group had "manipulated management" to stay an extra night so they could snowshoe and party. Here was the Ladder of Inference at work again, which gave us grist for discussion with not only the newcomers, but with Group 2 when we reconvened for a half-day follow-up session. What assumptions had Group 3 made about Group 2 that were inaccurate? Had Group 2 ever checked these assumptions out? What results had these inaccurate assumptions produced? How could Group 3 have conducted an effective reality check?

Client: Large Manufacturer of Easy-to-Use Imaging Products

Project Adventure Consultant: Mark Murray

Program Goal: Launch a cross-functional team.

The Challenge:

What do you do when an accident occurs, and how do you get the training back on track?

The Situation and Intervention:

It was late morning on the first full day of the training. As the woman I'll call Lisa approached the rope to swing across an expanse of taboo turf in an activity known as "Nitro Crossing," my critical trainer's eye made a last check. Everything appeared to be in order. People tested their strength by supporting their weight as they hung from the rope. People were in the correct positions for safe spotting. Ostensibly, all signals said "Go!"

Yet something nagged. Nothing I could put my finger on. Just a sense of uneasiness, an inchoate feeling that something more was required.

I ignored it.

Lisa's take-off was smooth. She sailed through the air and hovered over the hula hoop designated as the landing area, where spotters reached up to guide her landing. Before they could make contact, Lisa let go. Crunch! She landed in a heap, clasping her ankle.

Ten minutes later, a local rescue team arrived to transport Lisa to the hospital. After the ambulance pulled out, I was left facing a group of upset people with a day and a half of the training still to go.

Carefully, I proceeded to debrief the accident. Initially, the discussion focused on group members' immediate reaction to the accident. People voiced their concern for Lisa and expressed guilt for having failed to prevent the accident. As is typical of such situations, the conversation then cycled into expressions of anger, followed by a desire to affix blame. "What could we have done differently?" "What could you as facilitator have done?" And so forth.

After about 90 minutes of discussion, I asked group members if they felt ready to move on. They said they were, and we returned to the scheduled agenda. But Lisa, of course, remained on all of our minds. And at that point, we knew neither what was wrong with her nor how she was doing. When the group members who had accompanied Lisa to the hospital returned, we paused for an update. We learned that she'd compound-fractured her ankle and would require surgery. We were also told, "She's in good spirits, feeling positive." People seemed relieved by this and seemed to conclude, Okay, accidents do happen.

Still, I was mindful of the need for updates throughout the remainder of our hours together. We continued to get and share updates about Lisa's progress. And when we opened the next morning with an invitation for thoughts, observations, feelings, our conversation essentially recycled through the same emotions again before everyone felt ready to proceed.

As a result of Lisa's accident, group members were more attentive to each other during the activities that followed. Communication was stronger not only on issues related to physical safety, but on emotional issues, as well. The accident seemed to open people up and create an environment that felt emotionally safer.

We had one more discussion about the accident at the closing of the training. And I got permission from Lisa's manager to get in touch with her, post-training, to monitor her recovery and express my concern and support. That last part was for me as much as for Lisa. To be able to proceed effectively and not be frozen by self-doubt, adventure consultants also need to process such incidents. That includes talking the incident through with a trusted colleague and searching for lessons that might prevent a similar incident in the future.

Reflections:

In this instance, what wound up haunting me most was that I'd ignored the vague warning issued by my intuitive sense. Since then, I've learned to respect and heed my third eye for safety. When intuition sends up a flare, I simply ask participants to wait a moment before proceeding to swing or climb, jump or step. I've discovered that this brief pause gives me the opportunity to position myself for spotting more strategically if necessary. It also enables me to double-check the positioning of the other spotters and to reawaken the individual participant's attention to her own safety.

Client: Large Manufacturer of Easy-to-Use Imaging Products

Project Adventure Consultant: Steve Butler

Program Goals: Strengthen interpersonal skills, with an emphasis on facilitating meetings, giving detailed feedback, knowing when and how to make an effective intervention (particularly when managing difficult people).

Program Parameters: two three-day workshops, placed at the beginning (Phase 1) and end (Phase 2) of a larger 12-week curriculum, delivered in a succession of workshops, each with roughly 20 participants.

The Challenge:

What do you do when a group appears lethargic, unmotivated and/or detached from the experience?

The Situation and Intervention:

This was our first time delivering Phase 2 of the three-day workshops. This particular group, which we'd worked with two months earlier, had been energetic and engaged during the Phase 1 workshop and had exhibited stronger skills and understanding than most of the other groups. This time, we got off to a good start, with lots of encouraging feedback that the strong team performance owed much to the earlier workshop.

Then, in mid-afternoon, the workshop started to sag. We knew that business conditions were challenging and that was affecting employee morale, but the participants had indicated that they were eager to practice and further sharpen their facilitation skills. So we were baffled and disturbed by the group's lack of attention and obvious drop in energy.

"I'm observing less interest and involvement in this feedback process than I saw at the earlier workshop," I said during a post-lunch feedback session. "Is my observation accurate? And if it is, what's going on?"

Thankfully, this group was responsive and open. Over the next 15 minutes, the 20 group members laid out a number of concerns and issues, including: (1) after 12 weeks of straight training, they felt "trained out"; (2) this workshop felt repetitive of Phase 1; (3) they were expecting something new and more challenging; (4) they wanted more focus on facilitating meetings; (5) yes, the layoffs had harmed morale.

The feedback was as eye-opening as it was surprising. The challenge now was to make good use of that information. My immediate concern was how to enhance satisfaction so that participants would be more energetically engaged. Given the group's feeling that its members were at a higher performance level than the Phase 2 activities implied, I sensed that a directive approach would be ineffective. I also did not think that the addition of a single leadership practice session would fully meet their raised expectations for this workshop.

I opted finally to enlist the group as partners to determine how we should proceed. By inviting them to participate in solving the problem, I aimed: (1) to show them that the facilitator doesn't always have to have the answers or ideas, but in fact can be highly effective by assisting a team to develop its own capabilities; (2) to give them a feeling of empowerment to direct the training; (3) to re-establish commitment and enthusiasm for the program. To my mind, all of this was in keeping with the facilitation-building goals of the workshop.

"We have two remaining days together, and I don't want to simply go through the agenda and have it seem of little or no value to you," I said. "Tell me what you think we could do to make this phase more valuable for you. What would you like to see in the next two days?"

Their suggestions were specific and excellent, and generally had to do with tackling facilitation challenges. After that, we all agreed to call it quits for the day, an hour ahead of schedule. That gave the participants more time to rejuvenate for the next day. And it gave my colleague Nicki Hall and me more time to spend on the redesign for the next day's program. After working late into the evening, we arrived at a new design.

Making use of the request for a meeting format, we opened the next day with a challenge that had immediate, real value: we asked the group to generate five concrete recommendations for improving the 12-week curriculum, at least one of which had to apply to the Phase 2 workshop. Divided into four groups, they engaged the challenge enthusiastically and generated many recommendations. Each subgroup's presentation of its five priorities was informative and energetic. (The customer felt so positively about this piece that he requested it be integrated into all Phase 2 segments.)

This session was followed with an activity that practiced facilitation and feedback under complex circumstances, where a manager's needs and expectations had to be factored into the situation. Beyond those two changes, I adhered to the original agenda. But those additions made all the difference. The group was interested, engaged and highly productive for the remainder of the workshop.

Reflections:

By responding to what was actually unfolding in front of us, we were able to gather valuable information and offer a redesign that proved of value to the participants.

Of particular interest (and satisfaction) was participants' feedback that they felt we had modeled to them how to facilitate a difficult group. (Where we saw them as forthcoming, they saw themselves as difficult!) They identified as particularly useful our ability to: (1) listen and hear their information as feedback, rather than criticism; and (2) respond in a way that seemed receptive and valuing, rather than confrontational and defensive. Better than any adventure scenario, real-life events had presented the opportunity to enhance the participants' skills and understanding of facilitation.

Client: Large Manufacturer of Easy-to-Use Imaging Products

Project Adventure Consultant: Mark Murray

Program Goals: Achieve some clarification of personal values; achieve some common ground in the understanding and interpretation of the company's five key values; share ideas on how to bring those values to life; work on strategies for role-modeling the values; build coaching skills to help employees "live" the values.

Program Parameters: One-day, 10-hour workshop, to be delivered 50 times, with roughly 20 participants in each workshop, comprised primarily of managers and line managers, who in turn will deliver a 2.5-hour "Bringing the Values to Life" workshop to their work teams.

The Challenge:

What do you do when your activity props are not what you expected?

The Situation and Intervention:

Every adventure consultant has had the disconcerting experience of arriving at a location only to discover that they, the home office or their dog (a) packed the wrong gear, (b) packed a faulty piece of equipment or (c) packed in a manner that led to equipment damage while in transit. But this was a new one on me.

For the rollout of a pioneering values curriculum the design team decided that a "River" would be a rich symbol for the day's metaphorical journey. (Do you step into the river or watch from the bank? Do you go with the flow or fight the currents? Do you proceed cautiously with an eye toward what is buried in the riverbed and not within sight, or plow forward? And so forth.)

Despite the variety of our metaphorical musings, our anticipation of what this paper, 15-foot-by-2-foot artistic rendering of a River would look like was singular. Each of us envisioned that the final product would run horizontally, so that when unfurled, it could be hung on a wall in the conference center. That way, participants would be able throughout the day to stroll the "bank" and examine the River's contents. This seemed so apparent to us that none of us thought to share this particular aspect of our vision with our artist.

So a few days before the rollout, it was with a collective gasp that we unfurled the drawing to discover that the artist had rendered a beautiful River, rich with meaningful visual images—and a vertical orientation. That meant 15 feet of waters that could not be draped along a wall unless we wanted to run half of it along the 8-foot dropped ceiling and have people walking around with craned necks!

It's easy to work with what you get, if what you get is what you expect. Conversely, it is challenging to work with what you get, when what you've got is completely unexpected. This, of course, is what we ask our participants to do all the time. So, the challenge for us was to see if we could respond as partners in the process of adventure learning.

The obvious solution, of course, was to lay the River out along the floor. And, yeah, we got there—eventually. First, though, we had to let go of our expectations and disappointment. Only then could we begin to see some possible advantages to the vertical model. "We could put it right in the center of the room," someone suggested. "That way it'll capture people's attention right away."

On the pilot day, there was our River, running right up the middle of the room, with chairs placed to surround it. As participants entered the conference room and slowly made their way to their seats, they stopped and hung out along the "banks" of the River. Throughout the day, they admired, questioned and reflected on the various aspects of what quickly came to be known as "The River of Values."

Over the course of the workshops, which took us months to deliver, the River took on a life far greater than we'd anticipated during the design phase. Draped on a side wall, it might have been peripheral to the proceedings. Resting smack in the center of the room, it became central to what transpired.

People treated the fragile paper with care, treading gently along the banks, and drew interesting connections to the workplace. "Just as a river needs rain to keep it full and flowing, so a company needs new people, new ideas, to keep it alive," a participant observed. We added the raindrops immediately.

We also used our mishap with the River to advantage. We shared the horizontal-vertical blunder with the various groups, and it became a metaphor for shifting paradigms, trying on different perspectives, being open to outcomes.

Reflections:

I came away from that experience thinking that much as we'd all like to have perfection in every training delivery, perhaps we should think of perfection in a new way. The old paradigm holds that I have a vision of what will happen and, indeed, it happens. A new paradigm might hold that the perfect delivery is one where you are able to take the unexpected and learn something valuable from it.

Client: Large European-Based Oil and Chemical Company

Project Adventure Consultant: Ann Smolowe

Program Goals: Build cross-functional teamwork and trust within the Field Products Modernization Team, which comprises senior managers, support staffers, hourly union workers.

Program Parameters: Multiple presentations of a two-day workshop, involving low and high ropes elements, to cover 100 refinery employees in groups of 25. Co-led with the company's human resources manager.

The Challenge:

What do you do when an initiative provokes an unexpectedly strong emotional response?

The Situation and Intervention:

"The Wall" is an adventure classic. It challenges a group to cross an 8–14-foot barrier under a restrictive set of rules. Visually imposing, it arouses fear of physical harm and failure. It requires a group effort, carves out leader and follower roles and showcases the value of each. It demands attention to safety, pinpoints gender prejudices, requires spotting. Whether the pass is completed or not, the effort reinforces that success is measured by the quality of the attempt.

As this particular group drew up before a 12-foot Wall for the closing activity of the second day, I felt confident that the group members would have no problem safely navigating the initiative. They'd demonstrated a high level of responsibility adhering to safety guidelines in previous activities. Indeed, they'd been unusually vigilant about physical safety throughout the training, which I took to reflect their refinery culture, where physical hazards and attendant caution are constant.

After I finished laying out the safety guidelines, I said, "Now, I want you to take a minute to think about this Wall metaphorically. We all face Walls in our lives. Sometimes we go right over them. Sometimes, we try but don't succeed. Other times, we don't feel ready to try. I'd like you to reflect on what this Wall symbolically represents to you at work. Whether you choose to physically scale this Wall or not, I'd like each of you to step up to the Wall, identify and share with the group what the Wall represents, and share what you need from the group to help you try to get over the Wall."

As people approached the Wall, they spoke about a variety of issues. The Wall was "their lack of follow-through confronting one another when there was a problem," "poor communication," "not speaking their truth about their opinions back on the job," etc. While some felt challenged to articulate what the Wall symbolized, most were more anxious and focused on the dynamics of navigating the physical challenge.

Then an hourly worker I'll call John approached the Wall. As he stood in front of it, he choked up and began visibly to shake. Seeming to muster every ounce of inner strength, he said that the Wall symbolized his return to the refinery after a prolonged departure.

He went on to share his memory of an incident that had taken place in the refinery three years earlier when a tower caught fire. John recounted his fruitless attempts to rescue a colleague from the burning tower. He not only watched the man burn to death, but John subsequently spent many months in a hospital undergoing skin grafts to deal with multiple third-degree burns.

When John finished telling his story, the silence was heavy. Then he said, "I need your support in the form of being reminded and reassured that

I did everything possible to save my co-worker." The cheering and support that attended John's ascent over the Wall was . . . well, quite a few years later, I still well up thinking about it.

Framed as a personal closing activity, this exercise usually does not require a group debriefing. Needless to say, in this instance, the unpredictable not only demanded a facilitated discussion, but steered the dialogue right into the difficult emotional territory opened up by John.

Some members applauded John's courage and sympathized with his pain. Others hugged him. Those who had witnessed the fire summoned their own memories of the incident and shared feelings they had harbored silently for three years. In this manner, some people, senior managers among them, learned about the incident for the first time.

Everyone was intensely engaged. Each person seemed to take care to build upon and maintain the emotionally safe environment that was enabling them for the first time to collectively confront and discuss the tragedy.

At the end of the program, a few senior managers approached the company's HR manager and me to say that they'd been unaware of the fire and to ask if further processing of the accident seemed necessary. Shifting into the consultant role, I helped them further explore and articulate the learning points from the debrief. They concluded that at the refinery, where physical safety is a constant concern, not enough effort had been put into monitoring the emotional safety of the workers who had witnessed the accident. I helped them brainstorm possible strategies to continue dialogue about the accident back at the refinery.

Reflections:

Though three years had elapsed since the fire, guilt, grief and pain were still palpably in evidence. Healing had been impeded by the absence of a dialogue that allowed for and addressed the emotional scarring. Buttressed by the tenets of the Full Value Contract and the goodwill and trust that had evolved during the training's two days, the Wall provided the vehicle to revisit that tragedy and commence an open and honest discussion.

The experience made me appreciate anew the versatility and power of adventure. Never before had I seen the Wall so thoroughly reframed from a physical challenge into an emotional one. I was reminded that fears of scaling (physical safety) can pale beside fears of sharing (emotional safety).

Client: Luxury Car Manufacturing Company

Project Adventure Consultants: Steve Butler, Moe Carrick, Mark Murray, Ann Smolowe

Program Goals: Deepen understanding of the importance of customer satisfaction and its correlation to employee satisfaction; clarify vision and values; strengthen understanding and valuing of different behavioral styles and the benefits of working as a team for management, employees and customers.

Program Parameters: Participation included the management teams of 27 retail centers attending an initial five-day off-site experience, to be followed by on-site consulting; the initial five-day program was rolled out to over 150 retail operators and managers over a six-month period at a training location outside of Atlanta, Georgia.

The Challenge:

What do you do when you notice participants are mentally checking out before the program is actually over?

The Situation and Intervention:

The original program was scheduled to end at 3:00 p.m. on the final day. Prior to lunch, participants came together at the Wall for the closing initiative. Framing the Wall as a metaphor for the potential barriers of implementing Premiere Care back at the dealerships, each group was invited to approach the Wall as a team and individually announce what they were going to commit to doing differently upon their return to work. Then each team actively worked to get their members over. They would solicit support and safety spotting from other dealer teams as well, but the dealership team was front and center with this effort. Following lunch, there were some additional presentations and a more formal action planning session, closing remarks and final evaluations.

After the first few sessions, we noticed that the end of the workshop for most of the participants was mentally happening before lunch. We also discovered that participants were arranging their flights so that it would be difficult to stay beyond 1:00 p.m. Word had circulated within the dealerships that the departure time was flexible.

It was also evident that participants didn't feel there was an intention-al, planned and effectively implemented adjournment process. Somehow, it lacked a powerful and meaningful closing to the experience.

We went in search of an activity that would signal the end of our time to-gether by highlighting the interdependence of the dealers and supporting the importance of individual contribution to the success of the training ef-fort. There were some elements already in place for this to happen. We had a symbolic gift of a key chain carabiner for each participant. This was sig-nificant given their experience on the high challenge course during the first day of the training. The Wall created power, energy and, overall, positive emotions and attitudes.

By the third rollout, we put in place a new close that ended the training prior to lunch. As the participants left the Wall, they walked into a clearing and saw a 150-foot piece of KM 3 rope lying in a circle on the ground. They were asked to find a place on the perimeter of this rope and wait until all par-ticipants had found their area. As they looked to the center of the circle there was a purple stuff bag sitting on the ground. Curiosity was piqued and the usual jokes about being in a circle were heard. "Oh, this is when we hold hands and sing Kumbaya!"

When everyone had made their way to the circle they were asked to sit. The facilitator then showed the group a carabiner and asked them to remember back to their first day of the training. "The carabiner is a symbol of being on belay for each other. When we are taking risks in our business, remember to request the support of others. It is only with support and trust that we will be able to create what we desire in our dealerships and throughout our compa-ny. In the stuff bag there are carabiners for each of you. We invite each of you, one at a time, to come to the center of the circle and speak briefly about what you found to be most significant from this training experience."

With Challenge by Choice in place, participants were free to simply choose their carabiner and pass on making a statement. Participants were directed to place their carabiner on the rope when they returned to the perimeter of the circle. Most participants chose to make a personal state-ment. Much of it had to do with a renewed sense of trust and an anticipation of bringing this attitude back to the stores.

The group was then challenged with a last physical experience, the Yurt ac-tivity (see Appendix 1), as a reminder of the power that comes with sharing a common purpose. Participants were asked to pick up the rope and create the best balanced circle that they could. The Rope Yurt activity is designed to support a large group that is creating a significant amount of force on the rope. When participants simultaneously lean back in a coordinated fashion while holding the rope, they can literally feel the power of the collective group creating a tension on the rope that is a source of tremendous support. There is enough strength generated that the participants are able to move from a standing to a sitting position and back to a standing position in unison, allowing the rope to support them.

The activity proved to be a fitting ending to the training. After some final words, the evaluations were completed out in the field and participants were free to depart at their own pace. Some lingered to talk, others headed directly to lunch and some went directly to the airport. Whatever direction they took, there was a sense of closure.

Reflections:

The final few hours of the program looked radically different by the final delivery than it had early on in the rollout. It is often easy to overlook the closing aspect of delivery. Predictably, there is a lot to accomplish after the formal closure for all involved. There are calls to make, transportation logistics to coordinate, rooms to vacate, unfinished conversations to be had and training materials to be managed—all of which can distract from bringing a training to effective closure.

Such logistical considerations risk disrupting a final impression and message participants take away from an adventure experience. This training reminded us how critical final impressions are, particularly given the crucial culminating aspect of any training: the transfer of insights and learnings back to the workplace.

Summary

Unpredictable situations in the workplace are not always comfortable. And employees are often left frustrated and anxious in the face of the unknown. One of the many values of adventure learning is the opportunity to examine and explore unpredictable moments. What emerges from these moments is a wonderful parallel between the training event and the business world: embrace the unexpected as it offers opportunities to see new solutions, develop new ideas and create new structures.

This learning is amplified by the adventure consultant who is modeling creative approaches to difficult situations. Through his presence, discernment, action and intuition he is able to develop the adventure moment into a living example of how a learning organization works. And his effective use of the Experiential Learning cycle allows the group participants to transfer the learnings of the moment to their workplace, reminding everyone of the importance of Bringing the Adventure Home.

12 Bringing the Adventure Home

Always in the big woods when you leave familiar ground and step off alone into a new place there will be, along with the feelings of curiosity and excitement, a little nagging of dread. It is the ancient fear of the Unknown, and it is your first bond with the wilderness you are going into. What you are doing is exploring. You are undertaking the first experience, not of the place, but of yourself in that place. It is an experience of our essential loneliness; for nobody can discover the world for anybody else. It is only after we have discovered it for ourselves that it becomes a common ground and a common bond, and we cease to be alone.

—*Wendell Berry*

When an adventure training is effective, participants often return to the workplace with an afterglow. They may seem refreshed and exude a renewed enthusiasm. They may enjoy a heightened awareness of old behaviors and new possibilities. They may invite dialogue and talk excitedly about new tools for implementing changes.

That's the first hour.

Then the phone rings, memos land, workaday problems set in and—what happens? While operating out of the box, anything may have seemed possible: cooperation, exploration, playfulness, supportiveness, openness, introspection, risk. Now, back in the box of familiarity, with its demands and priorities, spoken and unspoken expectations, rewards and restrictions, will any of the meaning stick?

An adventure experience, of course, is only a beginning. It can hold up a mirror to old behaviors, create a forum for exploring new possibilities, suggest new pathways for navigating corporate waters. But the real work of behavioral change begins after participants emerge from the I.M.M.E.R.S.I.O.N. environment and return to their daily work lives.

An adventure consultant who has ongoing contact with a company may be able to identify further obstacles to behavioral change and encourage and expedite processes that help change along. But ultimately, for any change, whether individual or company-wide, to be meaningful and enduring, it must come from within.

The "Tipping Point"

The footprints left by adventure consultants are rarely perceptible or quantifiable. At best, an adventure experience unlocks the possibility for behavioral change by creating what theorist Margaret Wheatley aptly calls "disturbances" within a particular system. These ripples then are given room to begin to play out within a carefully cultivated environment that maximizes opportunities for penetrating insights and substantive learnings.

Ownership of these insights, however, belongs to the individuals within the participant group. What people do with those learnings, either individually or collectively, lies beyond our scope.

Moreover, in the hard-to-quantify area of behavioral change, cause and effect are rarely apparent. Even if change were miraculously as simple as "I saw that about myself yesterday, and as a result from now on I will behave this way," other factors intrude. Is the workplace primed to absorb that change? Are colleagues prepared to support it? Is the motivational spark strong enough to overcome resistance? Will it flame out? Does it need more gestation time? Will it reignite four months up the road, tripped by an incident that resummons and makes newly vivid the learnings of the training?

"Change can be very fleeting," warns Edgar H. Schein, a professor of management at M.I.T.'s Sloan School of Management. "We have all seen how clients can develop new concepts and points of view during training sessions and then revert immediately to their old point of view when they are back in the home environment if that environment does not support the new point of view" (Schein, 1988).

Like adventure, behavioral change is unpredictable. Usually, its trajectory demonstrates a greater allegiance to chaos than linearity.

In a fascinating article that explores how social problems often behave like infectious diseases, Malcolm Gladwell notes that epidemiologists speak of a "tipping point," meaning the point at which an ordinary and stable phenomenon veers into a public health crisis. "Epidemics aren't linear. Improvement does not correspond directly to effort. All that matters is the tipping point," he writes. "This is the fundamental lesson of non-linearity. When it comes to fighting epidemics, small changes . . . can have huge effects. And large changes . . . can have small effects. It depends on when and how the changes are made" (*New Yorker*, 1996).

An adventure experience is effective at creating the disturbances. It is also effective at designing memorable experiences that produce sustainable impact. But observable and enduring systemic change of a behavioral nature may not be forthcoming until a tipping point is reached. That said, let's examine some of the observable and traceable ways that the insights and learnings stirred by an adventure training are carried back to the workplace, both individually and collectively.

The Power of Symbols

Symbols can give powerful and poignant expression to the transfer of adventure learnings back to the workplace. They are something participants can point to, put their hands on, touch with pride. Moreover, brain research by Ned Hermann, Tennes Resengren and others indicates that symbols facilitate ready recall of a powerful experience, enabling impact and meaning to endure long after the event.

A particularly powerful symbol hangs in the entrance lobby of Hartford Life, Inc., the by-product of a training conducted in 1992 by the adventure company PlayWorks. The training, offered to all 1,300 company employees, had focused primarily on developing understanding and connection to the new corporate vision statement, and secondarily on team-building. At the closing of each of the four-hour trainings, each of the more than 100 teams was handed a box containing a 12-inch square of cloth, several other colored pieces of cloth and a variety of sewing supplies. The goal, they were informed, was to produce a quilt square that would convey a critical message about the vision statement and teamwork.

Not only did all of the teams comply with the instructions, but they completed the task on time. A crew of trainers and employees at Hartford Life then volunteered to stitch the squares together.

Six months after the training's end, all employees were invited to attend an unveiling in the cafeteria of the company's headquarters. To kick off the ceremony, the CEO articulated his feelings about the completion of the quilt and shared his impressions of how the company's work environment had changed in the half year since the training. He stated the quilt was "meaningful because everyone took part" and "each contribution was important." He read selections from several unsolicited letters that he received from employees about the Vision week training. The comments included: "the event was one of the most rewarding things I've done at the Hartford... our team was able to bring back ideas to our workplace... the content was excellent, and most important it was fun" (from the In Touch meeting, Lon Smith speaking, September 1992).

Then the quilt was unveiled, a spectacular effort that was roughly 40 feet wide and 10 feet high. Soon after, the quilt was moved to the lobby of the entrance, where it hangs to this day.

At first glance, this artful and heartfelt expression of lessons gleaned from an adventure experience may seem insignificant. But every day, employees see that quilt as they enter the building. It's a constant reminder of their own stake and pride in the company's vision, and a subtle prod to remember the importance of that vision and effective teamwork. It's a quiet memory jog that reminds employees how much they can accomplish when they work collaboratively and commitedly, with galvanized attention and energy. And when the company tour takes visitors and new employees through the lobby, the quilt is heralded as a symbol of what the company stands for. All in all, a simple yet prominent transfer for a training that lasted only a half day.

Visual reminders have served other companies well. As noted in Chapter 5, the creation of symbolic animal "beings" proved an effective way for employees of EG&G's Electro-Optic Division to move beyond the suggested set of norms described in PA's Full Value Contract in order to establish a set of operating norms and personal goals all their own. Five years later, employees still display the "beings" prominently on office walls. More importantly, the norms those beings were meant to symbolize have become entrenched. (Another visual reminder: on casual dress days, participants still sport the PA T-shirts and sweatshirts that were given as gifts at the end of the training!)

At BMW South Africa, the Dealer Support staff of the Sales and Marketing Division found a creative application for the results of a variation on a "Beings" exercise. In this instance, participants had been asked to identify an important aspect of teamwork, then create a symbolic representation that would hold meaning not only for the Dealer Support group as a whole, but for each of its five separate regional teams. The activity had been intended to bring closure to four days of team development work, before launching into eight days of skills building. But instead of tearing with relish into the supplies—markers, glitter, pipecleaners, colored paper, stickers—participants eyed the arts and crafts with seeming discomfort, perhaps even suspicion. The "Beings" activity seemed to fizzle.

Over the next eight days, the focus of the training shifted to strengthening the field teams' consultancy skills in such areas as contracting, diagnosis and resistance management. But as the participants continued to work with each other, the idea of the Beings continued to percolate. To promote a different outcome, the art supplies were left in plain sight and participants were periodically invited to revisit the task.

The extra time and thought made for a powerful final product. The five resulting representations, symbolizing the five regional teams, ranged from a lighthouse to Olympic rings to a train whose passengers included Albert Einstein, Mother Theresa and Snoopy. Participants then visually linked those five teams with their management team to create a unified field team.

Visually, the "Beings" were large, three-dimensional and provocative. More exciting, the meaning of those images was so powerful that the participants wanted, in some way, to preserve their creative effort. Ultimately, the group chose to photograph the final product and transfer it to a computer screensaver. Months later, it continues to fill screens and serve as a daily reminder that the regional teams, collective field team and their managers are part of one company, one division, one vision.

From Walk and Talk to Action

When a group returns from a training, they may walk a new walk and talk a new talk—for a while. The question is, once the residual exhilaration and excitement wear off, does anything remain? One of the best gauges of enduring impact is the efforts that participants make to translate the learnings into concrete practices. Again, EG&G serves as a strong example. The purpose of that 1993 training had been to identify behaviors that were impeding workplace efficiency, then to develop a new set of norms to improve the work environment. During the training, participants from the Electro-Optic Division in effect designed their own Full Value Contract.

Upon returning to work, those concepts became an active part of the work environment. When, for instance, Product Platform Teams were created recently to improve "cycle time," the new teams requested a meeting to develop norms of operation with each other. Interestingly, though only roughly half of the team members had attended the PA training, they were easily able to convince the newer employees that this exercise in norms-establishment was worthwhile.

The essential message from that training—the importance of establishing behavioral expectations of one another in the workplace—has now permeated the company. Sue Michel of the Human Resources division reports that armed with a norms tool, operations people find it easier to talk and work with not only their colleagues, but their managers as well. And managers now feel that they have a valuable tool for both establishing expectations and taking corrective action when warranted.

At other companies that worked on developing work norms, some have implemented process checks at the end of their weekly or monthly meetings. Others who identified "fun" as a key ingredient to workplace health have rotated responsibility for making meetings surprising and enjoyable. One company, interested in integrating the Challenge by Choice concept into the workplace, took a first step by ceasing to make the training mandatory.

Changes in group process are relatively easy to spot and document, Changes in the way group members interact with each other are harder to identify. (Six months after a training, is the growing consistency of giving and receiving feedback openly in a department an evolving result of the training? Or does it perhaps reflect the tone set by a new manager who regularly invites open dialogue?) Changes effected in individuals are the most difficult of all to pinpoint.

Think, for instance, about the Kodak manager in Chapter 6 who resisted a group juggling activity because he thought it was "a waste of time" and unconnected to the training goal of strengthening coaching skills. Over the course of that activity, Bob came to see that his balkiness mirrored resistant behaviors at work. He even went so far as to state that in order to be a more effective manager and coach, he was going to need to "get over some of my ideas about what's valuable and what's not."

No doubt, Bob returned to the office with a renewed sensitivity to and appreciation of resistant behaviors. But did his thinking change as a result? Did it result in behavioral changes that were apparent to others? Did those changes occur immediately and dramatically, or was it subtle, evolving almost imperceptibly over time? Adventure consultants are as unlikely to learn the answer to that as they are likely to know if the partner from the Big Eight consulting firm in Chapter 1 acted on his recognition that he was "too conservative" in the area of risk-taking.

After they've thrown the stones into a company's waters that create a disturbance, it is often a challenge for adventure consultants to gain access to see, manage and affect the resulting ripples. For that, the adventure consultant's best advocates and allies are the company's internal trainers and consultants, with whom they often form an ongoing relationship.

The Inside Track

Unlike an external consultant, the internal practitioner is in a position to impact the transfer of learnings back to the workplace. Over time, the internal consultant has a variety of means to further the aims of a particular training, among them:

- Soliciting, eliciting and working with feedback from the training to further support an individual, team or work group;
- Building on the experience to strengthen subsequent training designs; providing ongoing consultation on an as-needed basis;
- Integrating experiential methods into new or existing training programs;
- Leading or partnering in the design process for follow-up trainings;
- Facilitating process at internal meetings, as appropriate;
- Keeping the Full Value Contract and Challenge by Choice foundational concepts alive by integrating them as an ongoing practice and walking the talk;
- Promoting an experiential approach in other parts of the company.

The relationship with top leadership in larger-scale behavioral change efforts is critical for keeping a finger on the pulse of overall program effectiveness. Obviously, the tighter the external consultant's relationship to the person or people whose vision inform the company's direction—the CEO, the president, the divisional vice presidents—the better positioned the consultant is to know if the training has proved effective in furthering top management's goals. Moreover, when a consultant enjoys the trust of top management, the message—and corresponding trust and cooperation—often filters down through the ranks.

More commonly, however, the primary one-on-one relationship within a client system is between the adventure consultant and an internal consultant (i.e., the head of human resources, education and training or training and development). As these relationships mature and deepen over time, they mesh the strengths of internal expertise with the strengths of an external strategic perspective and adventure skills. When the partnership is fully ripened, the resulting synergism is enormous and the potential for effective transfer grows exponentially.

Both consultant and client benefit from such relationships. The adventure consultant's credibility, level of acceptance and ability to transfer and sustain his work within a company are all enhanced by a strong bond with an internal consultant. Conversely, when an internal consultant becomes active in the adventure process, training designs develop a richness, depth and continuity that is rarely achievable when the client contact is not actively involved in assessment, design, delivery and follow-up.

Project Adventure's relationship with Pam Jaeger, manager of training and development at Hasbro Games in Beverly, MA, exemplifies such a relationship. When Pam initially contacted PA in 1993, she wanted only to purchase a few game kits and initiatives. Over the next few years, PA consultant Mark Murray periodically checked in with Pam to see how things were going and to see if he could supply any additional props or ideas.

Then in 1995, after Parker Brothers (PB) and Milton Bradley (MB) were consolidated into the Hasbro Games Group, Pam requested a more serious involvement from PA. The merging of the PB and MB cultures, she explained, had raised some leadership and performance challenges among PB's many cross-functional product development teams, which take a product from conception to production.

PB's top management firmly believed that the next Monopoly sensation could only evolve in an environment where people worked together effectively and continued to feel a sense of product ownership. Pam was looking to design a training that would strengthen the teamwork of all 75 members of the cross-functional product development teams, including people from design, graphics, engineering, project management, the model shop, and sales and marketing.

During a six-month period in 1996, Mark and Pam co-ran five three-day workshops to handle all 75 people. With each successive workshop, Mark and Pam became more equal in the co-leadership as Pam became more active in the framings of the activities and the debriefings.

Back in the office environment, Pam managed the transfer from the workshops carefully. When groups returned from a workshop, they were greeted with a breakfast, facilitated by her and attended by people from earlier workshops, to ease the transition and transference of learnings. A picture gallery of workshops was hung to generate interest among those who had not yet attended. A weekly lunch was established to keep the spirit of the training alive.

The developing trust between Pam and Mark enabled the two of them to advocate internally for Mark to view various aspects of the product development cycle, a step crucial to strengthening each successive workshop as they rolled out over the five months. In the end, the five training groups each came up with a list of a half dozen operating norms that were then presented, winnowed down and adopted by all the teams. Mark and Pam's close collaboration ensured that all members understood the purpose of the norms and how they would be implemented in the workplace.

Since that rollout, Pam and Mark's collaboration has continued. It has included an in-house course on interpersonal communication skills, where Pam consulted with Mark to redesign the program, then delivered the one-day course herself; a Global Team Leadership meeting for Hasbro where Pam consulted with Mark on how to build a sense of community with an international flavor, then delivered the design herself; and a day-long high challenge course program, run by PA, to renew the spirit of the earlier product development team training.

Where Mark's efforts were initially focused on training PB product development teams, his primary focus now is on training PB's internal consultant to integrate adventure learning into her programs. For Hasbro, the adventure connection has meant not only the transfer of learnings from the workshop to the workplace, but the transfer of the skills associated with each of the adventure consultant's three roles—consultant, trainer, facilitator—to Pam. For Project Adventure, this enriches and deepens the meaning of its goal to Bring the Adventure Home.

The Long and Short of It

"Even if [a new idea] fits into the client's own personality and self-concept, it is possible that it will violate the expectations of significant others around the client—his boss, peers, and subordinates—to a sufficient degree that they will either not reinforce it or actually disconfirm it. The point is there is nothing automatic about this process. It must be managed carefully if the client's new perceptions, attitudes and behaviors are to survive."

—Edgar H. Schein, Process Consultation

It is hardly a secret that the more involvement a consultant has with a company over time, the better positioned the consultant is to help manage the change process. Obviously, the deeper a consultant's understanding of a company's processes, culture and internal relationships, the richer, more sophisticated and better customized the designs of any future programs.

Adventure consulting, in particular, is often an accumulative process. Initial workshops may be greeted with skepticism, reservation or outright resistance because of adventure's nontraditional approach. As a company's employees become familiar with adventure techniques, they become more open, more experimental, more accepting. That interest and trust builds on itself, in the contexts of both workshop and workplace.

When an adventure intervention is longer term, participants have an opportunity to practice and apply the new behaviors, then provide feedback for further strengthening those behaviors. The work climate enlarges to embrace and support the new behaviors. It also expands to place value on training efforts that are targeted at developing and strengthening these behaviors. Opportunities for self-exploration and learning develop a value that is no longer questioned.

While sustainable transfer in the area of behavioral change is most likely to flourish in situations where there is ongoing follow-up, transfer occurs in short, one-time programs, as well. The nature of the transfer, however, tends to be different. In a short-term relationship, the most salient impact tends to be a heightened awareness and recognition of behaviors.

However, adventure has many applications, and some of them thrive on short-term involvements. Frequently, adventure activities are integrated into a larger program to set a tone or to make vivid one particular point. In those instances, the training event, rather than the aftermath, tends to be the main focus.

Evaluating What's Behind, Looking Toward What's Ahead

It is difficult to pinpoint, evaluate and measure changes triggered or inspired by an adventure experience—or any other kind of behavior-related training, for that matter. Perhaps that explains why corporations, which spend an estimated $55.3 billion annually on training costs, make virtually no investment in follow-up attempts to quantify training results.

"Mainstream accounting practices do not require companies to document the investments they make in the learning and development of their employees," observes Curtis Plott, CEO of the American Society for Training and Development. "What data there is comes largely from such sources as training companies, training publishers, and other commercial enterprises seeking confirmation of a growing market segment" (*ASTD Journal*, January 1998).

In other words, consultants are largely left to their own devices to evaluate their own performance—often, without continuing access to the very people they are evaluating. A steep challenge, to say the least!

As a consulting effort proceeds from needs assessment to design to delivery, consultants constantly evaluate the process and its developing results, in much the same way that trainers and facilitators constantly monitor a training's process and results as it unfolds. Careful monitoring can be particularly useful in rollout situations where multiple workshops will be offered over time to accommodate a large number of participants. When evaluative information is used effectively, each successive training is strengthened, benefiting from the experiences of the preceding trainings. Moreover, the longer and more intimately the consultant works with the client, the stronger her ability to perceive the disturbances, effects and potentialities of the adventure experience.

Post-training, adventure consultants usually rely on evaluation forms that invite participant feedback. Often disparaged as "smile sheets," these forms have inherent limits. Typically, they are handed out just as participants are breaking for the day. Eager to go home, they sometimes speed through the evaluation without considered thought. They are also still in the mindset of the day's training and may offer a glowing review, whose effects are all but impossible to verify.

Commonly, participants are invited to fill out these forms under a cloak of anonymity. While the intent is to encourage forthrightness, it may result in gratuitous and unproductive nastiness and accusation. Anonymity also deprives both internal and external consultants of a context and the opportunity for follow-up. Sometimes, more useful results are produced when participants are encouraged to sign their names to the evaluation. If a client uses an evaluation form that limits opportunities for feedback by offering only options for circling ratings, participants can be encouraged to write additional comments at the bottom of the sheet.

Constructive evaluations of clients can also be very useful in an ongoing consulting relationship. Among the questions consultants need to address when providing feedback to clients: Did the client adequately prepare participants for the adventure experience? Did key corporate executives appear, as promised? Was the tone of these presentations in keeping with the rest of the training, and did they lend to the building momentum?

While none of these evaluative methods offer a quantitative measure of impact, they do provide qualitative assessments that help to refine programs, make design changes and so forth. Participant evaluations that are written weeks or months after a training ends can be particularly effective for gaining insight into the progress of the transfer from workshop to workplace.

Such was the case with a recent pioneering two-day leadership workshop for female Kodak managers that focused on balancing issues related to work, home and self. This workshop, which attempted to juxtapose public and private issues, felt new and daring for the internal and external consultants who co-led the sessions.

Evaluative information circulated one month later by participants affirmed that the impact had been strong, that a workshop for those who had missed the first one would be worthwhile and that a follow-up workshop was worth exploring. This feedback had particular value since the participants had the advantage of some hindsight.

The participant responsible for gathering feedback summarized the results this way in an e-mail: "All the feedback has been very positive, both from a personal and group dynamics standpoint . . . As an example of the workshop results, I have personally internalized: that I need to adjust my definition of success to be less perfectionist; that I should let people know what I need from them to be successful; and how my different personality profiles at home and at work affect my behaviors and choices. The workshop was a wonderful opportunity to build new relationships and strengthen existing ones."

Such feedback not only affirms the value and successful outcome of a particular training, but is a reminder of the larger agenda that underlies all adventure efforts: to unlock minds, stimulate fresh thinking, encourage meaningful dialogue. When that is the goal, an adventure experience is never an ending, but rather a never-ending beginning.

Summary

An adventure experience creates disturbances in a corporate field. But what any individual or group makes of those disturbances is neither predictable nor controllable. To encourage the transfer of insights from the adventure workshop to the actual workplace, adventure consulting relies on:

- visual symbols that represent outcomes and remind participants of the experience
- a close, evolving one-on-one relationship with an internal consultant
- ongoing interaction with members of top leadership
- written evaluations by participants that assess the impact of the experience
- contact with participants to solicit direct feedback
- further trainings that build upon earlier adventure experience.

I Design

The adventure approach to learning can come in many packages, from four-hour to multi-day programs, meeting a broad array of content and thematic needs. Whatever the package, the design is always customized to reflect the unique needs and expectations of the client group.

A comprehensive portfolio of designs is a valuable resource available from an organization with years of experience in the adventure field. This design portfolio was created by consultants who are knowledgeable about the adventure toolbox and have spent considerable time assessing the needs of many clients. Using this portfolio, adventure consultants can assess each client's needs and create from a palette of possibilities the program design that best ensures desired outcomes.

In this appendix are four sample designs from different client systems: a half-day program, a one-day program, a three-day program and a longer-term intervention reflecting a series of trainings. Each sample program design reflects the client's different presenting needs and parameters, stated goals and training flows.

Complementing the one-day customer focus design highlighted in Chapter 8, these examples illustrate the range of design templates from which adventure consultants can build programs. You may see some of the same activities in each of the designs. Upon deeper exploration, you will discover that the same activity, briefed differently, will generate different outcomes.

While this appendix describes the overall design flow in some detail, it is not intended to be a comprehensive trainer's guide. Rather, it is intended to illuminate common threads and marked differences in building program designs.

We continue to develop our knowledge and skills in the area of behavioral change. It is essential in this endeavor that we operate from a sound set of blueprints. In this spirit, this appendix is offered as a resource. It is our hope that these templates—broken down into convening, problem-solving and transition and closing components—will be helpful to your design efforts.

Values Management

Bringing the Values to Life, a one-day values management workshop

Presenting Issues

It is one thing to articulate a company's values, it is quite another to manage by these values on a day-to-day basis. The client requested that a "dynamic" workshop be developed to build awareness and skills in managers' abilities to lead in a values-driven environment. The company recognizes that unless management receives some form of practical training, the stated values of the company may not positively affect the quality of work and work life as originally intended. The workshop also needs to complement other leadership workshops in creating a performance-based culture, as well as an exciting and vibrant workplace.

Parameters

The scope of the program is to deliver a one-day training to all group leaders and supervisors in the company's manufacturing facility. This includes approximately 900 managers. The managers are then required to return and deliver two two-hour trainings to their teams. The training groups for this workshop are limited to 20–25 participants. The coordinating committee requested that an adventure approach be integrated, as a result of the company's previous success with this training approach. The delivery needed to be designed to be portable to meet the global needs of the company.

Participants

Participants are managers in a manufacturing environment with a broad range of years in the company as well as years in management. Most of the participants agree that they achieved their management position mainly due to technical expertise. Participation and attendance are required, so the level of interest and motivation vary within each training group. Each manager or supervisor leads his own group. Predictably, the different groups are at various levels of readiness to attend to values in the work environment. The readiness factor impacts the leaders' ability to transfer the skills from the training to their respective teams.

Goals

- Discover the meaning of the corporate values.
- Understand the dynamics of values and value systems.
- Assess personal value systems and determine where and how the corporate values fit.
- Develop clarity on the behavioral expectations for being a leader in this company.
- Develop clarity on the behavioral expectations for being a member of a team in this company.
- Design a values-training experience for each manager's team members.

The workshop is based on the belief that immersion in the process of understanding your own value system is critical. This personal understanding is important both prior and parallel to working with corporate value systems. The workshop flow moves from understanding of personal values, to awareness of corporate values, to team readiness and finally to developing the skills to manage effectively in a values-based environment.

The training combines the following: a series of short informational presentations supported by posters and/or overheads, adventure activities, small group discussions, large group discussions, self-report inventories, a training manual and a resource guide.

Training Flow

Convening the Group (3 hours)

The workshop begins with a warm welcome and orientation to how the workshop came into being. Anticipating some concerns as a result of the attendance requirement, attention is devoted early on to addressing participant questions, alleviating concerns and setting expectations for the day. Using simple get-to-know-you activities like Toss a Name Game, adding a value to the name as we toss, we infuse the values language. In a facilitated discussion, we begin to explore the meaning of leadership and values.

The workshop purpose is reviewed and parameters are established for discussing values, which can often be difficult and sensitive. A simple philosophy guiding the efforts of the workshop is presented to offer historical context to the purpose of the company's values. The "3H's" philosophy speaks to the importance of coordinating the dynamic relationship among the "3H's" of hand, head and heart.

The design asks participants to explore the power and meaning of values based on their own life experiences. A short presentation is given on "What is a value?" Participants are asked to think of a situation that helped them develop a value in their lives. This discussion explores the evolution of a value system. A brief go-round offers the opportunity for group members to share and further develop a sense of team among the group.

Toolbox Resources

- Toss a Name Game (convening activity)
- 3H Personal Integration Philosophy
- Large Group Presentation: Evolution of Values
- Dyad Activity (convening activity)

Problem-Solving (5 hours)

The concept of values is put into action with a series of values-focused activities. During the Stepping Stones activity, some of the "stones" are set up to represent the company's values, while other stones are just resources. Following the debrief focusing on how values were "lived" during the activity, participants are asked to reflect on how they are currently living the corporate values as leaders.

In a line-up activity, the power of deeply held values is explored. Participants are asked to take a stand on values-focused statements taken from business examples in the company. For example, participants are asked to strongly agree, agree, disagree or strongly disagree with statements such as "This company should institute random drug testing to ensure the safety of all its employees with three strikes and you're out for a consequence." Following this animated activity and discussion, a brief presentation is given offering a three-step values clarification model.

Once we have illustrated the process of values development and the potential power of a value, participants are asked to think about how values can be translated into behaviors to cause real behavioral change. Anomie, the state where values and normative standards of conduct are lacking, is defined and explored further in small groups in the context of working within a valueless workplace. As participants emerge from this discussion, they are guided in rotating small groups through a T-Charting activity. This activity focuses participants on making the abstract values become meaningful and relevant to workplace behaviors through exploring preferred responses to two critical questions: What does this value look like in action at work? What does this value sound like in action at work?

Using trust as the value central to all others, we move the group through a facilitated trust sequence. The traditional two-person leans are followed by a trust circle. The action culminates in a fall from a height. Throughout the sequence, the emphasis is on leadership styles and how different styles impact the development of trust. The connection between behaviors and values is illuminated. To conclude this section, the CEO of the company speaks on video about the importance of values in effective leadership.

Toolbox Resources

- Stepping Stones (see Toolbox Appendix, page 268)
- Values Continuum
- Large Group Presentation: Values Clarification
- Small Group Discussion: Anomie in the Workplace
- T-charting (group discussion/definition activity)
- Trust Fall Sequence (series of spotting and low ropes course activities)
- Video (from the client)

Transition and Closure (2 hours)

In this time period, we begin with a large group discussion of the major obstacles to values understanding and application at work. By beginning here, we help to set a positive framework for the second goal of this section—for each manager and supervisor to develop a plan for working with their teams. While some participants may choose to develop their plans independently, others may choose to work in small groups. The leaders are encouraged to think proactively about what they can do to change ambivalence to interest or resistance to compliance, depending on how they perceive the readiness of their teams at the current time. The large group reconvenes to share and enhance each other's designs. The program ends with a reading and evaluation.

Toolbox Resources

- Design Development Session
- Reading
- Evaluations

Team Development

A three-day team development model for product development cross-functional groups

Presenting Issues

The issues are several: teams and teamwork, people from various functions working together and people constantly moving from one product development team to another. The challenge for this organization is twofold—to develop a training program that will create a strong sense of team among sales, marketing, creative services, design and development functions, and to develop individuals' skills in moving in and out of teams effectively. The training manager has some knowledge of the adventure approach to learning and feels that it fits well with the company's business objectives. Personal skill development, knowledge of team concepts and creating cross- functional understanding need to be reinforced in this design.

Parameters

The scope of the program is to deliver a three-day training to the 75 employees who contribute to the product development function of this company. The training manager wants to be part of each experience so that the work transference will be enhanced. It is important that there not be a significant lapse of time between each session because creating a common ground of understanding surrounding behavioral expectations among participants is expected. Each training experience needs to replicate all activities and content to ensure consistency of the experience across the organization.

Participants

Participants are employees spanning all levels from vice presidents to model shop designers. They all have input into the creation of new products. The groups have a mixture of ages from mid-20s to late 50s, and a mixture of years in the company from three months to 30 years. The participants have a pre-meeting with the training representative prior to their three days, so they are generally positive about the experience. All participants have participated in some type of behavior-focused workshop so they are familiar with the nature of our goals.

Goals of the Training

- Increase understanding of components of effective teams as they progress along the team performance curve.
- Continue the process of building a consistent culture within all the product development teams.
- Improve participants' teaming skills.
- Develop a stronger sense of shared accountability in reaching performance goals.
- Offer an opportunity for personal renewal and a commitment to develop a proactive response in the work environment.

The training combines the following: a series of short informational presentations supported by overheads, adventure activities, solo reflection and partner reflection time, small group discussions, large group discussions, self-report inventories, a training manual and symbolic gifts.

Training Flow

Daily themes provide another way to link content areas, both within a specific day and across the program as a whole. The theme of the first day is How Effective Teams Work. We ask participants to think of themselves as a project team and, throughout the day, they have the opportunity to learn or relearn about some of the components of effective teams. The theme of the second day is I Can Make a Difference. Throughout the day, participants are given the opportunity to think about the question, "How am I as a member of a team?" The emphasis is on "How do I see myself and how do others view me?" Days one and two are awareness and skill-building days.

Day three provides different opportunities for participants to practice and apply their newly acquired awareness and skills. The application process is captured by the theme, Building Consistency and Predictability Across Product Development Teams. Finally, the last day of the program guides participants to look to the future and create plans to effect change within their product development teams. Each of the three daily themes supports and reinforces the underlying theme of team development.

Day One

Convening the Group (2 hours)

Daily Theme: How Effective Teams Work. After initial introductions and a re-view of workshop goals, participants are invited to introduce themselves through an activity using the Feelings Marketplace Cards (a set of cards with one feeling word on each card). Through a mingling process, individuals can select cards to use as springboards for their introductions, sharing information they would like the group to know as well as sharing the function they represent. Following this introduction, the Full Value Contract version of the Twelve Bits activity is used to actively introduce the Full Value Contract and initiate group problem-solving. The debrief of the activity focuses on the points of a Full Value Contract and how such a contract can enhance teamwork.

Toolbox Resources

- Feelings Marketplace Cards
- Twelve Bits (see Toolbox Appendix, page 277)

Problem-Solving (4 hours)

Using a set of activities that require team-based problem-solving skills, we cover the components of highly effective teams. By focusing on the team's own experience with the activities, we naturally bring to life the issues of teamwork. In the activity Full House, where the group must move along a set of boards without touching the ground, the focus in the debrief is on support, organization and problem-solving. A Teeter Totter, a large platform upon which the group must balance, is used to illustrate the balance between task and process. And finally, Nitro Crossing, an activity where the group must swing on a rope from point A to B, provides an opportunity to use a Team Effectiveness Rating worksheet and pulls together some of the components of effective teams. Finally, we provide time for personal reflection on teams.

Toolbox Resources

- Full House (see Toolbox Appendix, page 258)
- Teeter Totter (low ropes course element)
- Nitro Crossing (low ropes course element)
- Team Effectiveness Rating Worksheet

Transition and Closure (1 1/2 hours)

To close the day, group members participate in a puzzle activity to describe the current qualities existing in most product development teams. Participants write words or draw pictorial representations of the qualities of the existing work environment on a blank 20- piece jigsaw puzzle. Participants enter their thoughts and learning from the day in personal journals, which are then captured as a large group on flip charts. These learnings are posted and used as a reference as we begin to think about the qualities we want to have existing back at work. Finally, participants are given the DiSC behavioral styles inventory to take home to complete for day two. The day closes with a reading.

Toolbox Resources

- Puzzle Activity
- Journal writing
- DiSC Personal Profile System (see Toolbox Appendix, page 288)

Day Two

Convening the Group (1 1/2 hours)

Daily Theme: I Can Make a Difference. In order for the necessary personal reflection and skill development to occur, an atmosphere of trust and confidentiality continues to be paramount. A combination of understanding the DiSC behavioral styles inventory, setting a personal goal for the experiences of the day, and being open to both giving and receiving feedback is essential for meaningful learning outcomes. The day begins with an opportunity for participants to offer some quick reflections on the previous day. Time is also dedicated to addressing any concerns or questions that have emerged as reflection has taken place. To stay focused on team development, we ask the team to use the Team Effectiveness Rating Scale for day one.

This discussion is followed by a presentation on the DiSC Personal Profile System. The DiSC is a simple, easy-to-understand inventory that provides a picture of preferential styles. It also provides an opportunity for a team to view its group as a composite. The presentation and discussion are focused on helping participants better recognize their own behavioral patterns, strengths and opportunities for increasing their interpersonal effectiveness. By helping develop an appreciation for the different motivational environments required by those with different behavioral styles, it is also an opportunity for individuals to think about creating an environment that will ensure even greater individual and team success. Following DiSC, goal setting is done individually in journals.

Toolbox Resources

- Team Effectiveness Rating Scale
- DiSC Personal Profile System (see Toolbox Appendix, page 288)
- Personal Journals

Problem-Solving (4 1/2 hours)

The activities within this section of the training are framed and processed around the team performance, rather than on the problem-solving itself. The Human Camera activity is used to shift the focus to the individual. This partner trust activity helps to create "goal partners," twosomes who will work together to accomplish their personal goals.

The Relationship Traverse, an adaptation of the low ropes activity, the Wild Woozy, brings the whole group together to demonstrate the importance of interdependence and clear feedback and further develop the partnerships. The debrief focuses on the balance between team and individual needs.

From this activity, we move to a variation on the Spider's Web called "Prep for Management Line Review." The focus here is on how well the product development teams understand their internal customers, make decisions, communicate effectively and allow for individual initiative. Both the framing and debriefing of the activity are customized to accomplish these objectives.

We finish up the circuit with the communication activity, Minefield. The messages in this activity are strong and particularly poignant for a group working to develop clear communication and coaching skills. We frame and debrief the activity to help group members make connections to work—what limits are imposed on our communication, how we can work around these limits, which of these limits are self-imposed or intensified by our actions.

Toolbox Resources

- Human Camera (no-prop trust/communication activity)
- Wild Woozy (low ropes course element)
- Spider's Web (see Toolbox Appendix, page 264)

- Minefield (portable transport initiative)
- Personal Journals

Transition and Closure (2 hours)

There have been many experiences during the day where individuals are able to work on their goals. We begin the closing portion of the day with a Trust Fall from a height. This large group trust activity offers an opportunity for the group to physically demonstrate that when a member risks in an effort to grow the group will be there to offer support. The debrief allows time for personal reflection on the experiences and probes the issue of how risk-taking is supported in the business environment.

We move from this activity back into the "goal partners." Partners spend time together reflecting on the day and offering each other focused feedback. In the partner teams, group members reflect on how they made a difference today and how they can and do make a difference in their work team. We reconvene as a large group to share insights and to add to our flip chart Learning Journal.

Toolbox Resources

- Trust Fall from Height (low ropes course element)
- Personal Journals
- Flip Chart Learning Journal

Day Three

Convening the Group (45 minutes)

Daily Theme: Building Consistency and Predictability Across Product Development Teams. As with the previous two days, we begin by stating the goals for the day and restating the expected end-time. We follow with some reflection on day two. We remind the group that this is the final day and a good opportunity to work further on their personal goals. We also discuss the importance of the closing activities as an opportunity to integrate the learnings and insights from the previous two days.

Problem-Solving (5 3/4 hours)

This component of the program is intended to allow participants to put their newly acquired skills to practice. Since their creativity is the lifeblood of these teams, the Game Game activity is used to test their creative processes. The activity gives an opportunity for three subteams to develop a playable game with a minimum of props, present it to the two other groups and then reflect on their work process and hear from a process observer. The outcome looks at opportunities to continue to improve their team skills back at work.

Following the Game Game, we move to the high challenge ropes course. The concept of being "on belay" for each other at work is critical. Members of this group are often on teams of people operating from different geographical locations. They need to feel connected. The outcome of this activity is a strong, unifying bond that transcends geographical barriers. It also reinforces the themes of the previous days with a focus on role clarity, initiative, risk and support.

Toolbox Resources

- The Game Game (portable creative initiative)
- High Challenge Ropes Course

Transition and Closure (1 1/2 hours)

This is the final opportunity for pulling all the pieces together. The closing process is a multiphase approach. In the first phase, we debrief the high challenge ropes course experience. The different roles individuals assumed during the ropes course experience are discussed in the context of the strengths, challenges and rewards of each. Analogies are made to workplace roles. The areas of risk-taking on the job, asking for and giving support and taking initiative are also explored and transferred from the experience.

As the transference process from the ropes course experience continues, the discussion is guided to be more focused on the product development teams. We return to the puzzle activity from day one with an eye for how group members now envision the product development teams working in the future. The puzzle activity is followed with a small group norm activity. Each group creates a list of desired norms for the product development teams.

This closure activity is important both for the group that is here now and for our relationship with the larger group of product development teams. We use the puzzle and norming activity to collect information across many teams on the qualities and norms desired for the product development teams. The collective results are compiled and presented back to participants at a later time.

The group focus shifts to a personal one as participants reflect on the question, "How can I make a difference?" Goal partners commit to ongoing goal-setting and a continued relationship in the workplace.

The day concludes with a large group variation of Yurt Circle called Yurt Rope. This activity concretely illustrates the interconnected nature of teams—the roles of the individual and the need for the team. Lastly, carabiner keychains are given as a reminder of the goals defined in the training.

Toolbox Resources

- Puzzle Sets
- Yurt Circle (transition and closing activity)

Team Development

A half-day team development experience for a regional sales team

Presenting Issues

In this case, the organization is looking to develop a sense of team among people who contribute to the same company or departmental goal, yet who do not work directly with each other. In particular, communication issues are a significant stumbling block to building a coherent and efficient operation. Identifying this problem and developing some strategies for addressing it are important elements in the program design.

This is the second program we designed and delivered for this client. They like to add focused content and experiential sessions at the end of their regular meetings because of ease of scheduling. They also feel it is helpful to provide new and different experiences at the meetings to keep the format fresh and engaging (since so much of the meetings consist of didactic presentations with little opportunity for interpersonal interactions).

Parameters

This four-hour program is the final session of a three-day meeting for the company's regional sales team. The members of this group do not work directly with each other on a daily basis, but the company feels their efforts need to be coordinated better to achieve their overall sales objectives. This particular program coincides with the changing of the senior manager of the group. It is important to involve the entire group in some activities so that the new manager and the group have an opportunity to interact with each other.

Participants

Thirty-nine sales representatives and their managers come from across the sales region. There is a wide range in ages. Most people have been with the company for at least several years.

Goals

- Change a paradigm from "problem-solving" to "solution-seeking."
- Discover efficient strategies for everyone to have input.
- Review communication styles and their effect on external and internal customers.
- Present a "solution-seeking" model.

The training included a modified circuit design, where groups rotate through a series of activity "stations." The intent was to ensure that each group had the same activity experiences. Due to the brevity of the program, we set up three versions of every activity so each small group could do its activities on its own without having to worry about transitions with another group (as happens with a traditional circuit design where groups rotate to each station and there is only one setup per activity).

To create a sense of team in the large group, both the beginning and end of the program included everyone as a large group. The first problem-solving task also focused on the entire group. Then the smaller teams broke off to do their individual rotations focusing on the other goals.

The training combined the following: a series of short informational presentations supported by overheads, adventure activities, solo reflection, small group discussions, large group discussions.

Training Flow

Convening the Group (60 minutes)

We introduce the group to Project Adventure core concepts and review the training goals and agenda for the day. As tone setters, two activities are presented to the whole group: the first examines people's assumptions about competition and collaboration; the second invites individuals to share information—about a personal success at work and about the impact of personal styles on relationships and performance—as a way of promoting conversation and learning.

Toolbox Resources

- Overheads of Experiential Learning Cycle, Full Value Contract, Challenge by Choice
- Thumb Wrestling (convening/problem-solving activity)
- Look Up/Look Down (convening activity)

Problem-Solving (4 1/2 hours)

During this time period, the groups move from one large to three small groups. Before moving into action, we "frontload" the activity with a short presentation of a seven-step problem-solving model. The focus of this seven-step process is on moving beyond identifying problems to developing solutions.

The large group activity, Corporate Connection, requires the large group to accomplish a goal while divided into small subgroups. Each subgroup has its own goal, while at the same time the group must also attend to the objective of the large group—to achieve a high score. The debrief of this active ball-bouncing initiative is to examine the interconnectedness of the whole organization with the small subgroups.

After a short break, the group is divided into three teams. These new teams experience three initiative tasks, each lasting one hour. To provide a common frame of reference, every group does the same activities. Each activity is framed around a different issue facing this group at work: managing product quality and ensuring compliance with industry standards, reducing the cycle time of getting products to their customers and exploring how to create a successful relationship with a customer. At the same time, the debriefs examine the use of the problem-solving model and how successfully the group is implementing it.

At the close of the third debrief, the smaller teams are asked to identify three clear, practical and value-added "best practices" from the day and to record them for presentation to the larger group.

Between the second and third activities, the groups break for lunch.

Toolbox Resources

- Corporate Connection—large group activity (see Toolbox Appendix, page 246)
- Object Retrieval (see Toolbox Appendix, page 271)
- Cycle Time Puzzle (see Toolbox Appendix, page 255)
- Spider's Web (see Toolbox Appendix, page 264)

Transition and Closure (30 minutes)

Each small team presents the three best practices that it wants to transfer back to the workplace to improve performance. After hearing the reports, individuals have a final opportunity to state personal observations and insights from the day. A reading about teamwork brings the program to a close.

Focus on Team Development and Becoming a Healthy Organization—Multiple Event

This training series was originally created for an Information Services (IS) department of a leading company that produces computer software and games.

As we have discussed throughout this book, effective designs can often result in a lasting and deep relationship between a client and the adventure consultant. What begins as one thing can evolve into something else. In this way the consultant continues to add value and contributes to lasting change.

This design example shows what begins as a three-day retreat for a leadership group grow into a multi-day experience with follow-up sessions for all employees and close with a department-wide half-day celebration. A year later, new employees continue to be guided through a similar process.

Presenting Issues

The initial scope of work is a three-day leadership retreat for the intact information services leadership team. The overall goal is to strengthen both the team development skills of each leader and the group functioning of the leadership team. More specifically, goals include focused attention and dialogue about the process of becoming a healthy organization, developing increased cooperation and trust, developing operational functioning within and between I/S subgroups and reinforcing clarity on expectations, ownership and responsibility for roles and future business targets. The three-day design integrates discussion and analysis of the results from an all-employee survey that provided feedback on a variety of issues including specific leadership concerns.

After the Leadership Retreat and follow-up half-day meeting with the PA consultant, the team decides that *all* employees would benefit from a similar experience. A series of two-day retreats and half-day follow-up sessions results. The primary focus area for the department as a whole is on the creation of norms and behaviors applicable to every member of I/S.

Consultation continues with the leadership team throughout the subsequent trainings. As a result of the ongoing consultation and discussion, the leadership team makes a commitment to have a closing *department-wide* experience. Following the (four) two-day employee trainings and follow-up sessions, a half-day training is designed for the purpose of final ratification of the new I/S norms and behaviors. This half-day program offers an opportunity to celebrate the department's hard work and progress.

Six months after the culminating event, another two-day retreat is scheduled to bring new hires on board through a repeat of the initial two-day training. In addition, as the annual all-employee survey is prepared, questions are added that specifically reflect the work of the teams who participated in previous trainings. Finally, during annual performance reviews (on which all pay and incentive decisions are made), each employee and leader is required to add two goals that address how she can contribute to the ongoing development of the teams' effectiveness, morale and collective culture.

Parameters

To address time and cost constraints, we offer four two-day programs over a four-month period. Groups of 20 to 25 employees attend. The (off) sites do not have a Challenge Ropes Course. This rollout begins on the heels of the initial three-day off-site with the Leadership Team. Participants experience the same core content and activity flow. Each of the four attending groups also participates in a four- to five-hour follow-up session on-site at the company's offices. The follow-up sessions occur anywhere between three and six weeks after the two-day off-site training. Finally, the closing department-wide half-day experience is held at a company warehouse for the 125 I/S employees.

Participants

Participants are corporate I/S staff from both the programming and operations sides of the organization. A member of the Leadership Team attends each of the employee sessions to provide continuity and clarity about why the I/S department is investing such time, resources and energy in the culture change.

The Two-Day Employee Training

Goals

The overriding goal is to bring the entire I/S department together as one working group, with multiple interdependencies and common behavioral norms. All activities and content from the three-day leadership training are repeated to ensure consistency of the experience across the organization. Specific goals for the employees sessions include:

- Increase openness among members and increase team functioning.
- Decrease detrimental effects of "functional castles."
- Celebrate past and present successes.
- Continue process of aligning common values and norms (as begun by leadership team) and increase personal investment in building a stronger sense of I/S community.
- Review Stephen Covey's "Circle of Influence/Circle of Concern" and discuss its application.
- Explore the collective synergies and liabilities of different behavioral styles through the DiSC Profile System.

Training Flow
Day One

Convening the Group (1 hour 15 minutes)
Participants are engaged in a series of introductory activities focused on getting to know one another's names, learning some non-work—related things about one another, visiting potential preconceived paradigms about the experience and sharing their expectations about and interest in attending the training. The purpose is to engage the group in the adventure learning process, demystify it and create an upbeat, relaxed, open and honest learning environment. Additionally, participants are introduced to the tools undergirding the design, updated on the outcomes of

the leadership training and briefed on the defined program goals and logistics.

Toolbox Resources

- Name by Name, Categories, Snowflake, Vacationer/Prisoner Line-Up (convening activities)
- Experiential Learning Cycle, Challenge by Choice, Full Value Contract

Problem-Solving (4 hours)
Introducing the problem-solving elements into the experience, activities focus on heightening participant awareness of collaborative versus cooperative efforts within the I/S teams. Activity designs reward cross-team collaboration. Additional attention focuses on teaching the basic concepts of proactive behavior and brainstorming. Finally, smaller group initiatives focus on introspection on current team skills with particular emphasis on effective communication, feedback and problem-solving.

Toolbox Resources

- Corporate Connection (see Toolbox Appendix, page 246)
- Experiential Learning Cycle, Challenge by Choice, Full Value Contract, Program Goals
- Covey's Circle of Concern/Circle of Influence (see Toolbox Appendix, page 290)
- Pipeline (see Toolbox Appendix, page 261)
- Keypunch (problem-solving activity)

Transference and Closure (2 1/2 hours)
The closing portion of the day is designed to introduce the "Ladder of Inference" in the context of the assumptions people make and the damage assumptions can cause in the work environment. Discussion is intended to foster direct applications back to the I/S environment. Participants are encouraged to make their own work-related "ladders" visible to one another for the purpose of further analysis and understanding. A structured discussion is facilitated to capture the insights and learnings from the day.

Toolbox Resources

- Ladder of Inference (see Toolbox Appendix, page 291)
- Reflections

Training Flow
Day Two

Convening the Group (1 hour 45 minutes)
With an aim to capture any additional learnings, questions or concerns from the first day, day two begins with a check-in. Helping to maintain the environment and upbeat tone established the first day, a quick game of Have You Ever is played. This fast-paced game launches the day with high energy and allows participants to continue sharing on a personal level in a fun way. Another convening activity, Look Up/Look Down, is used to engage participants in paired discussions focused specifically on I/S concerns and other issues. The DiSC Profile System, a behavioral inventory, is completed and self-scored to provide a framework for exploring the impact of different styles at work. An initial interpretation is offered, lending further depth to the research behind the inventory and the dimensions upon which the tool is built to supplement the interpretive notes in the inventory itself.

Toolbox Resources

· Have You Ever (convening activity)
· Look Up/Look Down (convening activity)
· DiSC Profile System (see Toolbox Appendix, page 288)

Problem-Solving (2 hours 45 minutes)
Behavioral styles and Ladders of Inference are revisited through problem-solving activities designed to further heighten awareness, deepen understanding and develop appreciation for the I/S composite profile. Small group discussions focus on the strengths and weaknesses of individual profiles. These profiles are then investigated through an activity. The reflection is more introspective. The DiSC Profile serves to provide a common language and framework for the discussions and debriefs. A simple model for giving and receiving feedback is presented as a structure and tool and offered in the context of feedback as a "gift." A "two column" tool exercise is used to help participants practice becoming more aware of assumptions that may impact giving and receiving feedback.

Toolbox Resources

· Small Group Discussions
· Cycle Time Puzzle (see Toolbox Appendix, page 255)
· Feedback Model/Presentation
· Left Hand/Right Hand Column

Transition and Closure (1 hour 45 minutes)
As participants begin the closure process and consider re-entry back to work, they brainstorm to define the values and behavioral norms that the team desires within the I/S department, with the goal of rolling the compiled ideas into one final set of norms, including the leadership team and the other three employee groups. The two-day experience ends with an activity that symbolizes the power of working together.

Toolbox Resources

- Large Group Discussion: Values and Behavioral Norms/Goal Setting for the Workplace
- Yurt Circle (transition and closing activity)

3–6 Weeks Later: Half-Day Follow-up Session (On-Site/Small Groups)

Goals
- Renew key learnings from off-site retreat.
- Revisit norms and define specific behaviors.
- Develop strategies for keeping the learnings alive.

Convening the Group (1 hour)
A welcome and warm-up activity launch the follow-up session to recreate an atmosphere of learning and fun. This is an opportunity to reconnect with the group, re-establish rapport and provide a segue for revisiting and renewing the key learnings from the off-site retreat. Following a quick activity, a large group discussion offers the opportunity to record (via flip charts) the participants' responses to structured questions such as "What's been working well since the retreat?" and "What has been challenging, frustrating or not working well?"

Toolbox Resources

- Convening and Tone-Setting Activity
- Large Group Discussion/Brainstorm (flip-charted activity)

Problem-Solving (2 hours)
The group is updated on the progress since the leadership team retreat and other employee group retreats. The synthesis of the department's norms as defined by the leadership team is shared for the purpose of

soliciting further small group, department-wide input. The group is encouraged and engaged in adding further definition to the defined norms by defining specific behaviors to each of them using a T-Chart "looks like, sounds like" format.

Toolbox Resources

- T-Chart Activity

Transition and Closure (1 hour)
Revisiting the Ladder of Inference concept, a discussion is facilitated around the "ladders" that have occurred within the I/S department since the retreat and protocols for improving the balance of advocacy and inquiry. Participants are encouraged to share their own experiences, positive and negative, in applying this concept to work. Following this discussion, attention is focused on defining strategies for keeping the momentum of the learnings alive.

Toolbox Resources

- Ladder of Inference (see Toolbox Appendix, page 291)
- Large Group Discussion

Six Months Later: Half-Day Follow-up Session (Company Warehouse/Entire Department)

Goals

- Ratify department-wide norms and behaviors.
- Define and share personal commitments to behavior change.
- Celebrate the power of "linking up."

Convening the Group (1 hour)
To kick off this culminating event, a series of quick energizers is offered. The activities are intentionally colorful, physically active and varied to capture the diversity of the collective group. The theoretical underpinnings and content pieces undergirding the series of trainings are reviewed for the purpose of continuing where the small groups left off. The opening segment ends with a sharing of the leadership vision by the leadership team.

Toolbox Resources

- Boop (convening activity)
- Rock-Paper-Scissors (convening activity)
- Scattergories (convening activity)
- Basic Concepts: Experiential Learning Cycle, Challenge by Choice, Feedback Model, Ladder of Inference and Circles of Influence/Concern
- Leadership Vision

Problem-Solving (2 hours)
A small group discussion follows. In table groups of six plus, small teams review one norm topic and seek consensus on four specific behaviors that will support this norm. Department members agree to hold each other accountable for these behaviors. Small teams note questions or concerns they have in response to structured reflective questions. This is followed by presentations in which each small team presents a norm and accompanying behaviors, as well as any unresolved concerns they have as a group.

Toolbox Resources

- Large Group Discussion
- Small Group Structured Discussion

Closing (90 minutes)
A culminating four-way version of the Spider's Web activity launches the closing segment. The web is used to emphasize the validation process, encouraging participants to share aloud their personal commitment to behavior change as a way of moving the I/S group as a whole to new heights in a vastly different, team-oriented culture. Continuing the ceremonial celebration, the entire department is asked to gather around the Yurt Rope to experience the power and strength of working together. Carrying the symbolism a final step, carabiner keychains are presented as gifts of "linking together." At the end, we identify next steps and strategies for keeping the learnings of the training alive.

Toolbox Resources

- Spider's Web (see Toolbox Appendix, page 264)
- Yurt Rope (closing activity)
- Symbolic Gifts

II Toolbox

This appendix contains 10 sample activities and a reference list of instruments, inventories and models. The how-to write-ups for the activities are intended to add detail to your understanding of an adventure design. Thousands of activities and variations on activities can be used in an adventure design. These 10 are meant to offer but a brief glimpse into the cavernous adventure toolbox.

As we've discussed throughout the text, adventure consultants use their tools to meet the specific needs of clients and participants. In most cases, an activity or activity type is customized to accomplish a specific set of outcomes. The 10 activities that follow are from real-life consulting designs. Each is specifically tailored to meet a narrow focus. These activities have many other uses and variations.

To round out the toolbox, following the activities is a list of resources. The adventure consultant uses many effective and useful inventories, instruments and conceptual models to create a well-rounded design. The list is certainly not exhaustive, but represents some of the resources we have found useful.

Anatomy of the Activities

To bring some structure to the activity descriptions, we've used the following subheadings:

- Type—To add clarity and structure, we've categorized the activities into three types: Convening and Tone-Setting, Problem-Solving and Transfer, and Transition and Closure. The Problem-Solving and Transfer initiatives generally represent three types of activity:

> Transport —the moving of a group or object from point A to B

> Creation—the solution requires building something or finding an answer cognitively

> Retrieval—an object must be "recovered"

The type is meant to reflect how we used the activity in this instance, not to limit the activity to that particular use.

- Group Size—The number of people this activity is designed for

- Time Frame—Length of time for the activity and debrief. Time frames can change based on the specific goals for the activity as well as other factors—group size, overall program length, etc.—so this time frame is for this particular version.

- Outcomes—Expected outcomes for the activity as it is written

- Materials—Props needed

- Set-Up—Some activities require set-up before the action begins.

- Briefing—We've included a script of how we actually presented the activity. This briefing period helps the group begin to see how the activity connects to the content of the program.

- Rules—Step-by-step instructions for doing the activity

- Instructor's Notes—As an activity plays itself out, some predictable questions and pitfalls may occur. These notes offer tips for effectively facilitating the activity.

- Variations—Some ideas for using an activity in a different way or for making the activity more or less challenging

- Debriefing—In this final stage of an activity, the adventure consultant facilitates a dialogue around the activity and helps the group to generalize and transfer their learnings. We've included some of the types of questions an adventure consultant might use to encourage understanding of what happened, generalization and transfer.

- Other Thematic Connections...

Section One—Adventure Activities

The Being

Type: Closure and Transition

Group Size: 10–20

Time Frame: 1 to 2 hours, depending on group size

The creation of a "Being" uses the power of symbolic learning and tries to capture and define the desired work climate of a group.

Goals

- Describe the qualities of a shared work environment.
- Understand how the team and individuals are responsible for creating this environment.
- Develop team norms and personal goals.
- Create an awareness of obstacles to creating this environment.

Materials

Flip chart paper or a long sheet of butcher paper

A variety of Magic Markers

(More elaborate Beings can be developed with a range of arts and craft materials.)

Briefing

"During the last few days we have had the opportunity to view ourselves and our team in a different way. I imagine there are some qualities that you would like to bottle and bring back to the workplace. This activity is designed to create an opportunity for you to capture and transfer the positive work and learnings.

"The 'Being' is a symbolic representation that can keep the energy of this experience alive and meaningful at work. The power of our work together will not be evaluated by the excitement of the moment. Rather, the power is likely to be viewed in the results, especially the impact it has back in the workplace. In many respects, this is just the beginning.

"As a starting point, we ask that you think of something alive that best exemplifies the qualities that you desire for your team. This living example will become a symbol of the life we are giving to this process.

"The conversation may sound like this: *'We are hard working, persistent, enjoy working together, and we make things—perhaps we are like beavers.' 'What do you all think?'* Keep in mind that the qualities you attribute to this animal do not require biological verification. Be playful and creative and have fun.

"Finally, it is important to remain aware of the potential obstacles you have identified but not place too much attention on them. We are discovering more and more that what we choose to focus on is eventually what we create. We want to focus on the qualities we desire rather than on the obstacles we wish to avoid."

Rules

The Being is usually done in a four-step process. In each step the group will work together to create a shared understanding and visual representation of their responses to the following questions:

- Think of something living that would best represent your team. Come to agreement on this Being. Draw the outline of the Being on the piece of paper.

- What qualities of the work environment do you want to bring to life? (If near the end of a training, ask them to think about what they hope to transfer back to work after they leave the training experience.) Once you have agreed on the qualities, write them inside the outline of your Being.

- Identify the obstacles that may interfere with realizing these qualities. Write these obstacles around the outside of the Being's outline.

- Think now as an individual. Identify a personal behavior that you can commit to work on that will support the development of the qualities in the Being. Write your personal goals somewhere on the paper, being sure to sign your name.

Present all four steps at once to allow the group to see the big picture and progress through the activity within the time limits.

Debriefing

The workplace connections are visibly woven into the Being activity as it plays itself out, thus requiring little additional closure. In situations where multiple

Beings are being created by smaller teams within a larger business unit, it can be valuable for the larger group to come together and share the thought processes behind their creations for everyone to hear, appreciate and understand.

Instructor's Notes

· If this activity is to have significant meaning for the group, sufficient time needs to be allotted for the level of interest and excitement to build.

· The instructor is critical in managing the time during this activity, as the group needs to get through all the steps. There is a tendency for the group to spend an excessive amount of time on the living symbol and fall short on the other elements.

· The instructor may want to guide the group in identifying specific qualities and not let them become too general.

· A traditional Being is often the outline of a team member's body on paper. The qualities and commitments are written inside the outline and the obstacles outside the outline.

· In the Being examples in this book, including BMW SA, Hartford Life Inc. and EG&G, time was devoted outside of the formal training to creating the finished product. While groups may not be able to complete a finished product in the hour or two provided during a training, keep in mind that the meaning and transfer to work are the important elements. If you are able to get the basic information captured during the training, it is a great litmus test for the team to take the raw information back to work and create a more polished Being in which they have pride and ownership.

Corporate Connection

Type: Problem-Solving—Retrieval/Creation

Group Size: 24–60

Time Frame: 30–60 minutes, depending on group size

Goals

· Develop an understanding of collaboration versus competition.

· Explore the option of "win-win" outcomes when multiple groups or teams work together.

· Practice and understand "out-of-the-box" thinking.

· Examine leadership and communication issues.

Materials

· 8 containers (4 18 inches high and 4 12 inches high)

   Mark one small and one large container—front and back—with the color of each of the four teams' balls.

· 4 dozen hi-bounce foam balls

   There need to be one dozen balls per team of no more than 15 people; each team's balls need to be a different color (or marked somehow to identify with the team). We recommend hi-bounce foam balls for safety reasons.

· 4 boundary markers (10–15 feet in length)

Set-Up

For four subteams, it is recommended that the props be positioned as in the diagram below.

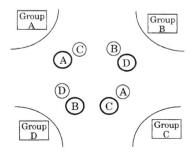

The smaller container is positioned 4–6 feet from its team's throwing area; the larger container can be 15–20 feet away.

It is generally helpful to position the containers so that there are clear throwing lines to each container.

Briefing

"Each of the four groups represents a different department of a retail operation. As experts in your respective areas, your primary goal is to leverage as many successful customer connections as possible for the whole operation in the time allotted. As is true in any business operation, each area delivers services to its own group of customers—both internal and external. It is these customer connections, represented by these different colored foam balls, that matter.

"Every time a ball successfully enters a can matching its color, it represents a successful customer connection. Those that land in the corresponding bucket placed closer to a team are worth 10 points each; those that land in the bucket placed farther away are worth 20. Any ball that lands in another team's container has no point value. Each team is responsible for getting its own balls into the appropriate containers. Finally, I'd like to ask each group to please designate a leader, and for the leaders to meet me in the middle of the area."

Additional Briefing for the Leaders

"You are responsible and accountable for your department's performance, as well as for the overall success of the whole operation. As the designated leaders, you can call a leadership summit or team meeting at any time. These meetings last for three minutes. Only two meetings may be called during the activity. Only the leaders may initiate a meeting. You do so by having any one of you come and request the meeting from me. If anyone asks for a meeting, the entire organization must stop its work. The meeting can include the leaders only, the entire organization or any configuration of people you choose. If a meeting is called in the middle of a round, the time for that round is suspended during the meeting, then resumed once the meeting has concluded. A final reminder that, as leaders, you are accountable. You need to organize your people and monitor the performance results of your own department in order for the organization to meet its overall goals."

Rules

Round One

1) The goal is for the whole organization to achieve the highest level of "customer connections." The closer container is easier (i.e., physically closer) but has a lower score—10 points; the larger container is farther away but has a higher score (hence a greater payoff)—20 points.

2) State that each department is responsible for ensuring that all of its balls end up in a container that matches the color of the balls.

3) The organization will have at least three rounds to achieve their best score. Each round lasts 90 seconds, or until all balls are in the containers.

4) All balls must start each round behind the boundary line where they are currently located. (Department A's balls must always start in Department A's area.) If the balls are in a bag to start, the bag may not be used as part of the solution.

5) Each small department divides itself into Throwers and Retrievers; the roles are permanent for that round. The department decides how many people are in each role.

6) Retrievers are only allowed to retrieve balls that are on the floor and roll them back to the Throwers. Retrievers may not do anything to assist a thrown ball into a container. Retrievers can roam anywhere in the area where the containers are. If a Retriever intentionally directs a ball into a container, the score for that container is nullified for that round.

7) Throwers must remain behind the boundary marker at all times.

8) To be included as a successful customer connection, any ball must bounce at least once on the floor before landing in a container.

9) The boundary markers and the containers may not be moved.

Facilitator Tip

It is generally helpful to move into Round One as quickly as possible with a minimal amount of planning and discussion. Typically, groups will assume they are competing with the other groups to produce the highest score. Allowing too much time for discussion at the outset may allow the teams to identify and organize a collaborative strategy.

If you hear such discussion, you may want to move into the action as quickly as possible. It's not that you want to prevent the teams from uniting behind a collaborative strategy, but the power of collaboration becomes even more evident and valuable if the first round evolves in a more chaotic, individualistic pattern.

Round Two, Additional Rules

Briefing: "Due to the success of our first cycle, the organization is investing in a new training program. We are creating a third job role: Backboard. Each department must now allocate its people into one of three roles. Due to the rushed nature of this training process, Backboards are not fully functional at this time."

10) Backboards may use their bodies to assist balls into a container. Backboards may not use their arms from shoulder to hands; they may only use their torso and legs.

11) Each role is permanent for this round.

Round Three, Additional Rules

12) For this round, all three roles are present and they are interchangeable. People can change roles at any time during the round.

Instructor's Notes

- If the teams are collaborating and have managed to get the highest possible score in Rounds 1 or 2, you might announce a new challenge by asking them to achieve the same score but in a shorter time frame. Another variation allows the departments to empty a container only after all the balls are inside it; the department could then attempt to increase its score by throwing the balls into the containers again.

- Record the scores for each small group and a total combined score for the four teams between rounds. For some people, recording the individual team scores pushes them to be more competitive. Be aware of this pattern and present the scoring in a manner that best matches the goals you are aiming for with this activity.

- This activity is a great example of an initiative that can work extremely well with large groups. A traditional view has been that problem-solving tasks work best with groups of 8–15 people; this activity tends to work better with much larger numbers. One consultant can comfortably lead this problem for up to 70–80 people.

- This activity can be used with two subteams as well as with four. The set-up is similar, only using materials for two teams.

- In general, 5–6 people on a subteam is the minimum in order for there to be sufficient numbers to fill all three roles. The upper limit of people per subteam depends on the number of balls and the amount of direct, active participation desired.

Debriefing

The goal of the debrief is to evaluate the interactions between the subteams as well as the impact of the leaders on the overall group's performance.

- How does the group feel about its overall performance?

- What factors contributed either to the organization's success or to its inability to achieve a satisfactory score and profit?

- What was the focus of each team during the activity? Did that focus change or stay the same? Why?

- What was the focus of the leaders? How did their role impact on the achievements of the separate offices? Of the overall company?

- What did it take for the four teams to unify behind a collaborative strategy?

- In terms of collaboration, how was this experience either similar to or different from what occurs at work?

- What would need to happen to create this type of collaboration in the workplace?

Other Thematic Connections...

This activity has been used to illuminate behavioral styles. For example, in one design where the DiSC Personal Profile had been used with a participant group, participants were divided into the four subgroups according to their "primary behavioral tendency" as indicated by their self-scored Profile. During the debrief, one of the goals was to evaluate the interactions within each subteam and their relative strengths, synergies and liabilities based on working with people who shared their same primary behavioral tendencies. Another goal was to explore the impact of different behavioral styles on overall effectiveness and end results.

Group Juggling/Warp Speed

Type: Problem-Solving—Creation

Group Size: 8–24

Time Frame: 20–45 minutes, not including debrief

Goals

- Increase skills in problem-solving and creative, out-of-the-box thinking.
- Practice listening to, testing and implementing ideas.
- Explore decision-making and goal-setting.

Materials

6–24 throwable objects (fleece balls, sqooz balls, rubber animals, etc.) in a bag

Briefing

"How many of you know how to juggle?" A few hands usually go up. Briefly demonstrate juggling three objects, if possible. After viewing hands, then ask, "How many of you do more than one task at a time at work?" Typically, all participants will acknowledge they do this. "So your response to knowing how to juggle depends on how we define juggling. You are all used to dealing with multiple demands on your time. This activity provides an opportunity for the team to examine how it performs when there are multiple tasks needing attention."

Rules

1) Ask participants to form a circle. Have a bag of throwable objects available.

2) Tell people that the first task is to practice the necessary skills of juggling, throwing and catching. Everyone will catch and throw a ball. In order to be ready to do these tasks, everyone should stand in the ready position—i.e., both hands extended in front of you.

3) "Once you have caught and thrown the ball, please put your hands behind your back to indicate you have done your job. This is the 'don't you dare throw it to me' position. There is only one rule here: don't throw to the person next to you."

4) "We will establish a pattern. As the ball moves around the circle, remember two things: who throws the ball to you and who you throw it to. We will need to repeat this pattern exactly."

5) Start by throwing the ball to a person and then allow the ball to move around the circle (reminding people to throw across the circle rather than to the person next to them). Watch to be certain that everyone receives the ball and that no one receives it twice. Encourage people if drops occur, trying to make it OK to make a mistake.

6) When the ball gets to the last person to catch, ask him to complete the cycle by throwing it back to you. After the ball returns to you at the start, tell people you want to practice again by repeating the exact same pattern. Start the ball by throwing to the same person and allow the ball to go through a second time.

7) Once you get the ball back again, stop and tell people you will now be introducing more objects. The team should do its best to manage all the tasks. Repeat that the pattern will remain the same at all times.

8) Toss the first ball, then add in others as appropriate. Usually aim to throw at least 6–8 objects in this first round. Use a variety of objects to make it more interesting and fun. The goal of this initial round is to immerse the group in a fast-paced and somewhat chaotic trial run.

9) After the activity has lasted several minutes (usually objects are flying everywhere and people are disorganized), stop and ask people to describe what the activity felt like for them. (Chaotic, like work, too many things to do, hard to concentrate, disorganized are typical descriptors.)

10) Now tell the group they will have several opportunities to create a more efficient, more effective operation. Tell them there are three factors they need to monitor:

> Volume—how many objects they can manage

> Speed—how fast they can move the objects to completion

> Quality—how many drops occur during each round

11) The rules are as follows:

> No one may be eliminated from the circle to improve performance.

> Objects must start and stop with the same person.

> Everyone must have contact with the objects as they move around the circle.

> Everyone cannot touch the objects simultaneously.

> The initial pattern/sequence that was created must be repeated; it cannot be changed. People will always pass the objects and receive the objects from the same person.

> The work process is to pass the objects through one complete cycle—starting and stopping with the same person—but halting the objects after one rotation.

12) Ask that someone else become the initiator of throwing the objects so that you can time the attempts.

13) Tell the team it is their decision to determine how many objects they want to attempt, how long it will take and how many drops they expect. Suggest that: choosing only one object may not be enough product for the company to survive; choosing many objects but needing an hour to complete the task will probably not be acceptable to customers; and multiple objects in a fast time probably will not be successful if there are too many drops. Remind the group it is up to them to determine how to proceed.

14) Once they have decided how many objects to use, tell them you will time the initial attempt. When they finish, announce the time and verify the number of objects and the number of drops.

15) At the end of each round, ask: "Does the group feel this attempt is its best possible effort?" If the answer is negative, allow the group to brainstorm, plan and continue its efforts until they feel satisfied with the result. As needed, refocus the group on the three factors: volume, speed and quality.

16) At the conclusion of the last attempt, put the objects away and begin the debrief.

Instructor's Notes

- This activity is the classic first initiative. It is short, almost always produces a "success" for the group and has a good "aha" when groups realize they can change positions. It is used in almost every program if people haven't seen it before.

- As a first initiative, this activity can be successful for exploring creativity and problem-solving. However, there can be a fine line between thinking out of the box and breaking the rules. The rules as stated are clear and need to be enforced. Allowing the group to struggle with and define the "gray areas"—Can we change positions? Can we pass all the balls inside the bag? What does having everyone touch the objects mean?—models the experiential learning process and encourages the group to think and interact on its own. Be careful of enforcing rules so strictly that you inhibit the group's thinking early on.
- Groups almost always want to know what is the "best" time you have ever seen. There is a risk when answering this question. If you don't answer, the group may feel you are withholding information. If you do answer honestly, the group may feel dissatisfied based on its comparative score, without knowing if the best group had the same rules, same number of people, etc. There are many ways of encouraging better performance during this activity. Identifying a best score and challenging the group to beat it may not always be a good idea.

Debriefing

The goal of the debrief is to identify what factors contributed to the team's performance.

- Did the group feel successful? Why?
- What did the team do that allowed this success to occur or prevented it from occurring?
- Which of the three factors (volume, speed, quality) is most important? Or is it a balance of the three? Does one need to happen first? Why?
- At work, is the same factor(s) most important?
- What lessons learned from this activity will be important to remember in the next activity and back at work?

Cycle Time Puzzle

Type: Problem-Solving-Creation

Group Size: 10–15 (standard set-up)

Time Frame: 45–60 minutes, depending on group size

Goals

- Further develop and practice problem-solving and communication skills.
- Increase understanding of the concept of continuous improvement.
- Exemplify the importance of roles and responsibilities.

Materials

A Cycle Time Puzzle—14 precut boards of various lengths (5' to 2') notched in two to four places along each board (see graphic)

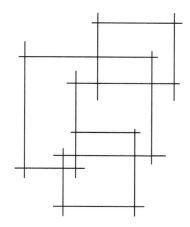

Briefing

"As you are aware, we are in a highly competitive market and our ability to meet the demands of the marketplace separate us from our competitors. You have been presented with a blueprint and raw materials for developing a new product that we believe will increase our market share substantially. Engineering believes you have what is necessary to complete the assembly of this product. Sales and Marketing are requesting that you provide a forecast for them on production schedule.

"This will require that this assembly team see how quickly this product can be assembled, moving from materials to completion. The materials are always delivered with the longest boards on the bottom ascending to the shortest on top. This will not and cannot change.

"At the end of 45 minutes, Sales and Marketing will need your forecast. We already have benchmark information which shows that our competition is assembling this product per unit in 40 seconds. Any questions? Good luck!"

Rules

The overall goal is to complete the assembly of the puzzle so that it matches the configuration on the photo. (Assembly teams receive a rough blueprint of the assembled puzzle.)

There are two goals to accomplish within one hour:

- Solve the puzzle within the time (that is, assemble the boards so they match the picture).
- Be able to assemble the product in less than 60 seconds under the stated guidelines. (Note: 40 seconds is a world-class operation.)

1) As you start to assemble the puzzle for the first time, working with various configurations is encouraged.

2) During the hour, you may attempt as many assembly iterations as possible.

3) When beginning each assembly iteration, the boards must always start in a stack, longest boards on the bottom to the shortest on the top.

4) The boards may not be marked or written on in any manner. No marking of the floor/assembly area is allowed.

5) In the finished design, the boards fit together without any significant bending or force fit.

Variations

Increase challenge

- Use two puzzles and two assembly teams with the best time being that submitted by the slowest team. Have the teams out of sight of each other.
- Do not permit any writing on the design blueprint given to the team.

Decrease challenge

- Allow more stated time for the demonstration of the "quick assembly" (2 minutes) or goal of achieving a "world-class operation."

Instructor's Notes

- Although you present the boards stacked on the floor, teams will begin to think of how best to start each assembly iteration. Some will want to start with boards on the table, some will have assembly team members touching their boards before the time begins. Allow for this creative process to emerge and encourage the team to identify what fits within the parameters of the rules.

- The activity seems fairly safe; however, preliminary caution should be given to the group that in the frenzied assembly process we need to be cautious of the Three Stooges phenomenon: rotating boards hitting people in the head.

- Early on in the process with larger groups, it may appear as though there is very little involvement by some members. The value is that at some point these people need to become committed to the activity in order to attain world-class time. Attend closely to the actions and conversations of the members on the perimeter of the activity and observe to see how or if they become involved with the work of the team.

Debriefing

The goal of the debrief is to evaluate both the overall team's performance and how individuals contributed to the team effort.

- As a team initiative, which elements of a high-performing team were evident and which elements needed more emphasis?

- Clarity of purpose and clarity of roles are essential for team performance. How did these two factors influence our performance?

- Often there were many voices competing for air time. Did people feel that their own voice was heard by the group? Whose voices were heard and why?

- What similarities do you see between this activity and the workplace? Is there anything we want to focus our attention on in future initiatives?

Full House

Type: Problem-Solving—Transport

Group Size: 8–24

Time Frame: 25–40 minutes

Goals

- Increase problem-solving and planning skills.
- Increase sense of support, trust and cooperation within the team.
- Develop a higher level of team communication.

Materials

Five 4"x4"x6' boards

Longer or shorter boards can be used for different size groups.

Arrange the boards in the configuration as shown.

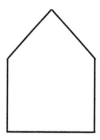

Briefing

"This activity is an opportunity for this team to create an environment that supports high-performing teamwork. The boards represent the structure of your organization. You are its staff. Your energy and skills make the organization function. During the activity, think about what characteristics and behaviors will best serve your team in achieving success."

Rules

1) Ask all the participants to stand around the boards on the outside of the "house."

2) Tell them that once the activity starts, they will need to step up onto the boards. Once they have stepped onto the boards, they may not

touch the ground again until they have completed the problem. They are not allowed to reposition themselves by walking on the ground prior to starting the activity.

3) The objective is to organize and line up in chronological order by month and day of birth (i.e., they will be in order as their birthdays fall in a calendar year—from January 1 through December 31). You may choose to establish where the start of the line should be (for example, at the peak of the house, moving clockwise around the frame).

4) No progress can be made until everyone has stepped up onto the boards.

5) All changes of position must occur on the boards. If two people attempt to pass each other, they may not pass at an angle (the point where two boards meet). The only acceptable pass is when both people start and finish the pass on the same board.

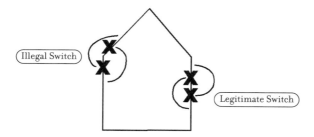

6) If anyone should touch the ground during a switch, the consequence is that the two people switching must do the switch again without stepping off.

7) If anyone should step off while not involved in a switch, the consequence is that the entire group must return to its starting position and begin the activity again.

8) Once the team has completed the task, have the team call out their birthdays to check for accuracy.

Instructor's Notes

· The consequence of touching the ground can significantly alter the challenge of this activity. Sending everyone back after a touch emphasizes doing it right, but it may also frustrate a group early in its development. Be deliberate about selecting the appropriate consequence based on the team's goals and its readiness to attempt the task.

- You may find once the group steps up that the criterion you have given them presents little challenge because they are already by chance almost in the correct positions. It would be appropriate to intervene and announce a new criterion to give the team a legitimate challenge.
- Other criteria that have worked:
  > arrange by how long you have worked at the company

  > arrange by height

  > choose an animal that means something to you; arrange by the size of the animals from smallest to largest

Debriefing

The goal of the debrief is to explore how the team worked together and what type of support was needed and offered during the exercise.

- How did the team approach the task? Did the team create a workable plan, and was it implemented?
- Did people work together effectively? What examples can you think of that demonstrated a high level of performance?
- How effective was the team at making switches? What techniques worked? What techniques were not effective?
- Did the team change its plan or approach during the activity? Was the change helpful?
- What characteristics of teamwork were most important in this activity?
- Do you find these same characteristics at work?

Other Thematic Connections...

Full House tends to require physical support and build trust within a team due to the need to work together to make switches successfully. Leadership is often a prominent theme that emerges as well. In a design focused on leadership, the goal of the debrief is to explore how leadership was modeled and whether leadership emerged in the form of a shared vision and understanding of how the task was to be accomplished.

Pipeline

Type: Problem-Solving—Transport

Group Size: 8–30

Time Frame: 45–90 minutes, depending on group size and variations used

Goals

- Explore relationship to customer expectations.
- Practice problem-solving skills.
- Practice goal-setting and attainment.

Materials

PVC pipe—15" sections of 2 3/4" pipe cut in half lengthwise (at least one pipe per person)

A variety of rollable objects that might include golf balls, small and large marbles, rubber eggs

One bucket

Border marker (preferably a rope or piece of webbing)

Briefing

"These balls, marbles and eggs represent products that you need to deliver to the customer. You have two primary tasks in this activity: 1) to set a realistic goal (a promise) that you can attain for the customer during the time allotted and 2) to deliver on that promise with 100% quality. There are some constraints as to how you handle the product during delivery . . ."

Rules

1) Set out the props so that the distance from the boundary marker (the start) to the container (the goal) is 3–5 paces more than the number of participants (i.e., 12 people = 15–17 paces). Adding a "dogleg" (the path to the container bends around an obstacle) adds more challenge.

2) Place the pipe sections and balls in the start area and assemble the group within this designated "work area."

3) Instruct the team that the balls, eggs and marbles all represent products needing delivery to customers.

4) Any object dropped safely into the container represents a successful delivery.

5) The only tools available to the team are the PVC pipe segments. No other props may be used for delivery purposes.

6) For the first delivery, all members of the team must start behind the boundary marker until the object has been dropped into the first pipe section. Once the object is in the pipe, people are free to move anywhere.

7) State that quality is extremely important to the customer; hence, there are strict controls for transporting the products to ensure a quality delivery. These rules are:

> objects may never stop

> objects may never roll backwards

> objects may not be dropped onto the ground

> objects may not be touched by any person after the first person drops it into a pipe section

> pipe sections may not touch each other

> when a person has an object in her pipe, she may not move her feet (she may move her arms and hands freely, and once the object has left the pipe she is free to move anywhere)

8) If any of these delivery guidelines is broken, any objects in the pipeline must be returned to the start area and transported again. Also, all members of the team must assemble behind the line to start the next delivery.

9) An object delivered safely into the container never has to be redelivered, even if a rule is broken afterwards.

10) If appropriate, ask the team to set a goal prior to making their first delivery. This goal represents the number of products the team feels it can successfully deliver in the time frame of the activity.

11) If asked, allow the group to practice moving objects to the container without monitoring infractions. However, any objects delivered must be returned to the start before they attempt to reach their goal.

Instructor's Notes

- Quality issues can be very challenging for groups, so make sure you are clear on what the customer wants from a quality perspective. The activity can be made easier or more difficult by modifying the rules.
- A variation for additional complexity is to break the marked area into segments with 2–3 people stationed at each segment (i.e., you must remain in your designated area). This dynamic tends to foster dialogue about handing off work and cross-functional communication and productivity.

Debriefing

The goal of the debrief is to evaluate how the team organized itself to achieve optimal performance.

- Did the team create a workable plan? How did this happen? Was the time spent planning adequate?
- Did you set a clear goal? Was it realistic? Did the group agree on it? Did you reach it? Why or why not?
- What factors contributed to the team's success? What factors made the task difficult?
- What about this activity is similar to or different from serving customers at work?
- On a scale of 1–10, 10 being high, how satisfied are you with your results? With your team process?
- What would you do differently next time to improve your effectiveness and performance?

Spider's Web

Type: Problem-Solving—Transport

Group Size: 8–100, depending on the number of webs and trainers

Time Frame: 40–50 minutes

Goals

- Explore and practice goal-setting and meeting expectations.
- Develop problem-solving, communication and planning skills.
- Examine "integrity" and willingness to explore ethical issues.

Materials

A fabricated "web." A web is typically made from some type of lightweight rope. It can be strung between two trees 10–14 feet apart or suspended within a frame. There are typically 14 to 17 open web sections. The top of the web should be no more than 7 feet from the ground.

Briefing

"The web represents a series of transactions likely to occur during the lifetime of a customer relationship. I (the trainer) will serve in the role of a lifetime customer in this activity." (Trainers can really have fun assuming a "demanding" customer "persona" and stating what they expect at the end of prescribed time period: e.g., integrity, whereby participants will monitor their own touches, etc.). "The group is challenged to meet or exceed my expectations by passing 'product' (bodies) through the web in a quality way. You have two goals:

1) To set an expectation (or goal) for me (the customer) as to how much quality product you can realistically deliver during the time allotted.

2) To meet or exceed the customer's expectations relative to that goal.

Each touch of the web indicates a business transaction in which the customer did not have his expectations met, requiring that the team revisit their process and make appropriate improvements."

Rules

The group's goal is to pass each member of the group through a separate web opening. The following rules apply:

- No body part may touch the web.
- No spotter may touch the web.
- Once a person passes through an opening, that section is closed to further passage.
- Participants cannot be passed over or under the web.
- If any participant at any time touches the web, the person being passed through at the time of the touch has to return to the beginning side, and the section which he attempted to pass through remains open.

Instructor's Role

- Check the area to be certain that the ground is safe (i.e., no objects or obstacles that could injure someone going through the web or cause a spotter to trip).
- Present the problem clearly, review spotting requirements and answer questions before the group begins the task.

Participants' Responsibility

- To be an active member of the group
- To give support to fellow group members both physically (spotting and passing) and emotionally (supporting and contributing ideas)
- To never drop or let go of a participant because someone touched the web

Variations

Increase challenge

- If *anyone* touches the web, the whole group returns.
- If *anyone* touches the web, half of those participants already across must return and pass through again (their holes reopen).

Decrease challenge

- Allow more than one person to pass through particular holes.
- Allow participants who have already passed successfully through a hole to come back around to the starting side to actively spot and lift.

Instructor's Notes

- This activity is very popular in the adventure field and has been written about in many PA publications. Please note the emphasis in the write-ups varies:

  > *Ropes Course Safety Manual* addresses safety and spotting procedures.

  > *Silver Bullets* describes the activity generically with some tips and safety considerations.

  > *Cows Tails And Cobras II* discusses leadership issues.

  > *QuickSilver* takes a different approach to building the frame for the web, along with some creative ideas for the activity.

Debriefing

The goal of the debrief is to explore how the team identified and attempted to satisfy the customer's needs, and to evaluate from a customer's perspective whether the team provided satisfactory service.

- Have group members discuss whether they were pleased or displeased with the results and explain the criteria upon which they made their judgment.
- Ask participants to place themselves in the customer's shoes. Ask each participant whether his expectations were met or exceeded and to explain why or why not from the customer perspective.
- How did the group prioritize their goals? Was it clear to everyone what the decisions were and how they were made?
- Was the customer approached to assess expectations and evaluate issues as they arose? Why or why not?

Other Thematic Connections...

Values Focus

Hanging from each hole is a laminated card on which is printed a behavioral value statement reflecting one of the company's core values, for example: *"I listen openly to input, ideas and suggestions because PEOPLE ARE OUR GREATEST ASSET."* When a participant member is preparing to be passed through a specific hole, she may remove the behavioral value statement hanging from that hole to symbolically represent her attentiveness to that expectation. If she or anyone else touches while she's being passed through, the card gets hung back up, as specified above.

Suggested linkages or potential connections for conducting a generic debrief with a values focus orientation include:

- Take a minute to ask the group to examine the value statements on the cards they successfully removed from the web. Did you feel that your process reflected the behavioral statements espoused by your company? If so, how? If not, where did you fall short?

- Take a minute to ask the group to examine the value statements on the cards they didn't remove that still remain on the web. What observations do you have about the value statements still remaining on the web? Do they in any way relate to your process or performance?

- Overall, do you feel your company values were modeled during this activity? If so, where did you see this demonstrated? If not, where did you as an individual, or the group, fall short?

Stepping Stones

Type: Problem-Solving—Transport

Group Size: 10–15 (standard set-up)

Time Frame: 30–40 minutes, depending on group size

Goals

- Practice and examine problem-solving and communication.
- Explore issues of integrity and accountability.
- Examine the role of trust and support in team development.

Materials

Stepping Stones (carpet squares, ethafoam pieces and small wood blocks all work well), enough for each person to have one, or one fewer than the number of people to increase the challenge level

2 boundary markers (2 long ropes)

Briefing

"The start area denotes the beginning of your current business cycle. The far boundary represents the goals for your organization during this cycle. Between the boundaries is the 'sea of confusion'—full of all the problems that make it difficult for you to achieve your goals on a daily basis. What are some of those barriers and problems that negatively impact your work?

"These stones represent the resources you use to be successful and to overcome the problems. These resources can be human, technical or mechanical, knowledge-based—anything that helps you do your jobs. What are some of those resources?

"Now that you have identified both some of the problems you face and some of the resources available to you, your task is to successfully transport your entire team through the cycle without encountering any problems that will prevent you from reaching your goals at the far boundary."

Rules

1) Set two boundaries; distance between them is typically one pace per person plus 3–5 additional steps.
2) Place the "stones" behind one of the boundaries as the starting place.

3) Assemble all the people behind this line.

4) Explain that the goal is for the team to move everyone safely from the start to the opposite boundary. No one may touch the ground between the boundary markers.

5) If a person touches the ground, that person *must* return to the start area and begin the activity again.

6) The "stones" are resources to assist the group in achieving the goal. Each stone may support as many people as can balance on it.

7) Once stones cross the boundary, there must be *constant contact* with them by a group member. If for an instant a stone is left untouched, the stone is *lost permanently* (i.e., it is taken away and may not be used by the group, nor may it be regained later).

8) If the group wants to practice its technique, it needs to do so behind the boundary or they risk losing "untouched" stones.

9) *Option:* Once the group begins, ask them to monitor quality issues (touching stones) and maintain accountability for abiding by the rules.

10) Give a time limit.

Variations

Increase challenge

- If someone touches the ground, the entire group must start over again.
- Decrease the number of stones so that two people do not have one at the start.

Decrease challenge

- If stones are lost, the group may regain any lost ones if they all return to the start area and begin the activity again.

Simulate multiple teams working

1) two groups crossing from opposite sides and passing each other;

2) three or more groups crossing from different points and having to pass through a small safe circle in the center of the area;

3) four groups crossing from different points to opposite sides with the option available for teams to assist each other; and

4) multiple groups starting from behind the same line and then being able to combine resources once they have traveled approximately 10 feet into the "sea."

Instructor's Notes

- This activity often brings to the surface issues of integrity and accountability. Many groups will attempt to ignore or avoid the consequences of people touching the ground or losing contact with a stone. In preparation for leading this activity, it's important to have a plan in mind for dealing with infractions. Do you enforce the rules? Do you point out the infraction and let the group decide to enforce the rule or not? Do you log the infraction to yourself and then use that information in the debrief to create an opportunity for learning?

- It is helpful to have "stones" that are a variety of shapes and sizes; the variety adds to the challenge level as the group must decide how and when to use the different sizes.

Debriefing

The goal of the debrief is to analyze the performance of the group and identify factors that can create improved performance.

- What factors allowed the group to be successful?

- How did the group work together to achieve its goals? What specific behaviors supported its effort? What behaviors or actions limited the team's performance?

- What happened if/when the group encountered a setback? What was the immediate response? What impact did it have on the end result?

- As you review the activity, what two or three lessons are most important for this team to carry forward to ensure improvement in performance?

Other Thematic Connections...

This activity has been widely and effectively used to address all five thematic drivers mentioned in this book: team development, leadership, customer focus, learning organizations and values. By having the stones represent important aspects of the themes, debriefing connections can address the importance of paying attention and staying in touch with these aspects while simultaneously exploring the pitfalls of losing sight of them. For example, if the stones represent values such as quality, learning or integrity, and contact is lost with a "quality" stone during the activity (e.g., the group loses the stone permanently and has one less resource), debriefing links might include:

- What was the impact when you lost touch with "quality" during this activity? How is this similar to or different from the workplace?

- How do you hold each other accountable for your values?

Site-Central Variation of Object Retrieval

Type: Problem-Solving—Retrieval

Group Size: 12–20 people

Time Frame: 45–90 minutes

The Site-Central variation involves dividing a group up into smaller units with specific roles. One unit is the *Management Team*; they are physically removed from the activity area and typically have their own problem(s) to solve. The second unit is the *Liaisons*; they are part of the management team but are allowed to move back and forth to the work site area where the activity is set up. The third group is the *Site Team*; they are the group that actually attempts to solve the problem. They remain at the work site for the duration of the activity.

Goals

- Explore and practice communication skills.
- Examine the role of decision-making in a hierarchical organizational structure.
- Develop skills in delegation and empowerment.

Materials

2 plastic buckets

enough assorted balls to fill one bucket

assorted lengths of rope

1 (or more) piece of bungee cord 18–24 inches long

2 spot markers (round rubber spots often used in physical education programs)

one boundary marker (to create a circle with diameter of 10–20 feet)

Management Team activity; for example, Twelve Bits (see page 277) or a pencil and paper puzzle

Handouts "Site Team Rules," "Site Team Guidelines" and "Management Team Guidelines" (see box on page 275)

Briefing

"There are three roles in this activity: Management, Liaisons and the Site Team. We need to divide up so that we have 3–8 Management people; from this group, we will select 1–2 Liaisons. The remainder of the group will become the Site Team. Management will stay in the Management area, which is separated from the work site. Liaisons may move freely back and forth between management's area and the work site. The Site Team will stay in the work area."

Move the groups to their designated areas, then offer the following briefings.

To Management

"This activity represents a business unit within this organization. The unit is responsible for shipping defect-free products to its customers. The products are currently in a container that indicates they have been fully assembled and inspected; they are ready to be shipped. Before shipment can occur, the products must be transferred to the shipping container.

"The Site Team is ready to perform that task and has been assembled in their work area. The 'Site Team Rules' contain essential information for that team in order for them to be able to successfully achieve their goal. They may not do anything without prior approval from Management. They are currently waiting for further instructions from you.

"Additionally, your Management Team has its own work to do, represented by these problems. You are responsible for completing these tasks as well as making sure that the Site Team completes its project successfully.

"Remember that only Liaisons can leave this area and go to observe what happens with the task team. Liaisons can help solve Management's tasks, but not the Site Team's problem. Liaisons may not switch roles after the activity begins.

"After I have answered your questions, the activity will begin and you will have ___ minutes to complete all the tasks."

To Site Team

"Your job is to complete this task. Management will be able to tell you exactly what the problem is and give you the necessary information to get the team started. Until Management arrives, you may not touch any of the materials. I suggest you spend some time discussing how you want to work together to achieve optimal performance during this exercise."

To Liaison

"As a member of Management, your job is to act as a liaison between the rest of management and the Site Team. You may move freely from the Management area to the work site. You may communicate freely with both groups of people. You may assist Management in solving its tasks, but you may not physically assist the Site Team with its work.

"Before you begin, you may need to clarify your responsibilities with the rest of Management to be certain that your role is completely clear and understood."

Rules

Management
1) Distribute to management the handouts "Site Team Rules" and "Management Team Guidelines" (see box on page 275). Review this information as appropriate. Also hand out any Management activities and present the rules as needed.

2) Be certain the Liaisons have been selected and that both Management and Liaisons know the limitations on their roles, as noted on the "Management Team Guidelines" handout.

3) Tell the Management team the time limit as the activity officially begins and repeat to them that the Site Team is currently waiting for them.

Site Team
4) Hand out the "Site Team Guidelines" (see box on page 276) to a member of the team; review the guidelines as necessary. While waiting for the arrival of Management, suggest that the team spend its time discussing how it wants to function together to achieve optimal performance.

Instructor's Notes

- Coordinate and confirm the time with your co-leader (if there is one) as the activity begins so that the overall time limit is known. Remember that Management is told the time constraints, but typically the Site Team is not informed by the instructors—that is part of Management's responsibility.

- Facilitating a Site-Central activity is a complex task. There are multiple groups of people interacting, sometimes together, sometimes alone. It is a challenge to monitor effectively all of what happens. This type of activity should be presented only if the instructor feels competent managing the full range of information that can emerge. For optimal management of the Site-Central variation, two experienced consultants are recommended. Many groups comment on how "lifelike" these scenarios are, and the emotions and frustrations that can erupt require high-level facilitation skills in order to ensure that a positive learning outcome results.

· Site-Central variations are excellent tools for involving larger groups in one activity. Where 20 people may mean too little participation with a standard presentation, with a Site-Central version the roles increase and more people can be actively engaged. Also this type of activity is another way to offer meaningful alternatives for people who, by using Challenge by Choice, decide not to participate actively in a problem. The Management and Liaison roles are important yet typically require little or no physical exertion.

Debriefing

The overall goal of the debrief is to explore the relationships among the three roles and assess the impact of each role on the performance of the entire group.

With a Site-Central activity, the debrief is often conducted in stages with the smaller units debriefing first, then making a report to the entire group before the large group engages in a discussion of the problem.

Small Group Questions (10–15 minutes)
· How would you describe your interactions with the other two roles in this exercise?

· What about the relationship with the other roles aided the ability of the larger group to successfully complete all the problems? What factors hindered the large group from being successful?

· What are the three most important observations this group learned from this exercise that you want to report to the other roles?

Large Group Discussion and Questions (10–30 minutes after small group reports)
· Having heard the observations from the three roles, what if any new insights emerge?

· What about this experience is similar to or different from situations you encounter at work?

· Based on this experience, what would you want to do the same or differently to be more effective in managing these types of situations in the workplace?

For Management Team

Site Team Rules

(Object Retrieval)

Objective:
To transfer safely all the objects contained in the defective container into the new, leakproof container. Any objects spilling on the ground are considered defects and cannot be shipped to the customer.

1) No person may touch the ground inside or extend a body part over the boundary marking the work zone. Any time this occurs, the team must start again from the start and the person may incur a physical limitation.

2) *Only* the props provided may be used to transfer the objects. The boundaries and spot markers may *not* be moved or altered. The transfer of the objects **must occur** with the new container on its spot.

3) The Site Team has a total of __ minutes to accomplish the objective.

For Management Team

Management Team Guidelines

1) Management may select 1–2 person(s) to act as liaison to the Site Team. A liaison may move back and forth freely to the Site Team planning area. All other Management personnel must remain in the Management area at all times.

2) Management personnel, including Liaisons, may *not* assist physically in solving the Site Team's problem.

3) The Management Team is responsible for ensuring that the Site Team achieves an acceptable outcome. Management is also responsible for completing its own tasks.

4) Important rules for the Site Team are contained on the Site Team Rules page given to your team.

5) The Site Team may not take any action without prior approval from Management. The Site Team is currently waiting for you.

For Site Team

Site Team Guidelines

1) All members of the Site Team must stay in the Site Team production area for the duration of the activity.

2) The Site Team may take no action without the prior approval of the Management Team.

3) None of the boundaries or spot markers for the activity in the production area may be moved or altered. The Site Team may not touch any props without authorization from Management.

4) While waiting for the Management liaison to arrive, your team may want to discuss how it wants to operate together as a high-performing team and what specific behaviors will be needed to do so.

Twelve Bits

Type: Problem–Solving–Creation

Group Size: 8–15 people

Time Frame: 40–50 minutes

Three different versions of Twelve Bits are included to illuminate the versatility and creativity the activity allows! The original version of the clues introduced by Jim Hassinger and Barry Carden, which was used in a team-development context, is included. A second version, used in the three-day team-development model in the Design Appendix, makes reference to PA's Full Value Contract. A third version, created around learning organizations, was originally designed to reinforce content themes from Peter Senge's *The Fifth Discipline*. We hope these examples will fuel your thinking and stir your creativity further.

Goals

- Explore the interaction of leadership and communication.
- Check underlying Ladders of Inferences and assumptions.
- Practice organizing information.
- Introduce and use problem-solving approaches to deductive reasoning challenges.

Materials

- 12 clues (see below)

  Note: The original version of Twelve Bits contains 12 clues. Other custom-designed versions contain varied numbers of clues.
- Pencil (or markers)
- Paper (flip chart or notebook)

Briefing

"Once you have your clues—small slips of paper—you will have all the information you will need to solve the problem. Your first challenge is to figure out what the problem actually is! The second task is to solve it within the time constraint.

"The problem you need to solve is found within the clues."

Rules

1) Pass out the slips of clues to the group (one or more to each person). Reiterate what is written on each slip: "Although you may tell your group what is on this slip, you may not show it to anyone else to read." Further clarify that this means group members can verbally share the information with one another but they cannot collect the clues or visually display them to one another.

2) Optional: Provide the group with pencil and paper. (If you want to make the problem more challenging, you may want to specify that no other props or materials may be used.)

Debriefing

The goal of the debrief is to examine how the team identified the problem and then attempted to find a solution.

- How did your group approach the problem?
- Did you develop a particular method of collecting, organizing and interpreting the information?
- Did a leader emerge in the process? If so, what did the leadership look like?
- Did individuals find ways to support the team process beyond taking responsibility for their own clues? How is this similar to or different from supporting one another at work?
- Did you verify or double-check your assumptions regarding the information you were given?

Twelve Bits—Original Version

Although you may tell your group what is on this slip, you may not show it to anyone else to read.

Of all the countries toured, Anne likes Austria the best.

Tom, Sheila and Jim spent the first evening discussing the day's countries and reviewing the maps.

Although you may tell your group what is on this slip, you may not show it to anyone else to read.

A part of the business trip was "country viewing," where the participants broke into four groups, which were led by four managers.

The new dictionaries did not seem to help with the languages in the various countries.

Although you may tell your group what is on this slip, you may not show it to anyone else to read.

The four groups toured different countries at the same time, and changed at the end of each country.

After inspecting the maps, the managers decided to replace all the rental cars with jeeps.

Although you may tell your group what is on this slip, you may not show it to anyone else to read.

Each manager toured through four countries in their own sequence.

Sheila's group toured Italy before they visited Austria.

Although you may tell your group what is on this slip, you may not show it to anyone else to read.

Each manager liked a different country best and arranged their itinerary so they would tour the country they liked best last.

Although you may tell your group what is on this slip, you may not show it to anyone else to read.

It was hard to tell which group was the most adept with the different languages.

Before the rental cars were replaced, they were tested and found to be incapable of enduring the rough terrain of dirt roads.

Although you may tell your group what is on this slip, you may not show it to anyone else to read.

Your team members have all the information they need to find the answer to the following question: (Only one answer is correct.) **In what sequence did Tom's group tour the countries?**

Communication problems and cultural gaps were common throughout the tour.

Tom's group toured France after it toured its first country.

Although you may tell your group what is on this slip, you may not show it to anyone else to read.

The first country that Jim's group toured was Austria.

The weather report predicted a clear, calm day.

Although you may tell your group what is on this slip, you may not show it to anyone else to read.

Jim toured Germany as his third country of the trip.

Working out a schedule was difficult because both Tom and Anne wanted to start with the same country.

Although you may tell your group what is on this slip, you may not show it to anyone else to read.

Some of the information our team has is irrelevant and will not help solve the problem.

Anne's group was the one to get up early and have breakfast that day. While Terry did not lead a group, he contributed much to the problem that day.

Although you may tell your group what is on this slip, you may not show it to anyone else to read.

Both Sheila and Anne agreed that the groups handled the language barriers and cultural gaps in a professional manner.

Although you may tell your group what is on this slip, you may not show it to anyone else to read.

The group that was up early to eat breakfast started their tour in Italy.

Before scheduling for the day, Anne solicited input from the tour guide staff.

Solution

ANNE	TOM	JIM	SHEILA
Italy	Germany	Austria	France
Germany	Austria	France	Italy
France	Italy	Germany	Austria
Austria	France	Italy	Germany

Twelve Bits Full Value Contract Version

Although you may tell your group what is on this slip, you may not show it to anyone else to read.

Of all the Full Value Contract elements studied, Marketing likes Open to Outcomes the best since they have been cited for this as an area of strength.

Representatives from Graphics, Engineering and Marketing spent the first coffee break discussing the various methods of implementing the tenets of the Full Value Contract in their respective product development teams.

Although you may tell your group what is on this slip, you may not show it to anyone else to read.

The focus of the seminar, where the participants were divided into their four functional areas, was learning the points of the Full Value Contract.

The Full Value Contract is a Project Adventure cornerstone of team development, as it provides specifics for the expected norms of behavior necessary to the development of effective work teams.

Although you may tell your group what is on this slip, you may not show it to anyone else to read.

The four product development team functions were in seminar sessions about different aspects of the FVC at the same time, and changed at the end of each session.

There are five elements to the FVC, only four of which were studied in separate sessions. The fifth element, Attending to Safety, was covered in a general session at the end of the day with all functions in attendance.

Although you may tell your group what is on this slip, you may not show it to anyone else to read.

Each function attended four FVC sessions in their own sequence. (Each session was about a different FVC element.)

Graphics learned about Showing Up before they learned about Open to Outcomes. They learned that Showing Up is an agreement to fully participate in the experience to the best of one's ability, while Open to Outcomes emphasizes the importance of keeping an open mind and suspending judgment until the end of an experience.

Although you may tell your group what is on this slip, you may not show it to anyone else to read.

Engineering learned about Speaking the Truth during their third session.

Working out a schedule was difficult because both Engineering and Marketing wanted to start with the same FVC session.

Although you may tell your group what is on this slip, you may not show it to anyone else to read.

Each function liked a different element of the FVC best and arranged their sequence so they would learn about their preferred element **last**.

The FVC has been used in a variety of learning settings and has proved to be a critical tool in enhancing both individual and team motivation.

Although you may tell your group what is on this slip, you may not show it to anyone else to read.

Your team members have all the information they need to find the answer to the following question (only one answer is correct): **In what sequence did Sales attend the FVC seminar sessions?**

Although you may tell your group what is on this slip, you may not show it to anyone else to read.

Sales learned about Paying Attention after attending their first session. Paying Attention is the agreement by participants to listen, not only to the words of others, but to their own internal thoughts.

Although you may tell your group what is on this slip, you may not show it to anyone else to read.

The first session that Engineering attended was about Open to Outcomes.

One of the most difficult elements of the FVC is Speaking the Truth. This element suggests that in order to learn from each other we must be skilled in the art of both giving and receiving feedback.

Although you may tell your group what is on this slip, you may not show it to anyone else to read.

The function that was up early to eat breakfast began their first session learning about Showing Up.

Although you may tell your group what is on this slip, you may not show it to anyone else to read.

All of the information your team has is important, yet only some of it is helpful in solving this problem.

The staff from Marketing was the one to get up early and have breakfast that day.

Sales and Engineering agreed that the FVC concept was fundamentally sound; however, they questioned its value in a business environment.

Although you may tell your group what is on this slip, you may not show it to anyone else to read.

Both Graphics and Marketing agreed that it would be worthwhile to practice and develop the skills necessary to implement the FVC in their product development teams.

Solution

MARKETING	GRAPHICS	ENGINEERING	SALES
Show Up	Pay Attention	Open to Outcomes	Speak the Truth
Speak the Truth	Show Up	Pay Attention	Open to Outcomes
Pay Attention	Open to Outcomes	Speak the Truth	Show Up
Open to Outcomes	Speak the Truth	Show Up	Pay Attention

Twelve Bits Learning Organization Version

Although you may tell your group what is on this slip, you may not show it to anyone else to read.

Of all the discipline components, Anne felt Team Learning was the most critical.

Tom, Sheila and Jim spent the first evening discussing how to create learning organizations in which people continually expand their capacity to create the results they truly desire and where collective aspiration is set free.

Although you may tell your group what is on this slip, you may not show it to anyone else to read.

Employees broke into four groups, which were led by four managers.

To move from the traditional controlling organizations to a learning organization means mastering five basic disciplines. However, only four were studied at this time.

Although you may tell your group what is on this slip, you may not show it to anyone else to read.

The four groups studied different disciplines at the same time, and changed at the end of each discipline.

The fifth discipline, which was not studied by the groups, is Systems Thinking, which is a conceptual framework, a body of knowledge and tools, that has been developed to make full patterns clearer and to help us see how to change them effectively.

Although you may tell your group what is on this slip, you may not show it to anyone else to read.

Each manager studied four component disciplines in their own sequence.

Sheila's group learned about Personal Mastery before they studied the importance of Team Learning.

Although you may tell your group what is on this slip, you may not show it to anyone else to read.

Each manager believed a different discipline was more critical than the others and arranged their order of study so they would study the discipline they felt was most critical **last.**

Mental Models are our deeply ingrained assumptions, our generalizations and images that influence the way we look at the world. These thoughts and perceptions are often limiting and should be brought to the surface and scrutinized.

Although you may tell your group what is on this slip, you may not show it to anyone else to read.

Your team members have all the information they need to find the answer to the following questions. Only one answer is correct.

In what sequence did Tom's group study the component disciplines of learning organizations?

The fifth discipline constitutes systems thinking because it is the discipline that integrates the other learning disciplines. It is the discipline that when practiced with the others, shows us that the whole is much greater than the sum of its parts.

Although you may tell your group what is on this slip, you may not show it to anyone else to read.

Tom's group learned about Building a Shared Vision after they studied their first discipline.

Although you may tell your group what is on this slip, you may not show it to anyone else to read.

The group that was up early started their day studying Personal Mastery.

Although you may tell your group what is on this slip, you may not show it to anyone else to read.

The first discipline that Jim's group studied was Team Learning. A learning team produces extraordinary results and its members grow more rapidly than they could have alone. The intelligence of the team surpasses the intelligence of the individuals.

Although you may tell your group what is on this slip, you may not show it to anyone else to read.

Jim studied Mental Models as his third component discipline.

Practicing a discipline is to become a lifelong learner. Lifelong learning is a process toward enlightenment but the end will never be realized.

Although you may tell your group what is on this slip, you may not show it to anyone else to read.

Some of the information our team has is irrelevant and will not help solve the problem.

Although you may tell your group what is on this slip, you may not show it to anyone else to read.

Anne's group was the one to get up early and have breakfast that day.

The five learning disciplines differ from the more familiar business disciplines such as accounting in that they are personal disciplines. They have to do with how we think, what we want, and how we interact and learn from others.

Solution

ANNE	TOM	JIM	SHEILA
Personal Mastery	Mental Models	Team Learning	Building a Shared Vision
Mental Models	Team Learning	Building a Shared Vision	Personal Mastery
Building a Shared Vision	Personal Mastery	Mental Models	Team Learning
Team Learning	Building a Shared Vision	Personal Mastery	Mental Models

Section Two—Inventories, Instruments and Models

In the following pages are examples of other tools that Project Adventure has employed in its trainings over the years. The intent is not to provide extensive detail about these tools, but to suggest resources for clients and practitioners to consider in designing and delivering effective trainings to corporate audiences.

We include this information to complement the activity descriptions in this appendix. These lists are not intended to be a comprehensive reference; many useful and valuable resources are not mentioned here. We have compiled these lists to highlight materials and content that have proved useful in a wide variety of programs.

Inventories and Other Instruments

Learning Style Inventory (LSI)

Based on the theory of experiential learning, Dr. David Kolb's research reflected in the LSI reveals an individual's strengths and weaknesses during the learning process. The LSI is particularly effective in helping individuals and groups explore opportunities of different learning styles present in managing others. **(David Kolb, Training Resources Group, Hay/McBer, Boston, MA)**

Leadership Competency Inventory (LCI)

Hay/McBer's research has identified four competencies essential to effective leadership: Information Seeking, Conceptual Thinking, Strategic Orientation and Service Orientation. This inventory measures an individual's use of these competencies, introduces the leadership model, analyzes motives and values and provides competency development strategies. **(Training Resources Group, Hay/McBer, Boston, MA)**

Personal Development Profile (DiSC)

This widely used tool helps individuals understand themselves and others. Responding to the Profile provides individuals with a framework for looking at human behavior while increasing their knowledge of their unique behavioral pattern. **(Carlson Learning Company, Minneapolis, MN)**

Dimensions of Leadership Profile

The Dimensions of Leadership Profile is an effective tool that helps to identify, develop and support our own and others' leadership potential. The instrument addresses 12 dimensions of leadership, highlighting ways in which leaders, because of their interests, abilities, experiences or preferences and the opportunities at hand, respond to situations. **(Carlson Learning Company, Minneapolis, MN)**

Situational Leadership Model (SL Model)

Ken Blanchard's *One Minute Manager* series of publications gave this model world renown. Useful in helping leaders effectively influence and develop others, this model also addresses how to build motivational climates that result in high levels of productivity, as well as human satisfaction in the short and long run. **(Ken Blanchard, Blanchard Training and Development, Inc., Escondido, CA)**

Managerial Style Questionnaire (MSQ)

Based on more than 20 years of research by Hay/McBer, the MSQ measures individuals' perceptions of how they manage—direct, motivate or control—in terms of six styles. Like the SL Model, no single managerial style is effective in all situations with all people, but the MSQ does stimulate thinking about which styles can be used most effectively to deal with various situations. **(Training Resources Group, Hay/McBer, Boston, MA)**

Organizational Climate Exercise (OCE II)

Exploring organizational climate—the atmosphere of the workplace—is a way to answer the question, "What is it like to work here?" The OCE focuses on assessing those climate elements critical to performance and productivity: an organization's structure, policies, procedures, norms and management practices. **(Training Resources Group, Hay/McBer, Boston, MA)**

Influence Strategies Exercise (ISE)

This is a valuable tool for understanding how individuals influence others. The ISE provides feedback on nine commonly used strategies and explanations of each, with suggestions on how to increase them. **(Training Resources Group, Hay/McBer, Boston, MA)**

Thomas-Kilmann Conflict Mode Instrument

Developed by Kenneth W. Thomas and Ralph H. Kilmann, this instrument is designed to assess an individual's behavior in conflict situations. It uses two different dimensions to assess behavior: assertiveness and cooperativeness. The resulting index describes five possible "conflict-handling modes": Avoiding, Compromising, Accommodating, Competing, Collaborating. **(Distributed by XICOM)**

Communication Styles Survey

Developed by Dr. Paul Mok, the Communication Styles Survey is based on Carl Jung's work, reflecting four basic communication styles: Intuitor, Thinker, Feeler, Sensor. A self-scoring instrument, it is intended to accurately reflect the ways individuals transmit and receive information. **(Distributed by Training Associates Press)**

Thematic Content and Models

Customer–Supplier Chain

This idea describes how every person in an organization is both a customer and a supplier in a continuous "chain" that produces the work of a company. This tool can be very helpful in highlighting how people interact with both internal and external customers, and how critical "pass-offs" from person to person or department to department can be in meeting the needs of customers who purchase a company's products or services. **(Organizational Dynamics, Inc., Seattle, WA)**

Situational Leadership

This concept views leadership as both flexible and responsive to the needs of the people and the situation. It can be useful in helping anyone who has leadership responsibilities understand the need to adjust their style to match the needs of the people they are leading. **(Blanchard Training and Development, Inc., Escondido, CA)**

Circle of Concern/Circle of Influence

This idea asks people to examine where they focus their attention and energy. It suggests that if people focus on things that they can influence, they will feel more energized and be able to increase their ability to influence even those things that initially they may have little or no influence over. **(Stephen Covey,** *The 7 Habits of Highly Effective People)*

Ladder of Inference

As a tool for improving communication, the Ladder of Inference asks people to examine how they create conclusions and beliefs based on assumptions, and then act—sometimes based on an inaccurate "meaning" attached to what is observed. It is helpful for people trying to understand and improve how they interact with others. **(Chris Argyris,** *Action Science,* 1985 **and** *Reasoning, Learning and Action,* 1982; **Peter Senge,** *The Fifth Discipline Fieldbook: Strategies for Building a Learning Organization)*

Contracting

Based on a definition of successful consulting, contracting examines the many people who may need to be involved in creating a workable situation when an individual is being asked to take responsibility for a project. It encourages people to take a step-by-step approach to determining what the project entails, who is responsible for it and what the outcomes will be—and to develop a collaborative relationship where both parties share responsibility for the success of the project. **(Peter Block,** *Flawless Consulting)*

Seven-Step Problem-Solving Model

This process helps groups and individuals understand and evaluate the way they solve problems. When matched with a variety of experiential activities, groups can explore the step-by-step approach and assess its effectiveness and usefulness for application in their work environment. **(Original source unknown)**

The Earning Model

Judith M. Bardwick's model explains how to overcome the lethargy of *entitlement* and the paralysis of *fear* and to move into the energy of *earning*. The Earning Model proposes that there are three psychological states in an organization or for individuals in an organization. These states are Entitlement, Earning and Fear. These states directly relate in this model to the research done by Yerkes-Dodson on performance anxiety and McClelland and Atkinson on motivation to achieve. It's a useful model for work in the needs assessment area. **(Judith M. Bardwick,** *Danger in the Comfort Zone)*

Stages of Group Development

While there are many models to draw from, perhaps the most commonly recognized is Tuchman's four stages: Forming, Storming, Norming, Performing. This model is simple to understand based on its four quadrants, and it matches well with other content such as Situational Leadership. In a corporate setting, however, a more detailed and focused theory, such as the seven-stage *Drexler-Sibbet Team Performance Model,* may be appropriate.

Understanding Teams

Again, there are many models and theorists to choose from when presenting a framework for understanding how teams function. When considering which model or theory to work with, consultants will want to explore the model for alignment with the unique goals and environment of each client. Certain models may offer a better match than others. Some resources to consider include:

- Jon R. Katzenbach and Douglas Smith, *The Wisdom of Teams.*
- Peter Scholtes, *The Team Handbook,* Joiner Associates, Inc., 1988.
- Ken Blanchard, Don Carew, Eunice Parisi-Carew, *Group Development and Situational Leadership II.*
- John Adair, Adair Model, *Effective Teambuilding,* Gower Publishing Co., 1986.

APPENDIX III

Risk Management Considerations

I n many of the preceding chapters, we have illustrated the importance of creating safe learning environments. Through our stories and vignettes, the significance of addressing the emotional and intellectual side of risk taking has been emphasized and underscored. Effectively putting the *Full Value Contract* and *Challenge by Choice* foundation tools to use, adhering to confidentiality guidelines, and seeking commitment to behavioral norms are some effective strategies we've addressed to create a positive learning atmosphere.

Yet, as we all know, adventure activities do include an element of real physical risk to those involved. Running, walking, jumping, climbing, swinging, using equipment, using ropes, leaning, touching, balancing, and playing are all essential elements of adventure and experiential learning—to a greater and lesser degree, depending on the design and scope of the event.

Clients considering hiring a vendor may be asking themselves, "Can I be assured this program or vendor is safe? What kind of insurance do they have? Will John Doe be able to participate with his disability? If it's safe, why do they require all participants to sign an assumption of risk and release of liability form? Do I need to run this through my legal or risk management department?"

Participants attending programs may be wondering or asking themselves similar types of questions, "Is this going to be safe? Why do they want medical information from me? Am I going to be forced to tell my colleagues I can't participate because I'm pregnant? I didn't even want them to know yet . . . Why do I have to sign a release of liability statement? I thought they were supposed to be safe? Will I get hurt?"

These questions, and others, perhaps can be addressed by examining eight fundamental risk management considerations and by briefly addressing some of the most commonly asked questions.

Fundamentals for Risk Management

1. Real and Perceived Risk

Many organizations have an image in their mind when they hear or think of adventure or experiential learning in terms of the actual activities. Often it is of an obstacle course type event or of high ropes course elements pictured in articles and advertising. In fact, there exists a great deal of mythology about adventure activities that at times is powerful enough to keep people from considering it as a training or consulting option in their company.

In actuality, most programs take place in a fairly controlled environment where, although there is always some risk, real incidents involving serious injury or death are rare. One must always consider the actual danger present in any given environment, as well as the level of control or management possible to prevent incidents, and try to avoid quick categorization of activities based on perception or initial impression.

The actual safety of any program is largely dependent on both the skills and knowledge of staff and the design of the activities in the context of overall program goals.

2. Consideration of Site-Based Programs and Wilderness Programs

When considering an adventure program, clients will likely find that they fall into two broad types: facility or site-based programs (which generally operate indoors or outdoors at a conference center, resort, or training center) and expedition or wilderness programs (which generally involve mobile travel through the wilderness via rafting, hiking, and other activity types). Wilderness-based programs typically take place in remote settings where they are further from emergency services.

Knowing the difference can be helpful in terms of both meeting program needs and assessing risk. The environment of a high ropes course or facilities based program is controlled, with fixed protection points and devices, as well as a high degree of redundancy (if the program is working within industry standards). The safety systems in a challenge ropes course are well tested.

Programs that operate in a wilderness or expedition environment, such as mountaineering or white water activities, operate in a more dynamic and changing environment. Unpredictable external factors such as the weather can increase the likelihood of an incident for participants even with seasoned and qualified staff. Clients considering these venues need to consider other variables than those included here to best analyze their safety.

Data collected from a wide range of adventure programs show fairly low incidence of accidents and injuries. In addition, risk is significantly diminished by following certain standards.

3. Spectrum of Activities

From a safety perspective, we often categorize the spectrum of activities in adventure training and consulting in order to better differentiate levels of real risk. Throughout the book, we have categorized the activities based largely on their use from a design perspective. In this case, we categorize based on the physical make-up of the activity, that is, is it on the ground? is it a constructed activity? does it use props? is a belay system necessary etc.?

Convening & Tone Setting Exercises

These include all activities done on the ground (versus at height) in any setting (meeting room, outdoor field space, client site, conference center, ropes course site). The activities may or may not use material props (e.g. balls, blindfolds, etc.). Physical activity ranges from low level (such as sitting in a chair and solving pencil and paper activities at a desk) through moderately active (such as walking slowly in a large group with spontaneous physical movements such as catching items or slow jumping) to relatively active (such as running tag games or jumping rope). This type of activity often has the lowest level of perceived risk but the highest actual or real incidence statistically of minor injuries (particularly running or fast moving games). Per participant hour, safety studies show that the risk of minor injury (abrasion, twisted ankle, small contusion) is highest for these activities, although it looks very safe and non-threatening to most clients.

Table 1 **Perceived Risk vs. Injury Frequency and Severity**

	Perceived Risk	Frequency of Injury	Potential Severity of Injury
Warm-Up Activities/Games	Low	Medium*	Low
Low Challenge Course Activities and Initiatives	Moderate	Low	Low to Moderate
High Challenge Course Activities	High	Very Low	Moderate to High

Portable Initiatives and Simulations

These include all activities done on or near the ground in a wide variety of settings (indoor and outdoor) that involve an element of group problem-solving and challenge. These can be portable versions of low challenge course elements such as the Spider's Web or stand-alone activities created for a particular design. This type of activity may require the use of spotters—people who use their own hands and bodies to safeguard other participants from potential injury, via breaking a fall from a low height (2–4 feet). Typically, spotting requires no specialized equipment and involves one or more persons working together to catch, lift and/or physically support the participants.

Low Challenge Course Elements

These include all fixed low element activities that are part of an indoor or outdoor challenge ropes course. In general, these activities require careful spotting on the part of other participants to ensure safety. They are all completed on or near the ground, and do not require the use of a belay system for participant protection. When spotting is taught and monitored well, the real risk to participants on low elements is low, although the perceived risk is moderate. Due to the more strenuous physical nature of these activities (swinging on rope, being lifted, balancing on a cable) they tend to challenge participants more physically and, therefore, do have some increased risk of incident.

---

* Compared with other Adventure activities injuries are *relatively* more likely to occur during certain types of warm-up activities and games. When compared with other comparable activities overall injury frequency is still very low.

High Challenge Course Elements

These include all activities conducted at a height requiring adequate fall protection beyond spotting to a climber. Protection is provided through the use of specialized equipment. There are a variety of belay types that are used both by participants and staff, depending on the program design.

In general, high elements have the highest perception of risk due to their height and the specialized equipment required. In addition, while accidents on the high course are rare, when they do occur, the consequences can be severe. This fact reinforces the need for established operational parameters, staff training, and equipment standards. See Table 1.

4. Insurance Issues

There are several types of insurance to consider:

- liability insurance to cover the practitioner.
- health insurance or workman's compensation to cover participants in the event of an injury
- ropes course site coverage if it is not owned or managed by the providing vendor

Liability Insurance

In the litigious society we live in today, it's not uncommon for companies to seek proof of liability insurance from vendors. The issues and decisions involved in liability insurance are often complex. Liability insurance is designed to cover the expense of a claim made against the provider of a service, including the cost of defense against such a claim. While it may make sense at times to use a vendor with limited liability insurance coverage, it should be understood that if a claim arises, liability would likely be held by the hiring organization.

Verification of liability coverage can generally be accommodated by the vendor simply providing a copy of their *Certificate of Insurance.* The decision of what amount is suitable for a vendor used by your organization is a complex one and best analyzed based on the specific needs of your company and the risks of exposure if a lawsuit or accident occurs. Although this should not be considered suitable for all cases, general liability coverage is usually found to be in the one to five million dollar range. As a general rule established vendors are more likely to have more coverage provided by reputable insurance providers.

Participant Health Insurance and Worker's Compensation

It is important that the vendor specify who is accountable for medical expenses incurred in the event of an accident or injury. If an injury happens during an employee's job related duties, worker's compensation usually covers related expenses. Project Adventure, Inc. and many other programs, require that all participants are also covered by health and accident insurance. If for some reason a participant has no health insurance, they are required to go on PA's supplemental health and accident insurance for the duration of the event at minimal cost.

Multiple or Varied Sites

If a vendor is using their own challenge ropes course, liability coverage may extend to all equipment and areas located on that site — it is prudent to check this coverage. Insurance needs for other site situations (such as a third party site at a resort) can be complex and are best analyzed in the context of the specific situation.

5. Verification of Program Safety

In analyzing program safety, there are two important areas to consider: the staff training and qualifications, and the equipment. For more discussion about staff training and qualification, see "Risk Management Plan." In considering the equipment, it is prudent for those companies seeking safety reassurances of a specific ropes course site to request a copy of the latest safety inspection report.

Annual safety inspections by a qualified professional are an industry-wide standard and are designed to review the physical elements of the course including the structures, hardware, materials, equipment and condition of the environment in the vicinity. Generally, a safety inspection report is generated that includes recommendations for repairs or modifications. It is important to verify that not only has an inspection been conducted, but that the recommended repairs have also been completed where needed.

Inquiry about a specific vendor's safety record is also helpful and should be available to a prospective client: has the vendor had significant injuries or deaths in their program and what were the circumstances? What is the level of risk management preparedness the vendor will bring to an event? What are staff credentials?

6. Trade and Membership Organizations

For general information about organizations in the Adventure business, as well as standards in the industry, companies often turn to different trade or membership organizations. *The Association for Challenge Course Technology* is a trade organization representing a majority of vendors who provide technical services such as installation and safety inspections. The "technology" in ACCT has traditionally meant hardware and engineering, however, its members include many trainers, facilitators and consultants. ACCT has established installation as well as training and operational standards specific to use of challenge courses.

The *Association for Experiential Education* is the membership organization in the Adventure field and publishes an Experiential-Based Training and Development Directory of Programs. AEE also provides program accreditation for a wide variety of experiential programs.

The *American Society for Training and Development* is the trade organization for corporate human resource and training professionals and publishes a monthly journal which has periodically published articles about the Adventure field citing Adventure providers.

7. Risk Management Planning

Risk Management Plans exist in most organizations that provide Adventure consulting services. Clients considering the use of Adventure for the first time should consider inquiring about the specific protocol and approach to risk of a given provider. There are two broad areas that adventure providers must think through and have plans for:

Prevention: What systems, equipment, staff training, protocol, documents, and logistics does the provider have to effectively attempt to prevent most, if not all, physical injury to participants? The best way to avoid harm is to take as many steps as possible to minimize the risk of real harm, without so controlling the environment that any element of perceived risk is eliminated— thus taking the adventure out of adventure!

Emergency Response: What will the practitioner do in the event of a near-miss or near-accident to capture the learning with participants and effectively avoid any resultant harm? What if, despite all prevention steps, an accident or injury does happen? Are staff trained? Is first aid equipment available?

Is the hospital route clearly defined? Are staff available to manage the non-injured group members? How will people be notified?

At minimum, plans should address:

- Site specific policies and procedures
- Maintenance schedules and inspection records
- Documented near misses, close calls, and accidents
- Documented staff credentials
- Clear evaluative criteria for staff
- Ongoing training and assessment plans for staff
- An emergency action plan and relevant equipment
- Medical screening procedures
- Ability to communicate the assumption of risk/release of liability form as outlined by the vendor
- Practical procedures for informing participants about the nature of the experience and inherent risks
- Staff ability to manage participant behavior to minimize risks
- Knowledge of specific rescue procedures for all elements
- Proper first aid and CPR training and equipment
- Accident/injury reporting systems
- Local hazard and weather knowledge as appropriate

Note: If you decide to manage a training site at your own location, there are additional things to consider that require additional knowledge and training.

8. Integrating a Vendor and a Company

In many programs, clients rely on the selected consulting vendor to follow their organization's safety and risk management protocol. At times, though, particularly when consulting and providing regular services in a client system, the process of safety management may best be shared and even co-created between the vendor and the client. In longer term relationships that evolve, it is important for the client to clarify their organizational safety protocol and to acknowledge and adapt to procedural differences if they emerge. The protocol to be used should be documented for all program staff.

An example of this is a client of ours that already had established risk management protocol for their internal training. Their process required medical clearance of a certain type for participants with certain conditions not typically a part of PA's screening process. Once this difference was acknowledged and discussed, a decision was documented in the jointly created local operating procedures.

Common Questions

What are the top things I should ask to assess a prospective vendors' safety experience and preparation?

- Describe your staff's training and experience?
- How much experience does the prospective vendor have with this type of programming?
- Are all ropes course facilities and equipment in good condition, and in compliance with current applicable ACCT standards?
- Has a qualified course inspector provided a professional inspection in the past year as required by ACCT standards?
- What references can speak to the safety of your program designs?
- Has your program received external review by another agency? Who? When?
- Do you have established Local Operating Procedures?
- What amount of liability insurance do you carry? May I have a Certificate of Insurance?

Why are medical information and assumption of risk/release of liability forms necessary?

Medical Information or Screening Forms and assumption of risk/release of liability forms are widely used and fairly routine in most adventure programs. Their fundamental purpose for Project Adventure, Inc., and why they have become an industry standard, is threefold:

1. Medical Information
The form helps to identify pre-existing medical conditions that may affect an individual's participation or their recommended level of physical activity. If certain pre-existing medical conditions are present, it is important to

advise participants to consult with their own physician prior to participating in a PA training program.

The medical information helps by providing relevant information for the program design as well as for medical personnel in case of an emergency. When staff have an awareness of participants' overall physical condition, they can then help participants make informed choices regarding their level of physical participation in the activity segments of the workshop.

It is also important for participants to understand the information provided is not shared without participant permission with anyone except Project Adventure staff delivering the workshop.

2. *Personal Responsibility*
Signature of the form implies that a participant has read the form about possible real risks and assumes personal accountability for their own level of participation. The release segment of the form can often be misunderstood. While it is not intended to release practitioners from responsibility, it *is* intended to ask participants to take responsibility for their own actions and acknowledge and accept that there is inherent risk of injury or disability in adventure activities. In Project Adventure programs, participants are reminded that *Challenge By Choice* is paramount and integral to the process.

3. *Health Insurance Verification*
PA requires that all participants have health/accident insurance coverage. Having the insurance information on the form can also be helpful if medical attention is necessary.

It is vitally important that corporate clients be made aware of the use and confidentiality of the forms prior to the delivery of a program. In some corporations the forms often undergo an approval process through the client's internal legal department. All participants are required to complete the form to physically participate in a Project Adventure program.

Do I need a Doctor's verification to participate in this event?

The level of medical information required by a vendor varies depending on the program design, location, duration, audience and level of activity involved. Most established programs have in place clear protocol for clients in specific situations. In some instances, limited medical information is required and it is sufficient for participants to respond to a few relevant questions. In other cases, for example where cardiac risk is elevated such as in climbing or high impact/more stressful activities, a doctor's consultation may be required. A key goal of most medical screening programs is the identification of those clients who may be at increased risk of suffering some form of heart failure. Identification of such individuals is usually based on established medical criteria which considers issues such as age, high blood pressure, sedentary life style, diabetes, smoking, and family history of heart disease.

Are there certain physical limitations that would limit involvement?

If a participant is at elevated cardiac risk our Project Adventure protocol is to recommend that they not participate in those activities that increase their risk and we work with them to find another, equally interesting role such as belaying without climbing.

Project Adventure's Challenge By Choice approach enables us to work closely with participants to find an appropriate level of challenge for their ability. In addition, we strive to design our activities to be fully accessible to all levels of physical ability.

Occasionally, though, there may be some physical conditions which would require modification of certain activities. For example, we once had a participant who had recently had brain surgery and was extremely sensitive to sun and prone to sun stimulated seizures. We were able to adjust most of our activities to be done inside, allowing his full participation.

When in discussion with a prospective vendor, it is important to ask how they will be able to accommodate multiple levels of physical ability.

What if an accident or injury does happen? How will it be handled?

The important areas to consider here are that a vendor has a clear and documented plan and process for handling an injury or accident. This should include adequate staff training and preparedness. Depending on the program, the audience, and the location, additional first aid or other preparedness training may be required.

Whenever possible, there should be adequate vendor staff to effectively tend to an injured person while someone else (trained) tends to the group. The site protocol directing an ambulance or transport of a patient should be understood and followed by vendor staff, if needed. How and to whom the incident will be communicated is important to know ahead of time.

Finally, there should be clear strategies aimed at managing the complex feelings, concerns, and opinions that are likely to occur after any incident. There should be time for groups to dialogue about what happened, their role in what happened, and what will happen next. Facilitators should be trained and competent at assisting a group through the complex reactions to an accident or injury.

How can I best prepare participants in advance of the event?

At Project Adventure, Inc. we make every effort to de-mystify the experience for participants as well as to align it with their overall organizational goals. We recommend that clients clearly articulate to participants the intent behind the event, as well as the key components such as Challenge by Choice and the actual physical level of exertion and weather exposure required.

Sometimes it is advantageous to have the vendor meet participants in advance of the program. Taking time on the front end to answer questions, clarify goals, and complete paperwork can save time during the program event itself. When this is not possible, we strongly encourage clients to proactively manage the expectations and worries of participants with open communication.

It is a good idea to ask prospective vendors how they like to prepare participants and what type of support they can provide.

Summary Thoughts

We consider the operation of a safe program as a critical value for any organization. In the workplace, companies pay attention to risk to minimize lost work time, low morale, and to maximize high performance. The adventure consulting services should further extend or maintain the elevation of safety as a core value. It only takes one breach for one individual to create hours or even years of work and frustration after safety has been violated. Prudence, proactivity and reasonableness are the key measures to ensure the long term operation of safe, effective programs.

When considering selection of an adventure provider, the following checklist may prove helpful:

Risk Management Checklist

Reputation: Call References

Ask about history and Safety Record

Inquire about Adherence to Industry Standards: such as A.C.C.T.

Liability Insurance? Amount? Site Specific?

Staff Credentials

Standard Protocol for Risk/Release of Liability Forms/Medical Screening

Safety inspection (if fixed site used)

Date and Vendor

Risk Management Plan

Type of Activity Utilized

References
& Suggested Readings

Argyris, Chris. (1993). *Knowledge for Action: A Guide to Overcoming Barriers to Organizational Change.* San Francisco, CA: Jossey-Bass Publishers.

Argyris, Chris. (1957). *Personality and Organizations.* New York: Harper Collins.

Armstrong, Thomas. (1994). *Multiple Intelligences in the Classroom.* Alexandria, VA: Association for Supervision and Curriculum Development.

Arrien, Angeles. (1993). *The Four-Fold Way: Walking the Paths of the Warrior, Teacher, Healer and Visionary.* San Francisco, CA: Harper Collins.

Bardwick, Judith. (1995). *Danger in the Comfort Zone: From Boardroom to Mailroom—How to Break the Entitlement Habit That's Killing American Business.* New York: AMACOM.

Belbin, Meredith. (1993) *Team Roles at Work.* Oxford: Butterworth-Heinemann.

Belenky, Mary Field and Clinchy, Blythe McVicker and Goldberger, Nancy Rule and Tarule, Jill Mattuck. (1986). *Women's Ways of Knowing: The Development of Self, Voice and Mind.* New York: Basic Books.

Blanchard, Ken and Bowles, Sheldon. (1998). *Gung Ho!* New York: William Morrow and Company, Inc.

Blanchard, Ken and O'Connor, Michael. (1997). *Managing by Values.* San Francisco, CA: Berrett-Koehler.

Block, Peter. (1981). *Flawless Consulting.* San Francisco, CA: Jossey-Bass Pfeiffer.

Bohm, David. (1996). *On Dialogue* (edited by Lee Nichol). Ojai, California: Routledge.

Bolton, Robert and Bolton, Dorothy Grover. (1996). *People Styles at Work: Making Bad Relationships Good and Good Relationships Better.* New York: AMACOM.

Bryner, Andy and Markova, Dawna. (1996). *An Unused Intelligence: Physical Thinking for the 21st Century Leadership.* Berkeley, CA: Conari Press.

Caine, Renate Nummela and Caine, Geoffrey. (1991). *Making Connections: Teaching and the Human Brain.* Innovative Learning Publications. Menlo Park, California: Addison-Wesley.

Caine, Renate Nummela & Caine, Geoffrey. (1997). "Meaningful Learning". *Zip Lines: The Voice for Adventure Education.* vol. 31. pp 10-16. Hamilton, MA: Project Adventure.

Capra, Fritjof. (1996). *The Web of Life.* New York: Doubleday.

Clemmer, Jim. (1995). *Pathways to Performance: A Guide to Transforming Yourself, Your Team, and Your Organization.* Rocklin, California: Prima Publishing.

Colvin, Geoffrey. (1997). "The Changing Art of Becoming Unbeatable." *Fortune Magazine.* pp 299-300. November 24, 1997.

Cousins, Norman. (1979). *Anatomy Of An Illness.* New York, New York: Bantam Books.

Covey, Stephen R. (1989). *The Seven Habits of Highly Effective People.* New York: Simon & Schuster.

Csikszentmihalyi, Mihaly. (1975). *Beyond Boredom and Anxiety.* San Francisco, CA: Jossey-Bass.

Csikszentmihalyi, Mihaly. (1991). *Flow: The Psychology of Optimal Experience.* New York: Harper & Row.

DePree, Max. (1989). *Leadership Is An Art.* New York: Dell Publishing Group.

Dewey, John. (1938). Experience and Education. New York: Macmillan.

Funches, Daryl. (1989). "The Three Gifts of the Organizational Development Practitioner." *The Emerging Practice of Organization Development.* Edited by Walter Sikes, Ph.D., Allan B. Drexler, Ph.D., Jack Gant, Ph.D. Alexandria, VA: co-published by NTL Institute for Applied Behavioral Science and University Associates, Inc.

Gardner, Howard. (1990). Multiple Intelligences: Implications for Art and Creativity. In William J. Moody (ed.), *Artistic Intelligences: Implications for Education.* New York: Teachers College Press.

Gass, Michael A. and Goldman, Kathy and Priest, Simon. (1992). "Constructing Effective Corporate Adventure Training Programs." *Journal of Experiential Education.* 15 (1), p. 36.

Gass, Michael A. (1995). *Book of Metaphors: Volume II.* Dubuque, IA: Kendall/Hunt.

Gladwell, Malcolm. (1996). "The Tipping Point." *New Yorker Magazine.* June 3, 1996.

Helgeson, Sally. (1990). *The Female Advantage —Women's Ways of Leadership.* New York: Doubleday Currency.

Hock, Dee Ward. (1996). "Writings for the Chaordic Alliance." p. 48. text of speech from Systems Thinking in Action Conference, San Francisco, CA.

Jamison, Kaleel. (1984). *The Nibble Theory and The Kernel of Power.* New York: Paulist Press.

Jaworski, Joseph, (1996). *Synchronicity, The Inner Path of Leadership.* San Francisco, CA: Berret-Koehler Publishers Inc.

Katzenbach, Jon R. & Smith, Douglas K. (1993). *The Wisdom of Teams.* Boston, MA: Harvard Business School Press.

Kolb, David A.. (1984). *Experiential Learning: Experience as the source of learning and development.* Englewood Cliffs, NJ: Prentice-Hall.

Kouzes, James M. and Posner, Barry Z. (1990). *The Leadership Challenge.* San Francisco: Jossey-Bass.

Kuczmarski, Susan Smith and Thomas, D. (1995). *Values Based Leadership.* New Jersey: Prentice-Hall.

Lebow, Rob and Simon, William L. (1997). *Lasting Change: The Shared Values Process That Makes Companies Great.* New York: Van Norstrand Reinhold.

Lippitt, Gordan and Lippitt, Ronald. (1978). *The Consulting Process in Action.* San Diego, CA: University Associates, Inc.

Noddings, Nel. (1992). *Caring: A Feminist Approach to Ethics and Moral Education.* Berkeley, CA: University of California Press.

Oakley, Ed and Krug, Doug. (1994). *Enlightened Leadership: Getting to the Heart of Change.* New York: Simon & Schuster.

Pribram, Karl. (1987). *A Systematic Analysis of Brain Function, Learning and Remembering.* Paper presented at Educating Tomorrow's Children. San Francisco, CA: Neuropsychology Services.

Prigogine, Ilya and Isabelle Stengers. (1984). *Order Out of Chaos.* New York: Bantam Books.

Rohnke, Karl E. (1984). *Silver Bullets.* Dubuque, IA: Kendall/Hunt.

Rohnke, Karl E. (1989) *Cowstails and Cobras II.* Dubuque, IA: Kendall/Hunt.

Rokeach, Milton. (1973) *The Nature of Human Values.* New York: The Free Press.

Schein, Edgar H. (1987). *Process Consultation Volume II: Lessons for Managers and Consultants.* MA: Addison-Wesley.

Schultz, Howard and Yang, Dori Jones. (1997). *Pour Your Heart Into It.* New York, New York: Hyperion.

Secretan, Lance H. K. (1997). *Reclaiming Higher Ground.* New York: McGraw-Hill.

Selye, Dr. Hans. (1978). "On the Real Benefits of Eustress." *Psychology Today,* pp. 60-67. March, 1978.

Senge, Peter. (1990). *Fifth Discipline: Mastering the Five Practices of the Learning Organization.* New York: Doubleday.

Sewell, Carl, and Brown, Paul B. (1990). *Customers for Life: How to Turn That One-Time Buyer into a Lifetime Customer.* New York: Pocket Books.

Snyder, Neil H., Dowd, James J. Jr. and Houghton, Dianne Morse. (1994). *Vision Values and Courage: Leadership for Quality Management.* New York: The Free Press.

Spears, Larry C. (1998). *Insights on Leadership: Service, Stewardship, Spirit, and Servant-Leadership.* New York: John Wiley & Sons, Inc.

Taylor, Craig R. and Wheatley-Lovoy, Cindy. (1998). "Leadership Lessons from the Magic Kingdom." *Training and Development.* pp. 22-25. July 1998. Alexandria, VA: American Society for Training & Development, Inc.

Tichy, Noel and Cohen, Eli. (1998). "The Teaching Organization." *Training and Development.* pp. 27-33. July 1998. Alexandria, VA: American Society for Training & Development, Inc.

Tuckman, Bruce W. (1965). "Developmental Sequence in Small Groups." Psychological Bulletin, 63, 384-399.

Vail, Peter B. (1995). "The Rediscovery of Anguish." *Rediscovering the Soul of Business: A Renaissance of Values.* p. 73. Edited by Bill DeFoore and John Renesch. San Francisco, CA: New Leaders Press.

Vail, Peter B. (1989). *Managing as a Performing Art.* San Francisco, CA: Jossey-Bass Publishers.

Weaver, Richard G. and Farrell, John D. (1997). *Managers as Facilitators.* San Francisco, CA: Berret-Koehler Publishers.

Wheatley, Margaret J. and Rogers, Myron Kellner. (1996). *A Simpler Way.* San Francisco, CA: Berret-Koehler Publishers Inc.

Wheatley, Margaret. (1992). *Leadership and the New Science: Learning About Organization from an Orderly Universe.* pp.144-145. San Francisco, CA: Berrett-Koehler.

Zohar, Danah. (1997). *ReWiring the Corporate Brain.* San Francisco, CA: Berret-Koehler Publishers Inc.

Challenges Solutions

Section 1

Word Puzzle #1

Starting in the lower left corner with the letter "I", draw your line to spell the word IMMERSION.

Wordles

From left to right, the answers are: paradigm . . . excellence . . . team building

Section 2

Word Boxes

Top row: Challenge By Choice

Bottom row: Full Value Contract

Letter Equations

1) Experience + Reflection + Generalization + Transfer = Four Stages of the Experiential Learning Cycle

2) Caring + Competence + Common Purpose + Consistency + Confidentiality = Five C's of Trust

3) Pay Attention + Be Present + Speak Your Truth = Tenets of the Full Value Contract

4) Challenge By Choice = The Right to Choose—When and at What Level to Participate

How Many F's

5—don't forget the one in the title.

Section 3

Pie Pieces

The solution requires that one line is curved. A couple of solutions include:

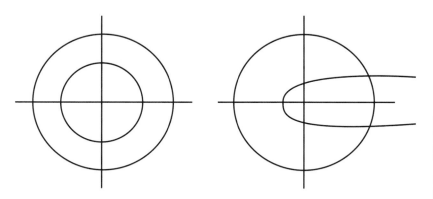

Volume, Volume, Volume

Fill the five gallon container; then pour three gallons (from the five gallon container) into the three gallon container. After emptying the three gallon container, pour the remaining two gallons from the five gallon container into the three gallon container. Fill the five gallon container again. Pour one gallon into the three gallon container to fill it. You now have exactly four gallons remaining in the five gallon container.

Section 4

Word Puzzle #2

Start in the middle of the top row with the letter "A", then draw your line to spell the word ADVENTURE.

Bringing Learning to the Surface

Find a water source and fill a glass with sufficient water to fill the bottle. Pour the water into the bottle and the pen cap will float to the surface. As it nears the top where the bottle narrows, you may need to pour more slowly and carefully to prevent the cap from getting stuck.

Project Adventure Training and Consultation Services

Catalog Trainings

Over 25 different open enrollment workshops are offered multiple times across the United States. The curricula of the workshops are designed for professionals using Adventure in the school, camp, community organization, therapeutic and corporate settings. Divided into different categories with each category offering entry level to advanced workshops, they vary in length from one to five days.

Custom Programs

Custom corporate trainings and program designs are offered in a broad range of areas including leadership development, team development, customer service and change management. Catalog workshops are also available on-site at your location on a custom basis. Many organizations opt for a custom approach because it can be more cost effective, program specific and time efficient.

Consulting Services

Project Adventure consults in all areas of its business. Consulting services are offered in our school and community, therapeutic and corporate markets. Services include ongoing consultation for companies involved in process redesign and change efforts, schools undergoing restructuring, communities implementing prevention strategies and therapeutic professionals working with youth labeled adjudicated, court-referred and at-risk. The consulting services offered by our risk management and installation specialists cover many areas include accreditation, safety inspections, site evaluations, indoor and outdoor installations, technical skills verification and testing, rescue review and training and risk management and medical screening.

Partnering

Project Adventure has partnered with other consultants, institutions and agencies to deliver integrated services in our market areas since our inception in 1971. With over two decades of networking with other consulting organizations with special market expertise, our experience runs the gamut and includes acting in the service of someone else's design, leading a design where we've enlisted the services of other consultants, co-designing and co-delivering full programs with in-house training staffs and designing around other consultants' design needs.

Challenge Course Design and Installation

Project Adventure has been the leader in designing and installing Challenge Ropes Courses since 1971. PA's installation specialists have planned and installed thousands of courses globally. Courses have been installed by companies in a range of settings including training and education centers, conference and resort centers, private reserves and at corporate headquarters.

Catalog and Publications Services

Membership

Staying up to date with the latest in program development, safety standards and equipment options are but a few of the many unique benefits available through our membership program. Becoming a PA Member helps you stay in touch through on-going access to a cross-market consulting team as well as other practitioners and experts in the field. Membership also provides you with discounts and exclusive member-only programs available on-line.

Publications/Zip Lines

Project Adventure Publications offers the most extensive library in the adventure field. Our titles cover all aspects of Adventure in most markets. Inclusive of engaging activities, PA philosophies, model curriculum, leadership discussions and thematic variety PA's collection of publication offerings is second to none in the field. *Zip Lines: The Voice of Adventure Education*, PA's quarterly vibrant magazine, is also available through Publications.

Equipment Catalog

Project Adventure is committed to providing field-tested products, a variety of tools and materials, props and Challenge Course gear through our equipment catalog. New products are featured each year which include new games, additional props and the latest in breakthrough pulley, equipment and installation materials.

Please send information on the following:

❒ Catalog trainings

❒ Custom programs

❒ Consulting services

❒ My company is interested in partnering with PA.

❒ My company is interested in PA's Challenge Course Design and Installation services.

❒ My company is interested in exploring different training venues.

❒ Membership

❒ Publications

❒ Equipment Catalog

❒ Please send your promotional materials.

Comments/suggestions for the book

Name _____

Organization _____

Work Address _____

Home Address _____

Phone _____

E-Mail _____

To get further information about Project Adventure services and programs, contact one of the offices below, or visit us on the web at www.pa.org.

P.O. Box 100	P.O. Box 2447	P.O. Box 1640	P.O. Box 14171
Hamilton, MA	Covington, GA	Brattleboro, VT	Portland, OR
01936	30015	05302-1640	97293
978/468-7981	770/784-9310	802/254-5054	503/239-0169
FAX 978/468-7605	FAX 770/787-7764	FAX 802/254-5182	FAX 503/236-6765

Project Adventure also has several offices overseas: Australia, New Zealand, Singapore, Japan and Taiwan. For more information, call 978/468-7981.